EUROPEAN PORTUGAL

Also by José M. Magone

THE CHANGING ARCHITECTURE OF IBERIAN POLITICS

European Portugal

The Difficult Road to Sustainable Democracy

José M. Magone
Lecturer in European Politics
University of Hull

Hull 25/5/2001

To Nancy and
her perceptive spirit and
studies.
A critical overview of
the origins of the First
Wave of Democratization
continued. In friendship
All the best

palgrave

Published by
PALGRAVE
Houndmills, Basingstoke, Hampshire RG21 6XS and
175 Fifth Avenue, New York, N. Y. 10010
Companies and representatives throughout the world

PALGRAVE is the new global academic imprint of
St. Martin's Press LLC Scholarly and Reference Division and
Palgrave Publishers Ltd (formerly Macmillan Press Ltd).

ISBN 0–333–65415–3

This book is printed on paper suitable for recycling and
made from fully managed and sustained forest sources.

A catalogue record for this book is available
from the British Library.

Transferred to digital printing 2001

Printed and bound in Great Britain by
Antony Rowe Ltd, Chippenham, Wiltshire

To

**Tó Louçã, Bibiana, Carlos and
Dona Domitilia**

for wonderful adventures in
the peripheries of Lisbon

Like to a ship that storms urge on its course
By its own trials our soul is surer made.
The very things that make the voyage worse
Do make it better; its peril is its aid.
And, as the storm drives from the storm, our heart
Within the peril disimperilled grows;
A port is near the more from port we part-
The port whereto our driven direction goes.
If we reap knowledge to cross-profit, this
From storms we learn, when the storm's height doth drive-
That the black presence of its violence is
The pushing promise of near far blue skies.
    Learn we but how to have the pilot-skill,
    And the storm's very might shall mate our will.

(Fernando Pessoa, *Poemas Ingleses*, Lisbon: Atica, 1987, p. 166)

Convaincre les hommes de parler entre eux, c'est le plus qu'on puisse faire pour la paix. Mais il y faut plusieurs conditions, toutes aussi necessaires. L'une est que l'esprit d'égalité préside aux conversations et qu'aucun ne vienne à la table avec la volonté d'emporter un avantage sur l'autre. Cela implique que l'on abandonne les soi-disant privilèges de la souveraineté et l'arme tranchante du veto. Une autre condition est que l'on parle bien du meme objet; un autre, enfin, que tous s'attachent a rechercher l'intérêt qui leur est commun. Cette methode n'est pas naturelle aux hommes qui se rencontrent pour traiter des problèmes nés précisément des contradictions d'interets entre les États nationaux. Il faut les amener à la comprendre et à l'appliquer. L'experience m'a enseigné que la bonne volonté n'y suffit pas et qu'une certaine force morale doit s'imposer a tous: c'est celle des régles que sécrètent les institutions communes supérieures aux individus et respectées par les États. Ces institutions sont faites pour unir, pour unir complètement ce qui est semblable, pour rapprocher ce qui est encore différent. Les Européens ont decidé de vivre sous les memes règles dans une Communauté que rendent possible leur densité culturelle et leur développement homogène.

(Jean Monnet, *Mémoires*, Paris: Fayard, 1976, pp. 558–9)

Contents

List of Tables

Preface

One of Portugal's most famous literary works is *História do Futuro* (*History of the Future*), written by Father Antonio Vieira in the seventeenth century. In it Vieira predicted that a new king would liberate Portugal from Spanish annexation (1580–1640) and transform it into a glorious empire. This prediction failed to materialise and the process of decline continued until the 'Revolution of Carnations' in 1974–5.

This peaceful event heralded Portugal's first steps on the path to democracy, the first of a string of countries seeking a more just and free society. This book is a modest contribution towards an understanding of the democratisation process and the difficulties political elites and the population may encounter on the way. Democracy is not an easy ideal to achieve and maintain, and before it can work it needs much investment in people. This is the main message of this book, which describes the Portuguese road to democracy within the context of Europeanisation and globalisation.

The process of globalisation started as far back as the sixteenth century, but since the early 1970s we have experienced a large global shift towards more flexible forms of production, labour and capital movement. The nation-state has lost considerable autonomy in policy making. When Portugal embarked on its project of democratisation this loss was overshadowed by the transition towards more flexible forms of production and trade. This affected Portugal more severely than many other countries, because in the decade prior to 1984 it had to adapt its political, social and economic structures to the demands of the world economy.

This work relates these pressures of globalisation to the process of European integration and Portugal's place in it. The Europeanisation of West European political systems, and perhaps later the East and Central European ones too, is both an economic and a political project to gain a collective autonomy. Here we concentrate on the effect Europeanisation has had on the Portuguese political system. The whole message of the book is positive, but it nevertheless casts a critical eye on the present situation in Portugal.

'European Portugal' refers to this process of Europeanisation, which is leading to a massive change in attitude and thinking at both the elite and the popular level. The emergence of civil society in the 1990s is a positive sign that Portuguese democracy may evolve towards a qualitative new stage. 'The difficult road to sustainable democracy' addresses the premise that popular participation at all levels of the political system is essential to improving the quality of life in Portugal. Such a commitment is laid down in Article 2 of the Portuguese constitution and may be used as a reference point when fashioning a participatory democracy based on sustainable development. It will be a long road as well as a difficult one, but the journey is crucial if democracy is to be made to work (Putnam, Leonardi and Nannetti, 1993).

I would like to thank all the people who helped me during my three years of research. In Lisbon, I am very grateful to Clemie Nogueira Lobato for her help when I was a lecturer at the Instituto Piaget in Lisbon and for the material she sent to me during my time in Hull. My thanks go to Professor António Oliveira Cruz, president of the Instituto Piaget, who gave dignity to a young academic in Portugal, and to all the other persons with whom I worked. I also wish to thank Professor Manuel Braga da Cruz for his continuing moral support.

In Britain, I am very thankful to my dear friend and mentor Geoff Pridham, who helped me during some bad times in Lisbon by phoning me up or including me in his research projects. This was very important, because young political scientists in Southern Europe can feel very isolated from mainstream political science.

My greatest experience of all has been membership of the Department of Politics at the University of Hull, which motivated me to search for and cross new boundaries in political science. The excellent political theory and European integration research seminars helped me to formulate many of the thoughts expressed in this book.

Last but not least, I wish to thank my mother for helping me throughout my research. Apart from her patience, she made me aware of many things that a political scientist tends to ignore.

JOSÉ M. MAGONE

List of Abbreviations

AD	Aliança Democrática (Democratic Alliance)
APU	Aliança Popular Unitária (United People's Alliance)
ASP	Acção Socialista Portuguesa (Portuguese Socialist Action)
CAP	Common Agricultural Policy
CAP	Confederação de Agricultores Portugueses (Confederation of Portuguese Farmers)
CCP	Camâra do Comércio Portuguesa (Portuguese Chamber of Commerce)
CDS	Centro Democrático Social (Democratic Social Centre)
CDS–PP	Centro Democrático Social–Partido Popular (Democratic Social Centre–People's Party)
CDU	Coligação Democrática Unitária (Union of the Democratic Coalition)
CGTP-In	Confederação Geral dos Trabalhadores Portugueses (Intersindical/General Confederation of Portuguese Workers)
CIP	Confederação da Industria Portuguesa (Confederation of Portuguese Industry)
CM	Comissões dos Moradores (residents' committees)
CPCS	Conselho Permanente para Concertação Social (Permanent Council for Social Harmonisation)
CSF	Common Support Framework
CT	Comissoes dos Trabalhadores (workers' committees)
EC	European Community
EU	European Union
FRS	Frente Republicana e Socialista (Republican and Socialist Front)
IMF	International Monetary Fund
Inamb	Instituto Nacional do Ambiente (National Environment Institute)
Ipamb	Instituto para a Promoção do Ambiente (Institute for the Protection of the Environment)

MDP	Movimento Democrático Popular (Democratic People's Movement)
PCP	Partido Comunista Português (Portuguese Communist Party)
PDR	Plano de Desenvolvimento Regional (Regional Development Plan)
PPD	Partido Popular Democrático (People's Democratic Party)
PRD	Partido Renovador Democrático (Democratic Renewal Party)
PS	Partido Socialista (Socialist Party)
PSD	Partido Social Democrata (Social Democratic Party)
PSN	Partido de Solidariedade Nacional (National Solidarity Party)
SEA	Single European Act
SEM	Single European Market
TEU	Treaty of the European Union
TNC	Transnational corporation
UCP	Unidades colectivas de produção (collective production units)
UGT	União Geral dos Trabalhadores (General Workers' Union)

1 The Rise of Democratisation Studies

INTRODUCTION

In the 1976 Summer Olympics in Montreal a modest Portuguese bank employee named Carlos Lopes won a silver medal in the 10 000 metre race, coming in second after the Finn Lasse Viren. This, together with a silver medal for shooting, were the first Olympic medals ever won by Portugal.

This was a joyful surprise in the wake of the revolution that had ended 48 years of authoritarian rule. The Constituent Assembly had agreed on a constitution and the first constitutional government and president had been elected into office, but a painful decolonisation process was underway and as a consequence the economy was in disarray.

Carlos Lopes used to run in the evening in the stadium of the well-known sports club in Lisbon – the Sporting Club of Portugal. He trained during the revolutionary period and afterwards, preparing himself for Montreal, while the uncertain transition to democracy was being fought out between different political groups and the revolutionary military. Carlos Lopes became famous throughout Portugal and a symbol that success in sport can be achieved by hard work. He was the first in a chain of Portuguese to symbolise the newly gained freedom of this small country on the western fringe of Europe.

At the economic level a similarly joyful moment was Portugal's accession to the European Community in 1986 after eight years of negotiations. The decision to join the EC had been a major factor behind the implementation of several drastic measures that had been imposed by the International Monetary Fund in 1978–9 and 1983–4. The political elite had been impatient about the slow pace at which the negotiations were being conducted, but on 1 January 1986 Portugal at last became a member of the European Community and six years later was fully integrated into its institutional framework. Portugal's presidency of the EC during the first half of 1992 enhanced the international prestige of this small country – for the first time the Portuguese government was representing the largest trading bloc in the world and was in charge of coordinating and announcing the policies of the EC.

1

On the whole, one can say that Portugal provides a good example
of successful development towards democratisation. This point is quite
important, because although it has often been overlooked by democratisation theorists, Portugal was the first country to participate in the
so-called *third wave of democratisation.*[1] On 25 April 1994 the twentieth anniversary of the 'Revolution of Carnations', which had led to
the end of authoritarian rule, was celebrated by all parties in Portugal.
This marked two decades of democratisation in a country whose per
capita GDP in 1994 was still only 56 per cent of the EC average and
in which 15 per cent of the adult population were illiterate. Nevertheless, during these twenty years considerable progress was made in all
aspects of life and the standard of living in Portugal changed considerably for the better.

This chapter will analyse certain problems inherent in present democratisation studies, which tend to emphasise political and economic stability when discussing countries embarking on the transition to democracy
and define democratisation as the process leading towards it. Consolidation, according to these studies, is the point when a country achieves
a high level of political, economic and social stability.

After this analysis a differentiation will be made between formal
democracy and qualitative, sustainable democracy, which is essential
to understanding the current situation in Portugal and other recently
democratised countries such as Spain and Greece.

THE *ZEITGEIST* OF THE THIRD WAVE OF DEMOCRATISATION

Democratisation theory has experienced a boom since the mid 1980s.
The excellent collection of essays edited by Geoffrey Pridham on
Mediterranean democracies seems to have been the starting point of a
qualitative development in this area of research (Pridham, 1984a), although the third wave actually started in 1977 with the launching of a
large project by the Woodrow Wilson International Center (Washington) to compare political transitions in Southern Europe and Latin America
(Agh, 1993, p. 231). According to Samuel P. Huntington, the third
wave of democratisation followed those between 1828 and 1926 in
Europe and Latin America and between 1943 and 1962 in the 'developing' world (Huntington, 1991).

This new wave started in southern Europe with the Portuguese Revolution of the Carnations, followed by the democratisation of Greece

and then Spain. Although the Greek and Portuguese transitions to democracy were completed in 1975 (Bruneau, 1984; Diamandouros, 1994), it was the later Spanish transition that most interested democratic and consolidation theorists. The main attraction of the Spanish transition was the fact that it was a negotiated process that led to a politics of consensus between actors of the previous regime and the opposition. This process, initiated and completed by Prime Minister Adolfo Suarez and his faction-ridden *Unión de Centro Democrático* (Union of the Democratic Centre – UCD) became a model for many countries in Latin America, Asia and Eastern Europe. The language of political scientists was enriched by Spanish words such as *dictablanda*, *democradura* and *ruptura pactada*, which characterised the period before, during and after the constitutional settlement. The mixed nature of the political codes, comprising elements from both the authoritarian and the new democratic languages, attracted the attention of political scientists.

Now the deterministic functionalist theory of the 1950s and 1960s is being contested by the new democratisation theorists. The new approach crities the previous one for its attempt to relate democracy to economic and modernisation indicators such as literacy, basic infrastructure and market behaviour. The trend in the 1980s and 1990s has been to concentrate research on the dynamics of transition and consolidation. In particular the interaction between political actors and negotiation processes during transitional periods has become a central concern of the new wave of democratisation theorists. Moreover it is now commonly accepted that the process of democratisation can fail and be reversed. The uncertainty of the outcome has become an accepted fact upon which one has to build (O'Donnell and Schmitter, 1986; Przeworski, 1988, 1992; Santiso, 1994; Manuel, 1995).

A 'genetic' approach to democracy, emphasising the distinctiveness of democratisation processes in individual countries, has been set against the functionalist approach of earlier democratisation theorists such as Seymour Lipset, Gabriel Almond, Sidney Verba and Daniel Lerner (Pridham, 1991, pp. 5–12; Shin, 1994, p. 139). Although comparative politics has been challenged by the globalisation thrusts of the 1990s and the growth of international relations (Erickson and Rustow, 1991; Hix, 1994), one can assert that the third wave of democratisation has facilitated the return of comparative politics. The so-called 'comparative revolution' does not ignore the international dimension of democratisation processes. On the contrary, it stresses that international actors are important in impeding or promoting successful transitions to democracy and diffusing uncertain situations. According to Agh:

The significance of the direct involvement of the Western European countries in the democratisation process of the Southern European countries, in my opinion, cannot be emphasised enough. Without their massive financial assistance and large-scale investment, solution of the debt-crisis and accomplishment of the structural changes in the national economies might not have been possible at all. The direct political assistance of the Western European states has also to be seen as a very important factor in the whole political democratisation process. While Latin America has failed, Southern Europe has succeeded in the transition to democracy, above all because of the predominance of external factors in the transition, which will also determine the fate of further democratic transitions.

The European Community needed this Mediterranean extension to improve its own performance on a global scale and the Mediterranean needed Europe in order to overcome authoritarian rule and relative backwardness. In this historical bargain 'Europeanisation' has not been an empty political slogan but a catch-up and effective safeguard against sliding back into authoritarian rule. Europeanisation has also meant the reinforcement of the European tradition of parliamentary system with its leading role in the political transition (Agh, 1993, p. 234).

Democratisation processes have become linked to developments at the global level. Since the first oil crisis in 1973 the world has experienced a macro transition and consolidation process, which is primarily targeting national economies and consequently the political, cultural and social systems of nation-states. Agh's excellent analysis brings this aspect to the fore and shows that Europeanisation followed the globalisation process that started in the early 1970s. The logic of the 'great transformation' (Polanyi, 1944) had repercussions on political systems across the world.

The thrust towards globalisation started in the United States. Internationalisation of the financial and service sectors put nationally oriented markets under strain, and cross-border raids by transnational corporations (TNCs) on smaller firms increased considerably in the 1980s. Since the 1986 Punta del Este General Agreement on Trade and Tariffs (GATT), attempts have been made to reach a settlement between north and south. While the countries in the southern hemisphere agreed to open their markets to services and financial transactions – the new stage of capitalism – the north would open its markets to textiles and farming products. Such a division of world trade would naturally perpetuate the continuing hegemony of the northern hemisphere over the countries of the developing south.

Technologically, new production technologies have speeded up the processes of manufacturing and changed the organisational structure of factories. A more flexible form of production, subject to constant adaptation in line with technological change, has emerged. The Fordist model of production based on assembly lines is being steadily replaced by a post-Fordist one based on flexible, lean production methods. The former homogeneous situation whereby working time was synchronised and each worker performed a single task is being replaced by a more heterogeneous workforce with different time–space routines. While in the Fordist system most workers had permanent contracts, were protected by extensive labour legislation and were represented by strong trade unions, post-Fordism is characterised by workers with different types of contract – permanent, temporary, part-time – and a wider field of representation (Muller and Wright, 1994; Wright, 1994; Cerny, 1990; Esping-Andersen, 1993).

This has had two main consequences for the class structure of nation-states. First, social stratification has been reorganised around educational qualifications and access to information. Expertise in the new technologies is a crucial factor in moving forward in the social structure. Second, it has led to globalisation of the class system, because the highly mobile new middle classes are monopolising the high skill jobs in the services sector (Esping-Andersen, 1993, pp. 24–5).

In the transitional period the nation-state has experienced an erosion of its autonomy. The globalisation process has put nation-states under strain because they are now competitors in the international economy. The need to offer better conditions to TNCs and to liberalise financial and services transactions has led to a retreat of the state *vis-à-vis* the economy. Privatisation, deregulation and marketisation have become the main catchwords of this development. The 'changing architecture' of politics has meant that states have had to adapt to the globalisation process and become more flexible, resulting in strategic state intervention in certain sectors and the rise of the regulatory state (Majone, 1991). In the course of this the welfare state has been replaced by the 'competition state' (Cerny, 1990, p. 53).

Total Europeanisation of the national economies of Western Europe started to become a necessity in the mid 1980s. Between 1984 and 1992 the president of the European Commission, Jacques Delors, initiated several projects to build up a single European market, so that the EC could compete more efficiently. The single European market

(SEM), designed and implemented by Lord Cockfield between 1985 and 1992, the introduction of the Single European Act (SEA) in 1987 and the ratification of the Treaty of the European Union (TEU) in November 1993 were direct responses to the globalisation process.

What was once a purely economic alliance, the EC, is now attempting to create a new political identity: the European Union, a powerful trading bloc and participant in the G-7 summits. The Europeanisation of national systems has been seen by many as leading to a loss of national autonomy in all fields of policy making (Notterman, 1993). However in reality the formation of the EU was an attempt to enhance regional, and consequently national and subnational, autonomy *vis-à-vis* the globalisation process. A collective effort can increase the ability to control processes that threaten to undermine the role of the state in Europe.

The 'great transformation' of the nineteenth and early twentieth centuries reached its climax with the emergence of nationalist and fascist nation-states in the 1920s and 1930s as a reaction against the economic crisis of the time and a perceived loss of national autonomy as a result of the globalisation process (Polanyi, 1944). We are part of a similar wave, which is leading to a multitude of reactionary strategies, for example Islamic fundamentalism, nationalism and regionalism. It seems that an ideological *Zeitgeist* (spirit of the time) acts as a sustaining force for medium-term reactionary models. As Juan Linz asserts for the interwar period:

> There is also what the Germans would call a *Zeitgeist*, a feeling shared across national boundaries, that a particular type of political system is the most desirable or the most questionable. This feeling tends to be reinforced or weakened by the positive or negative perception of other more powerful states or nations that are successful with a particular type of regime. In the interwar years the *Zeitgeist* was deeply affected by the success of Fascist Italy, and later Nazism, and this helped weaken the commitment to democratic legitimacy in many countries. As Weber noted, no type of legitimacy is found in pure form in any society. Most people give allegiance to a regime on the basis of a complex set of beliefs. Democratic legitimacy, therefore, is often reinforced by becoming a form of tradition, and the personal charisma of democratic leaders committed to the regime tends to reinforce its institutions (Linz, 1978, p. 18).

The most recent 'great transformation' has been sustained by a neoliberal *Zeitgeist*, based on the works of such writers as Milton Friedman and

Friedrich von Hayek. The so-called 'Chicago boys' were asked by General Pinochet of Chile to advise the military junta on how to stabilise the economy. At the end of the 1980s the Chilean dictator was able to present a sound, liberal macroeconomic policy and his economy became one of the most stable in Latin America. The authoritarian conditions in Chile seemed propitious for the implementation of drastic austerity measures and for the Hobbesian model of rule to become a reality (Huneeus, 1987, pp. 120–2). Ordinary citizens would no longer play a part in politics, but would confine their actions to market relations. Moreover the authoritarian structure would provide them with a stability that had been absent before. The ideological think tank of the time was the Mount Pellerin Society, which had been founded in 1947 and had built up a network of over 600 neoliberal scholars around the world. Moreover it had the support of the Reagan administration and was a major ideological element of Thatcherite politics.

The neoliberal idea of 'freedom to choose' (Milton Friedman) was strong enough to erode the welfare-statism and social democracy of the 1970s, which was based on the principle of solidarity and equality of opportunities. On the one hand this conservative project idealised the nuclear family and its values and assigned to all its citizens the anthropological qualities of a *homo economicus*, who saw economics, politics and society in market terms. On the other hand it overemphasised national security and national assertiveness, recalling old victories such as that over Nazi Germany and Japan and transferring this spirit to the British intervention in the Falkland Islands, the US intervention in Grenada and the Allied participation in the Gulf War (Calleo, 1994, pp. 24–30; Overbeek, 1990, pp. 162–5). The reemergence of the nation-state at the international level and its internal erosion became a striking contradiction against the background of accelerating globalisation following the advance of information technology.

The 'overmarketisation' of everyday life during the 1980s found its way into democratisation theory. Liberalisation and democratisation became intertwined processes that fed each other during the transition to democracy. The role of political actors was emphasised, but in the mid 1980s the predominant model was democratic liberalism. This became even more so with the collapse of communism in Eastern and Central Europe and the Soviet Union.

The transition to democracy is closely linked to the introduction of a liberal market economy, together with an economically defined civil society that sustains both market and society as a whole (DiPalma, 1991a, pp. 88–94, 1991b, pp. 28–30; Poznanzki, 1992).[2] This linkage contradicts the original idea of the founder of transition and consolidation theory, Dankwart Rustow, who postulated in his well-known essay of the 1970s that there are many roads to democracy (Rustow, 1970, p. 345), and signals a return to one-world theory, based on Almond's concept of the political market behaviour of the citizens of Anglo-Saxon democracies (Almond, 1956, p. 398; Heinrich, 1985).

Interestingly, it was Seymour Martin Lipset, one of the most prominent representatives of the functionalist school during the 1960s and 1970s, that restored the validity of a differentiated approach towards the study of democracy in different countries. After conducting a long and sophisticated regression analysis in an attempt to find a correlation between economic development and democratisation, his team came to the conclusion that economic development, though playing an important part, can only partially explain the democratisation process. Lipset maintains that cultural factors condition the development towards democracy, and that cultural differences in different regions of the world, such as the Arab world or Asia, are variables that must be taken into account in the study of democratisation. He concludes that while there are distinctive trajectories to the democratisation process (Lipset, Seong and Torres, 1993, pp. 196–9), the two theoretical approaches to it are complementary (Lipset, 1994, p. 16).[3]

Such a critique has been always inherent in Przeworski's work. In his *Democracy and the Market* he clearly states that the social market economy may be the best economic arrangement to ensure successful democratisation. The necessity to structure the market and the polity, to devise rules of the game and implement them, and to take into account any contingent outcomes makes the social-democratic model quite attractive, in that it introduces market forces in a moderate form and is socially oriented. Political liberalisation should be linked to a social project that assures a less traumatic transformation of present forms of social organisation. Disruption of collective forms may in the end prevent successful democratisation because some social groups will be denied access to democratic procedures and equality of influence in the political, social and economic arenas (Przeworski, 1991, pp. 133–5).

The social dimension of transition has been emphasised recently by the Latvian political scientist Feliciana Rajevska, who brought to the fore the social costs of transition. The painful process of introducing a market economy can cause disarray among the population. (Such social costs were experienced during the Portuguese transition and many other transitions around the world.) In particular the older members of the population can be severely hit in transitional periods because they have to exist on extremely low pensions. The economy of transition and consolidation is a *compositum mixtum*, combining elements of market behaviour and distorted patterns of the former planned economy, or what has been called 'market fascism' in the case of former authoritarian regimes (Arrighi, 1985, p. 265). Furthermore the markets of the Baltic states and the republics of the former Soviet Union have been occupied by the Russian 'mafia', because the new market economy was inadequately prepared for and there is a lack of institutional control (Rajevska, 1994; Rodin, 1994; Steen, 1995; Arter, 1994; Ishyama, 1993; Semanis, 1994; interview with Andris Runcis, March 1995).

All this points to the fact that, although transition and consolidation may be successfully achieved at the economic and political levels, cultural and social transformation may be a far more difficult and lengthy process. This has been put forward by Ralf Dahrendorf, who emphasises that social and cultural democratic transformation will take more than a single generation to accomplish (Dahrendorf, 1990, p. 99). During this period representation by patronage may arise, which gives certain groups special access to public goods and is characterised by a high level of apathy among the population. Such forms of intermediation may persist for a long time after transition and consolidation and seriously impede the emergence of true democracy. Moreover new democratic structures may become subject to patrimonialist patronage and lead to inequality of influence on political processes (Lemarchand and Legg, 1972; Ozbudun, 1981, p. 252). The explosion of patronage in postwar Italy and the results of the investigation initiated in 1992 by the Italian judge Antonio di Pietro show that patronage can arise suddenly and patrimonialism may have persist for a long time. The Italian *tangentopoli* (kickback city) affair, which led to the collapse of the postwar political class, was not an isolated case (Guzzini, 1994) and it is a widespread but little studied phenomenon in new democracies.

As a general rule of thumb it seems that the cultural ethos sustaining the democratisation process is a mixed one, whereby past forms of authoritarianism and patrimonial behaviour coexist with, democratic forms of behavior. 'Post-communist', 'post-Francoist', 'post-Salazarist' are accurate descriptions of new political systems. The old structures remain, but democratic institutions and culture slowly emerge (Pridham, 1984b, p. 12). The democratic ideal may require several generations of socialisation to become a reality (Perez-Diaz, 1993, p. 29).

On the whole, one may conclude that the international *zeitgeist* tends to reduce alternatives during the process of democratisation. A particular

model may be deemed the most desirable one for transition and consolidation, and as a consequence national particularities may be
put aside.

The social costs of converting an authoritarian or planned economy
to a free market can destroy all prospects of total democratisation, and
adaptating to the globalisation process has more negative social implications in emerging democracies than in the more developed ones –
the lack of socialisation towards economic market behaviour may be
one reason for this. The elitist approach to democratisation has to be
followed by a more participatory one that is concerned with developing a qualitatively sustainable democracy.

INSTITUTIONALISATION: THE QUALITATIVE DIMENSION OF DEMOCRACY

In an excellent essay on democratic transitions called *To Craft Democracies*, Giuseppe di Palma (1990a) expressed some critical thoughts
on the nature of 'consolidation'. What does it mean? Is it the process
of institutionalisation described in Samuel Huntington's *Political Order
in Changing Societies* (1968) or is it the process of socialisation, which
in the long run will make the new democracy a more secure one
(DiPalma, 1990a, pp. 138–44)? DiPalma presents the image of a half-
way house, where remnants of the old regime may reverse the whole
process of democratisation. He clearly emphasises the role of human
choice in keeping the democratic project alive. This is the meaning of
crafting democracy (ibid., pp. 156–82).

Until now this human factor of democratisation has been confined
to the performance of the political elite. Although 'civil society' has
been a buzzword in transition and consolidation theory, in reality it
fulfils an ancillary purpose by creating market behaviour and greater
efficiency in the political system.[4] In this work we want to go beyond
the minimalist approach of DiPalma and regard institutionalisation as
a qualitative new phase that follows consolidation. Democratic consolidation is defined as the process of stabilising the institutions of a
new political system, particularly at the economic, social and political
levels. It creates a network of 'routinisations' at different levels of the
political system, which in the end will feed the process of consolidation.

In the consolidation period new socialisation and participation structures
have to be devised and adjusted to the new political system. Such a
process is uncertain, may take longer than one generation and is a

multilayered phenomenon of group, regime and social structuring. As O'Donnell and Schmitter rightly assert, some 'partial regimes' need a longer period of time for democratic consolidation than others. In this sense one has to speak of a multitude of consolidation times (Durão Barroso, 1989). Both authors compare it with running parallel chess games, each with a different rhythm – some lasting a short time, others longer (O'Donnell and Schmitter, 1986, pp. 66–7).

Institutionalisation goes beyond consolidation. It is the qualitative dimension of democracy and is central to the process. It is present during consolidation, but becomes quite dominant after, say, one generation of stable democratic consolidation. While regime consolidation refers to the process of stabilising of the new constitutional settlement in theory and practice, institutionalisation is adjustment to an emerging civil society that was socialised into the new democratic system during the consolidation phase (Perez-Diaz, 1993, p. 4).

During institutionalisation, political structures have to be tailored to the needs of the population, so that the institutional framework facilitates participation. The purpose is to strengthen democracy by increasing the population's involvement in public affairs. This can only be achieved by decentralising the political system. The formal political institutions have to be steadily adjusted to the demands of civil society. Central to this is transforming the institutional framework into a participatory one. Such 'participatory institutions' have to be seen as citizen-friendly, and proactive in increasing the participatory possibilities of the citizen, in enhancing the level of transparency and democratisation in decision making and in developing people-oriented policies (Pateman, 1970, pp. 110–11).

Moreover it is committed to identifying and reducing the inequality of power distribution that is inherent in mass-society institutions (Galtung, 1975, pp. 19–23), and moving towards 'likestilling' (equal rights) policies in the labour market, with its implications for equality in gender relations, as exists in the Scandinavian countries, particularly Norway (Schneider, 1990). Such a programme is compatible with the necessity to shift at the world-system level from a quantitative exponential growth model based on a liberal market economy to one based on environmentally friendly, sustainable development (World Commission on Environment and Development, 1987). Sustainable development could be based on a model of 'strong sustainable democracy' (Barber, 1984). Sustainable democracy creates the optimal conditions for women and men to develop their individual potential in a participation-friendly social and material environment.

Is this Utopia? From a political, sociological and philosophical point of view the answer is of course no. As one can craft democracy, one can also craft better institutional structures and create the psychological conditions for such a transformation. From an economic and political point of view, this has become a necessity. The new technologies are leading to the transformation of everyday life, to the disruption of former routines and to a culture of violence and discontent due to lack of work and adequate social programmes (Virilio, 1986).

'Quality democracy' has become a general demand across the world and not only in new democracies. A 'society of organisations' tends to exclude people outside organisations and to create an anthropologically distinct 'organisation woman/man'. Participatory democracy could contribute to a steady transformation of the spatial no-man's land between organisations, where school drop-outs, the unemployed and other disadvantaged social groups fall through the net and lose their dignity as citizens.[5]

Democratisation, according to the definition used in this work, transforms a rationality based on money and power into an emancipatory one (Horkheimer, 1987). Such an emancipatory rationality predisposes socialisation into a more tolerant 'communicative action', which emphasises a respect for 'otherness' and the building up of a multitude of flexible intersubjective agreements. Moreover it leads to the internalisation of a critique of ideology of modern mass society. It could also reverse the process whereby everyday life is dominated by the mechanisms of the consumer industry and lead to the complete transformation of 'people' into a 'public' and redirect it towards the emergence of 'the responsible citizen' (Ribeiro, 1986, pp. 14, 20; Costa, 1992, pp. 81–98). As Schlosberg discovered, this Habermasian ideal is no longer a Utopia, but has become part of the way of life of new American social movements. He summarises the move towards intersubjective forms of communication as follows:

> Intersubjectivity as a practice calls not for instrumental, dominating relationships, but rather for interactions based on the continued tension of mutual recognition. Instead of the manipulative relations of instrumental rationality and the isolation and alienation that result from lack of recognition, we communicate to develop a continual balance between our need for recognition and the like need of others.
>
> The full realisation of intersubjectivity in practice would be a situation free from domination and strategic motivations. Participation would be open to all those capable and interested; each could ques-

tion others' proposals or make their own; and anyone could freely voice opinions, attitudes, or needs. Habermas acknowledges that 'a speech situation determined by pure intersubjectivity is an idealisation', but at least, with a mastery of the skills of communicative competence, we can attempt to redeem its potential (Schlosberg, 1995, p. 295).

A transformation of the cultural rationale of liberal democracy is needed, so that one can begin to develop a post-liberal democratic theory (Parekh, 1992). Such an effort will require a worldwide rethinking of the viability of the political and economic foundations of democracy. In this sense we come closer to the concern of C. B. Macpherson, who in the early 1970s insisted that we should overcome the models of democracy defined by the Soviet Union and the United States and move towards a post-liberal democratic theory.[6]

Because of the collapse of communism in the Soviet Union and Eastern and Central Europe we are facing a unique chance to move towards a form of post-liberal democracy, based on the principle of communicative action, the creation of participatory institutions and the corresponding psycho-social qualities among citizens that will be required to sustain it. A strong, sustainable democracy may lead to a different kind of economic system based on environmentally friendly and human-development-friendly sustainable growth.

These macroeconomic and macrocultural transitions are crucial to understanding the background of the Portuguese institutionalisation processes. The next section returns to the Portuguese case and attempts to use these theoretical thoughts as a heuristic construct to investigate the 'great democratic transformation' of Portuguese politics.

REGIONAL MONITORING OF THE DEMOCRATISATION PROCESS: THE EUROPEAN UNION AND PORTUGAL

Article 2 of the Portuguese constitution clearly states that the Portuguese Republic aims to deepen participatory democracy. The full text runs as follows:

> The Portuguese Republic is a democratic State that is based upon the rule of law, the sovereignty of the people, the pluralism of democratic expression and democratic political organisation, and respect and effective guarantee for fundamental rights and freedoms, and *has as its aims the achievement of economic, social and cultural*

democracy and the deepening of participatory democracy (Constitution, 1992, 1995, Article 2 – emphasis added).

This definition of democracy and its aims comes very close to the heuristic construct outlined above. Democratisation means a continuing effort to extend democracy to all areas of political, economic, social and cultural life. The constitution defines it as a long-term project. Therefore institutionalisation – the process of creating effective, citizen-friendly participatory institutions – may be an open-ended process. The new definition of Article 2 in the revised constitution of 1992 replaced the former article of 1976, where participatory democracy was linked to the ultimate goal of completing the transition to socialism. In the first revision of 1982, Article 1 even postulated that the Portuguese Republic would transform itself into a classless society.

The watering down of expectations after the second and third revision of 1989 and 1992, respectively, reflected the global *zeitgeist*. The Portuguese Revolution happened at a time when the left-wing *zeitgeist*, influenced by the emergence of revolutionary movements in different countries of the southern hemisphere, was shaping the vocabulary of Portuguese leaders, particularly the military incumbents. This faded away in the 1980s and was replaced by the 'neoliberal revolution'.

The integration of Portugal into the world economy impacted on both its constitution and its political choices. Moreover the alternating Portuguese governments were bent on joining the European Community as soon as possible. Europeanisation was regarded by the political elites as a means – if not the only means – of consolidating democracy. Impatience about the time it was taking to be accepted by the EC was quite evident in 1983–4 during the implementation of the second IMF stabilisation plan (Magone 1995a, 1995b, 1996). Nevertheless this period of regional monitoring gave the structures of the new political system time to stabilise.

Accession to the EC represented a new stage in this monitoring process, and furthermore the EC provided the necessary material, legal and cultural framework to strengthen democracy in Portugal. The integration of Portuguese civil servants into EC institutions, the exchange of ideas with their counterparts from other countries, and the democratic rationality inherent in EC programmes, based on accountability and procedural transparency, had a spillover effect on the Portuguese administrative culture, so that it became part of the vocabulary. The Europeanisation of Portuguese civil servants and dissemination of a more transparent approach to administrative procedures are, even almost ten years after accession, still in their beginnings, but nevertheless they do matter in the institutionalisation process.

Although there is much questioning of the democratic accountability of institutions in the present-day EU, the policy-making processes of the EU do emphasise the necessity to involve citizens in decision making and implementation. The Environmental Impact Assessment (EIA) directive provides a good example of how citizens can become involved in the pre-implementation stage of larger projects that directly affect their lives. Protests by environmental associations and the Commission led to change of position by the Portuguese government in relation to implementation of the EIA directive in the 1990s (see Chapter 8). It seems that regional monitoring of democratisation processes may be a way towards a safer world, where solidarity between nations may replace the logic of competition. Presently this is being applied by the EU to the countries of Eastern and Central Europe as well as the Soviet Union. 'Political learning' becomes a crucial factor in the instilling of democratic behaviour, so that new internalised codes of political activity are based on more humane future.[7]

This book is only a modest contribution to the study of third-wave democratisation processes. Although the democratisation process has been very painful for Portugal, developments after Portugal's accession to the EC/EU suggest that the country has already entered a phase of qualitative democratisation, which implies that institutions will become citizen-friendly and based on the principles of strong, sustainable democracy outlined above. The following pages are an empirical attempt to assess how far Portugal is from achieving a strong and sustainable democracy. We stress that Portugal's further democratisation is intertwined with further Europeanisation.

The EU's Fifth Environmental Action Programme clearly stresses the linkage between sustainable development and changes to cultural patterns of consumption. Such changes will require stronger, more proactive participation by the people. Furthermore the programme wants to contribute to a more united world based on the findings of the Brundtland Report. The EU member states have been asked to include environmental education in their national curricula until the year 2000 (Commission of the European Communities, 1992), and it has become a general trend across all member states and in the new democracies of Eastern and Central Europe. The double process of democratisation and Europeanisation may take a long time, but it is necessary to the development of strong and sustainable democracy based on European and international solidarity.[8]

2 The Portuguese Political System: From Democratic Transition to Europeanisation

THE HISTORICAL BACKGROUND OF DEMOCRATISATION IN PORTUGAL

In eighteenth-century France, before the revolution of 1789, market women used to shout 'Portugal' when selling oranges (Braudel, 1979, pp. 441–2). Even today 'Portugal' in the Greek and Kurdish languages is synonymous with oranges, an illustration of the extent to which this small country projected itself on the world.

Portugal, the mighty sea power of the fifteenth and sixteenth centuries and technologically one of the most advanced countries in Europe, declined during the seventeenth century to a second-rate power that depended on the protection of other countries such as England. During its annexation by Spain (1580–1640), Portugal had to face several losses to its empire, particularly in Brazil and along the African coast. In the eighteenth century several reformers tried to restore Portugal's independence, for example Count Ericeira and the Marquis de Pombal. Nevertheless the Methuen Treaty of 1703 established a dependency relationship between Portugal and England in that Portugal would export wine to England in exchange for textiles. This was a severe blow to the infant Portuguese textile industry, and indeed all Portugal's domestic development strategies were vulnerable to the emerging dominance of the international economy (Ligthart and Reitsma, 1988, pp. 359–60).

It was also becoming increasingly difficult for this small country to maintain its empire, which required ever more human and material resources, so Portuguese colonialism remained superficial and was restricted to the coastal fringes. This was the case even in its largest colonies – Mozambique, Angola and Brazil. The Portuguese colonial administrators tended to follow the pattern of settlement in continental

16

Portugal: a relatively developed coastal fringe and complete neglect of the interior.

The nineteenth century was a time of political instability. The invasion by Napoleon and his troops in 1807 forced King João VI to flee to Brazil with his court. English troops under command of Lord Beresford were able to push back the French from Portuguese territory and to establish a regency on behalf of King João. Then in 1820 a liberal revolution deposed Beresford and the new Constituent Assembly adopted a radical constitution based on political liberalism, popular sovereignty and universal suffrage. The new political elite demanded that the king return home as soon as possible (Marques, 1981).

In the first half of the nineteenth century Portugal was also stricken by the struggle between the pretender to the throne, Dom Miguel, who wanted to restore the absolutism of the ancien régime, and Dom Pedro, the son of João VI, who strove to introduce a more moderate, liberal constitution.

Only in the second half of the nineteenth century did the Portuguese constitutional monarchy become more stable and a two-party system modelled on the English example was established. The Regeneration Party (*Partido Regenerador*) and the Progressive Party (*Partido Progressista*) alternated in power between 1841 and 1910. This system of alternation was called *rotativismo* and was based on patronage. An 'electoral machine' consisting of influential local bosses, called *caciques*, ensured that the elections would bring the desired results. In this regard *caciquismo* was a major pillar of the constitutional monarchy and was possible because more than 70 per cent of the population lived in rural areas and were illiterate. Illiteracy and lack of income were the major reasons put forward for the exclusion of the general population from the political system, backed up by a very restrictive electoral law.

In the first decade of the twentieth century political violence and instability rapidly eroded the power of the political regime. In 1907 King Carlos I empowered Prime Minister João Franco to establish a dictatorship. One year later the king and his son Luis Filipe were assassinated by republicans. In the latter phase of the constitutional monarchy republicanism became increasingly stronger in urban areas (Sobral and Almeida, 1982–3; Mónica, 1994).

On 5 October 1910 the Portuguese Republic was proclaimed. The new political regime was perceived as a panacea for all the major problems of Portugal and the establishment of the republic was seen as the dawning of a new age. However in practice the republic was stricken by the same problems as the constitutional monarchy. The masses were not incorporated into the political system; nor were the land labourers in the southern province of Alentejo and the emerging working class in the urban centres supported by the new republican government (Oliveira, 1975; Pereira, 1982, pp. 21–76). The elite remained mainly middle class, supported by the lower middle classes in the urban centres. The new republican political system was based on urban patronage to avoid the rural *caciques* influencing the outcome of elections (Lopes, 1994). Anticlericalism and political violence were major factors behind the increasing antagonism between republicans and monarchists.

The sixteen years of Portuguese democracy was based on a very restrictive electoral law that was changed several times during the period of the republic. *Personalismo* (the personalisation of politics and the dominance of personal conflicts in the political field), party factionalism, short-term dictatorships, attempted coup d'états and political violence eventually led to the collapse of the First Republic in Portugal (Wheeler, 1978; Marques, 1980; Vidigal, 1988; Schwartzman, 1987, 1989).

The military coup of 28 May 1926, led by General Afonso Costa, was an attempt to end the unstable and conflict-riven First Republic. It had as its major aim the restoration of political and economic stability. But the inexperienced military found it difficult to establish stability in the first two years of its dictatorship. Then António Oliveira Salazar was appointed finance minister. Salazar asked for absolute power over the financial budgets of other ministries and within a year he had stabilised the economy – within two years he had become the most important member of the cabinet. He built up his personal power inside the cabinet and became prime minister on 28 May 1932 after the resignation of the government of General Júlio Domingos de Oliveira.

Salazar advocated a strongly authoritarian state along corporatist lines and explicitly rejected totalitarianism. The constitution of 1933 enshrined the family, the corporations and local government as the pillars of the *Estado Novo* (New State). The corporatist state saw the family as the first unit of the political system and stroved to present a different model from that of the individualism and liberalism of the First Republic. Salazar's framework was based on the idealised model of the 'paternalist family'. This was possible, because about 70 per cent of the population lived in rural areas and already typified the model. But the harmonious natural order it was supposed to instil was more wishful thinking than reality. Nevertheless the concept of the family and family relations was extended to all fields of political, social and economic life. Salazar contrasted this 'harmonious' corporatist system with the unstable First Republic, which had been stricken by class conflict and liberal individualism (Kay, 1971; Figueiredo, 1976; Lucena, 1976).

However the authoritarian dictatorship of Salazar was in reality based on a 'political economy' of repression (Martins, 1968, p. 329), intended to control all political opposition inside and outside Portugal through censorship and – well into the 1940s – mass illiteracy. Nevertheless one has to acknowledge that the political, economic and social stability achieved during Salazar's dictatorship did improve the standard of living of the population and several long-term projects were launched to improve the Portuguese economy.

The forty-eight years of authoritarian dictatorship can be subdivided into several periods, each lasting up to a decade. The first encompassed the 1930s and involved building up a distinctive corporatist political regime and initiating major campaigns to improve the standard of living of the population (such as the wheat campaign, *campanha do trigo*). It was a period of national autarky and streamlining.

In the second period, 1940–6, Portugal's neutrality during the Second World War brought relative wealth to the country. The political regime was well entrenched in both continental Portugal and the colonies.

The third period coincided with the start of the Cold War in 1947–8, and the creation of Cominform in Warsaw gave the authoritarian regime a feeling of respectability. Although the opposition – consisting of republicans, monarchists and communists – was able to challenge the government in elections, this was without effect because the elections were controlled by the Salazarist electoral machine.

In the fourth period, the 1950s, Portugal joined several international organisations such as the United Nations (UN) and the North Atlantic Treaty Organisation (NATO). The Portuguese economy became more integrated into the world economy.

In the 1960s, the final period, Salazar had to face the rise of anticolonial movements in Mozambique, Angola, Guinea-Bissau and East Timor. Several economic development plans were prepared to bring Portugal up to the level of most West European countries and further improve the standard of living in continental Portugal and the colonies. Economic and social development, tourism, increasing interdependence with other West European countries and media exposure changed the whole social structure of the authoritarian regime. Salazar's successor, Marcelo Caetano, tried to reform the political system after 1968 but failed because of resistance on the part of conservatives in the government, such as president Américo Tomás and the former foreign minister, Franco Nogueira.

The colonial wars could not be won militarily – a political solution was needed. But such a solution was strongly resisted by hardliners in the authoritarian regime and the wars became a decisive factor in the collapse of the regime. A much deeper reason lay in the inability of the dictatorship to deal with the increasing complexity of modern society. The corporatist political structure was inadequate to deal with the dynamic and highly complex society that was emerging, and closing the rift between political structure and social reality was a challenge that the Salazarist regime was unable to meet (Passos, 1987; Schmitter, 1975).

DEMOCRATIC TRANSITION AND REVOLUTION (1974–6)

Transitional processes are characterised by a high level of uncertainty, and the Portuguese case can be cited as one of the most salient examples of a difficult transition to democracy. Developments during the pretransitional period already indicated that the incumbent regime was in permanent crisis, particularly as a result of the colonial wars in Africa. The failure to think of a solution of the colonial problem other than the military one had a negative impact on continental Portugal. This problem had to be solved before Portugal could start to focus on a transition to democracy.

The military coup of 25 April 1974 by the *Movimento das Forças Armadas* (Movement of the Armed Forces – MFA) was primarily a protest against the war policies of the authoritarian regime. The MFA consisted of middle-ranking officers who were fighting in the war theatres of Angola, Mozambique and Guinea-Bissau and following the orders of higher-ranking officers based mainly in Lisbon. They had direct contact with the enemy and knew that they could not win the war, mainly because the colonial liberation movements were highly motivated in their fight against the Portuguese troops. The *Movimento Popular para a Libertação da Angola* (People's Movement for the Liberation of Angola – MPLA), the *Frente Nacional para a Libertação de Angola* (National Front for the Liberation of Angola – FNLA), the *Uniao Nacional para a Independência Total de Angola* (National Union for the Total Independence of Angola – UNITA), the *Frente para a Libertação de Moçambique* (Front for the Liberation of Mozambique) and the *Partido Africano para a Independência de Guiné-Bissau e Cabo Verde* (African Party for the Independence of Guinea-Bissau and Cape Verde Islands – PAIGC) were generally supported by other African anticolonial movements. In addition Western Europe and the United States were broadly sympathetic to Third World independence movements, and Portugal's three-front war was exhausting its human and material resources. The low morale of the Portuguese troops made them more sympathetic to the cause of the African liberation movements. Africa politicised some of the officers into becoming the main protagonists of the revolutionary period in Portugal. They began to reflect on their status as citizens of the authoritarian regime and came to the conclusion that they were in the same situation as the peoples of the colonies. Several secret meetings in Portugal led to the decision to launch the coup d'état.

The coup, organised by Major Otelo Saraiva de Carvalho, unexpectedly turned into a revolution. The people took to the streets, although the MFA had expressedly advised them to stay at home. The authoritarian regime fell like a house of cards (Carvalho, 1986; Harvey, 1978).

Surprised by their own success, a *Junta de Salvação Nacional* (Board of National Salvation – JSN) was constituted under the leadership of the two highest-ranking officers, General António Spinola and General Costa Gomes, who had opposed the regime during its latter phase. Although the real power holders of the movement were middle-ranking officers such as Melo Antunes, Vitor Alves, Otelo Saraiva de Carvalho and Vasco Lourenço, the figurehead during the first months was Antonio Spinola. He was well known for his book *Portugal and the Future*, which advocated the transformation of the Portuguese colonial empire into a Lusitanian Commonwealth, whereby the colonies would become an integral part of Portugal with equal rights (Spinola, 1974). This suggestion was regarded by the regime as highly subversive and by the MFA as highly reactionary (Bruneau, 1984, p. 35). Nevertheless dictator Marcelo Caetano declared he would surrender to the MFA only if he could hand over power directly to General Spinola.

In its first days the new junta announced a programme based on three main aims: decolonisation, democratisation and development. This MFA programme was quite moderate and was intended to become more radical during the revolutionary process (Praça *et al.*, 1974, pp. 184–5).

The first provisional government was not formed until 15 May. A law professor, Adelino de Palma Carlos, was appointed prime minister. All the major political groups were incorporated into the government and even the Communist Party was represented by a minister. Spinola became provisional president.

From the start the new provisional government, though supported by the MFA, was not the only centre of revolutionary power. Already in May social movements were dominating the political field. In the shanty towns of Lisbon, Porto and Setúbal groups of dwellers began to occupy empty houses and establish what would later be called the 'revolutionary legacy'. In enterprises the workers began to establish *comissões de trabalhadores* (workers' committees). These first months of euphoria and power vacuum complicated progress towards democracy in Portugal and it was not certain which kind of democracy would eventually emerge (Ferreira, 1983, pp. 180–2).

The civilian politicians – some of whom had returned from exile, such as the leader of the Socialist Party, Mário Soares, and the leader of the Communist Party, Alvaro Cunhal – from the start were in a disadvantageous position in relation to the revolutionary political actors. In the course of time the members of the MFA became increasingly engaged in the political process and the relationship between the government and the MFA deteriorated, particularly when Palma Carlos put forward a plan to the State Council (the provisional legislative body) to advance the date of the presidential elections so that António Spinola could achieve democratic legitimacy during the transitional process. This was blocked by the MFA members of the State Council and Palma Carlos decided to resign from office on 11 July (Harvey, 1978, p. 22; Eisfeld, 1984, p. 136).

Subsequently the transition to democracy became even more uncertain and the radical faction of the MFA gained even more influence. The new prime minister was brigadier Vasco Gonçalves, who Spinola believed would be more moderate than the other members of the MFA. Some in the MFA were astonished by this appointment because Gonçalves was not one of the leading members and had not been involved in the planning of the coup. It turned out that Gonçalves had been a member of the Communist Party in the 1950s and was still sympathetic to the party.

In the summer of 1974 the relationship between the MFA, President Spinola and the moderate political parties – the Socialist Party (*Partido Socialista* – PS) and the People's Democratic Party (*Partido Popular Democrático* – PPD) deteriorated. The growth of social movements, the steadily decline of industrial production and the increasing politicisation of the MFA had transformed the atmosphere of euphoria that prevailed during the first months after the coup into a revolutionary one that divided the political actors into antifascist and fascist factions.

Spinola was increasingly the prime target of the MFA because he continued to pursue his aim to hold the presidential elections in the summer. Furthermore he disagreed with the decolonisation negotiations of the socialist foreign minister, Mário Soares, and still hoped to achieve a political solution to the colonial problem. The climax of his efforts was his call for a demonstration of the 'silent majority' in Lisbon on 28 September in order to show that the majority of the population supported him. The MFA completely opposed Spinola's plan and believed that he wanted to stage a coup against the government. All roads to the capital were closed and all cars, were searched for weapons. The demonstration, which the MFA called an *intentona* (little coup), did not take place. On 30 September Spinola resigned from office. General Costa Gomes became the new provisional president and a new government under the continuing leadership of brigadier Vasco Gonçalves was formed (*Expresso*, 28 September 1974, p. 1; *Expresso*, 12 September 1974, p. 1; Gallagher, 1983, pp. 206–8).

During autumn 1974 relations between the Socialist Party and the Communist Party deteriorated. The Socialists accused the party of Alvaro Cunhal of trying to dominate the state apparatus and the media. On several occasions Mário Soares expressed his discontentment with this situation. In reality Alvaro Cunhal was not disposed towards radicalisation of the revolution. On the contrary his position was quite moderate in comparison with that of Prime Minister Vasco Gonçalves.

In January 1975 the Socialist Party organised demonstrations against the MFA to prevent the introduction of a single trade union for the working population (*unicidade sindical*). The Communist Party responded with a counterdemonstration supporting the trade union policy of the MFA. The introduction of a single trade union would give a position of monopoly to the Communist Party because the only trade union that existed at that time was the Intersindical, which had been founded in the late phase of the authoritarian dictatorship and was very close to the Communist Party. The Socialist Party was defeated in the 'battle of demonstrations' (Soares, 1975a, pp. 189–201; Zenha, 1976).

The military institutional framework was increasingly becoming the dominant decision-making centre. After 28 September several new organs were founded by the MFA: the Higher Council of the Movement (*Conselho Supremo do Movimento*) and the MFA Assembly (*Assembleia do MFA*). The rapid decolonisation process led to the MFA being closely identified with the African liberation movements.

On 11 March 1975 the revolutionary process entered a new phase. A supposed coup attempt by General Spinola led to further radicalisation of the revolution. Socialisation of all enterprises occupied by workers' committees, legalisation of all land estates occupied by land labourers and an extensive catalogue of social policy measures changed overnight the configuration of forces (Ferreira, 1983, p. 202). The parties were forced to accept the 'Platform Parties–MFA', that is, to accept the leadership of the MFA in the supposed process towards democratisation. To this end the radical faction of the MFA, the Gonçalvists, attempted to devalue the importance of the forthcoming elections.

At that time, the transition to democracy was more uncertain than ever, the revolutionary command was not subject to democratic accountability and the MFA and the 'Platform' agreed that this would continue to be the case in spite of the elections. During March and April they continued to discredit the forthcoming elections. Shortly before the elections the Gonçalvists advised the electorate to leave their ballot papers blank (Harsgor, 1975, pp. 172–3).

In spite of all this the first free elections based on universal suffrage were held without major difficulties. The results were speculated on television and political leaders were interviewed about their expectations. This long night of excitement and novelty had an incredible impact on the population and the whole revolutionary process.

The elections resulted in a resounding victory for the moderate parties. The Socialist Party gained a majority with 34.71 per cent of the votes, followed by the PPD with 24.25 per cent, the Communist Party with 11.44 per cent, the CDS with 7 per cent and the UDP with 0.79 per cent. In the aftermath of the elections the political scene became even more conflictual. The MFA described the elections as a necessary step towards socialism, while the moderate parties increasingly distanced themselves from the emerging revolutionary political system installed by the military. The Socialist Party opposed the MFA's plan to create a Higher Revolutionary Court based on the principles of the 'revolutionary legacy' (Hespanha, 1986).

The seizure of the Socialist Party newspaper *A República* on 19 May by a tiny left-wing party called the Movement for the Reorganisation of the Party of the Proletariat (*Movimento para a Reorganização do Partido do Proletariado* – MRPP) led to a more full-frontal opposition by the Socialists against the MFA (Eisfeld, 1984, pp. 124–6).

Due to this polarisation between the Socialist Party and the Communist Party on the one hand, and the Socialist Party and the MFA on the other, the military movement began to split apart between June and August 1975. The different factions inside the MFA – the communist-influenced Goncalvists; the supporters of the left-wing popular-power model, represented by Otelo Saraiva de Carvalho and the special police force (COPCON) under his command; and the Third-World-socialist followers of Melo Antunes – began to present their individual models of pluralist socialism. This split in the MFA led to the downfall of Prime Minister Vasco Gonçalves, who in August 1975 tried to form a government consisting mainly of members sympathetic to the Communist Party. Gonçalves was forced to step down in September (Louça, 1985, pp. 149–61).

A sixth provisional government, under the leadership of Prime Minister Admiral Pinheiro de Azevedo, restored the broad coalition of political parties that had existed before August 1975.

The new government was confronted with a high degree of political, social and economic instability. While the political field was still dominated by the social movements, at the elite level the impasse continued between the political parties, representatives of the new democratic legitimacy, and the MFA, the guarantor of the revolutionary legacy. Military indiscipline in the barracks was growing steadily. The appearance of a soldiers' movement during the autumn added to the radical atmosphere. The *Soldados Unidos Vencerão* (United Soldiers Will Win – SUV) tried to reverse the process towards democratisation.

Moreover the government was continually challenged by social movements during the autumn. Political strikes, demonstrations and the occupation of houses and landed estates led to increasing anarchy in Portugal. No centre of power was able to gain a position strong enough to swing this uncertain situation in its favour.

The climax of all this was the one-day sequestration of the government in the Palace of São Bento on 12 November by 20–30 000 construction workers demanding higher wages. Even the revolutionary police force, COPCON, under the leadership of Otelo Saraiva de Carvalho, was in sympathy with the construction workers. Only Captain Jaime Neves was able to dissolve the demonstration.

The growing number of strikes during this period caused the government to go on strike too, on 19 November, in protest at the continuing obstruction of their work by the different political actors in the revolutionary process, and in particular at the demands of the social movements (OS SUV, 1975; Downs, 1989).

On 25 November 1975 a supposedly left-wing coup, supported by some members of the MFA, was crushed by a countercoup under the command of Lieutenant-Colonel António Ramalho Eanes. This led to the collapse of the revolutionary process and the steady normalisation of political life (Antunes, 1979).

The sixth provisional government continued its work until 22 July 1976 and made preparations for the final transition to democracy. During this period the parties signed a second agreement with the MFA, whereby the revolutionary council would continue to supervise the process of democratisation for the next five years.

The next big event was the legislative election of 25 April 1976. This confirmed the majority of the Socialist Party, which gained 34.87 per cent of the votes and 106 seats. The PPD/PSD gained 24.38 per cent and 71 seats, the CDS 16 per cent and 42 seats, the PCP 14.35 per cent and 40 seats and the UDP 1.67 per cent and one seat.

The first legislature of the new political system was to convene after approval of the constitution on 2 July 1976. On 27 July 1976 the presidential elections were held and Lieutenant-Colonel Ramalho Eanes ramped to victory with 61.5 per cent of the votes. The left-wing candidate, Otelo Saraiva de Carvalho, gained 16.5 per cent, Pinheiro de Azevedo 14.4 per cent and the communist candidate 7.6 per cent. Ramalho Eanes was to become crucial to the consolidation of democracy in Portugal.

The new constitution was based on a semipresidential form of government, so that a repeat of the political and parliamentary instability of the first republic at the beginning of the century could be avoided. The new president represented the military power still embodied in the MFA, which intended to take its supervisory role, defined in the 'Platform Parties–MFA', very seriously. The polarised atmosphere of the revolutionary process would continue to persist throughout the consolidation period. The constitution, which reflected to a high degree the different political designs put forward during the revolutionary period, became the main target of these polarised politics until 1982 (Constitution, 1976).

In sum, the transitional period was quite uncertain until the constitution was approved. The struggle between the different political actors to gain control over the political field led to a general impasse in late 1975. Even after the successful coup by General Ramalho Eanes the political field remained quite unstable.

The only person to provide stability during the early stages of the consolidation period that followed was Ramalho Eanes, now president of the republic. This was an important period in which to overcome differences, judge the strengths and weaknesses of the new political system and guage its boundaries. The prerequisite for this was consensus on democratic attitudes and behaviour. The crafting of democracy is an open-ended process.

DEMOCRATIC CONSOLIDATION REEQUILIBRATING THE POLITY (1976–82)

The economic policies of the first constitutional government, under the leadership of socialist Mário Soares, were aimed at stabilising the economy. A major element of Soares' strategy was integration into the European Community, so in 1977 Portugal submitted its application for membership. However the main priority of the government was to restore international confidence in the Portuguese market. The government's austerity policies were quite controversial, both in parliament and in society as a whole, and there was a collapse of the assumption that the government would emphasise purely socialist strategies aimed at long-term changes to society and the political system. Those in power had to acknowledge that their policy options were very restricted. The excesses of the revolution had led to a collapse of the Portuguese economy, which was now very vulnerable to global economic processes. Broadening the scope government policy options in an open economy has to be based on international actors' confidence in the national market. This principally means that the first priority of a government has to be the restoration and preservation of stability (Kolm, 1975–6, 1977; Rother, 1984).

This was the main problem for Soares. In a sense he was between the devil and the deep blue sea. On the one hand, as his government was a minority one it was highly dependent upon the support of parliament, which was very fragmented. On the other hand he had to keep the Socialist Party united behind the government's programme. In reality he was unable to achieve the continuous support of either. Moreover the government team was inexperienced and lacked a sufficient number of qualified personnel, and the government as well as the party was split into revolutionary and reformist factions (Rother, 1985). Many government members, such as the minister of agriculture, António Lopes Cardoso, were quite supportive of the new revolutionary institutions (Magone, 1995a, p. 98). All this was exacerbated by the fact that the actors in the new political system were still in the process of gauging the boundaries of their political activities. The end result was that this first constitutional government resigned at the end of December 1977 due to lack of parliamentary support.

The climate of uncertainty and policy inconsistency did little to improve the Portuguese economy. On the contrary, the economic and social situation became even more dire. The second constitutional government, again under Mário Soares and supported by the conservative

Christian-Democratic Party (The CDS), attempted to stabilise the economy with the help of the International Monetary Fund. However this coalition was doomed to fail because of its ideological diversity. It lasted only until July 1978.

Because of the governmental impasse, President Ramalho Eanes decided to nominate an independent as prime minister. The three so-called 'presidential governments' between August 1978 and December 1979 did not manage to stabilise the economy. On the contrary, the situation was worsened by the implementation of IMF austerity measures. In addition the autumn 1978 budget of the second presidential government was rejected, and only after intervention by Eanes was it finally approved in May 1979. All this contributed to political as well as economic instability. The only stable factors were the president and the semipresidential form of government defined in the constitution.

The presidential governments were not supported by parliament and governmental work was constantly obstructed by the political parties. Behind this was resentment that General Ramalho Eanes was bypassing the legitimate democratic processes of the country. On 13 October 1979 he finally announced that interim elections would take place on 2 December. These elections brought victory to a centre–right coalition, the *Aliança Democrática* (Democratic Alliance – AD), consisting of the liberal PPD/PSD, the Christian-democratic CDS and the People's Monarchic Party (*Partido Popular Monárquico* – PPM). The AD gained 44.9 per cent of the votes and 158 seats, the PS 27.33 per cent and 74 seats, the PCP 14.35 per cent and 40 seats and the UDP 1.67 per cent and one seat.

The AD's victory was repeated in the legislative elections on 5 October 1980 with a further gain in votes and seats: 47.36 per cent of the votes and 166 seats. The socialist alliance, the *Frente Republicana Socialista* (Republican Socialist Front – FRS), gained 26.65 per cent of the votes and 71 seats, and the communist alliance, *Aliança Povo Unido* (United People's Alliance – APU), 16.75 per cent and 41 seats. This repeat victory promised greater stability for the political and party systems. On the whole one can indeed say that the level of instability decreased substantially because of the absolute majority of the coalition government.

Nevertheless disputes between the coalition partners increased over time. Between January 1980 and June 1983 the coalition formed four governments. The death of the charismatic leader of the PPD, Francisco Sá Carneiro, on 4 December 1980 in a plane crash led to even more disputes within the coalition. Governmental work was also constrained by the dominant role Ramalho Eanes was playing in foreign and defence policy. The reelection of Eanes as president on 7 December 1980 with 56.4 per cent of the votes meant that the new government would have to take his position into consideration at some point in the future. Therefore one of the main constituents of the new government's programme was revision of the constitution.

The Council of the Revolution's five-year supervisory role was almost at an end, so the civilian politicians saw an opportunity to diminish the role of the military in the political system.

The new prime minister after Sá Carneiro's death was the media tycoon Francisco Pinto Balsemão, who had great difficulty in keeping his party and the PSD members of the government behind him. On 9 September 1981 the government resigned (Stock, 1985a, 1989a).

The second government of Pinto Balsemão (September 1981 to December 1982) was successful in achieving its main aim: revision of the constitution. The main changes to the very socialist constitution of 1976 were abolition of the Council of the Revolution and its replacement by the Constitutional Court, and a weakening of the presidency in the Portuguese political system (Gomes, 1982, pp. 38–9).

Abolition of the Council of the Revolution meant the end of the supervisory role of the MFA and the 'civilianisation' of the political system. The power to monitor the constitutionality of law making and application were transferred to the new Constitutional Court, and thus the coexisting principles of revolutionary legacy and democratic legitimacy came to an end (Bruneau, 1984, pp. 81–2).

Experiences in this early consolidation period led to the conviction that the 'semipresidential' nature of the political system was impeding governmental work. Accordingly the AD and the PS agreed to reduce some of the powers of the president, such as his right to veto legislation and other aspects of government. The revised constitution was approved on 14 August 1982. Interestingly, the majority of the population were completely unaware that there had been a constitutional revision (Eisfeld, 1984, pp. 183–204; Bruneau, 1984, pp. 89–106).

The coalition government was facing several difficulties in different policy areas. Inertia in some of the ministries – for example, health, social affairs and education – prevented an overall reform of the state. This was exacerbated by internal divisions in the coalition government. In view of all these problems and the permanently poor economic situation, Pinto Balsemão resigned from office in December 1982. New elections were called for April 1983.

To sum up, this early period of consolidation was characterised by a high degree of instability in the political, economic, social and cultural spheres, a legacy of the revolutionary period. The search for a new democratic idiom was a major obstacle of the government, due to the fact that Ramalho Eanes interfered quite often in political life. The turbulence was also a reflection of the intensity of the activities of the political elite.

However, it was also a time of political learning, and in particular the actors had to learn to deal with and act within the new political structures set up by the constitution. Inexperience in political life, a tendency to personalise politics, antagonism between the revolutionary legacy and democratic legitimacy, the mixed cultural idiom – of patrimonial practices, of radical politics and of incipient democratic behaviour – were major factors preventing the stabilisation of the political system. Vulnerability to external influences, particularly in the economic sector, can be regarded as a major destabilising factor as well, for example the growing disappointment among the political elite and the population that membership of the European Community was continuously postponed.

REGAINING POLITICAL STABILITY (1983–7)

During the early consolidation period major advances were made in the formation of the political and party systems, and the first outlines of the new political regime were drawn. Having experienced socialist minority governments, presidential governments and alliance governments, the political elites were confronted with a wide range of governmental options. The narrow victory of the Socialist Party in the legislative elections of 1983 added a further option to this list: the *Bloco Central* (Central Bloc). In the elections the PS gained 36.12 per cent of the votes and 101 seats, the PPD/PSD 27.24 per cent and 75 seats, the communist alliance (APU) a surprising 18.07 per cent and 44 seats and the CDS 12.5 per cent and 30 seats. The communists offered themselves as coalition partners to the socialists, but Mário Soares preferred to form a coalition with the PPD/PSD so that a government of national consensus could act to resolve most of the problems of the Portuguese economy. After negotiations between the two parties a coalition agreement was reached on 4 June 1983. The new prime minister would be Mário Soares and the deputy prime minister Mota Pinto.

The main priority of the government was to stabilise the economic situation. The PS had already announced before the elections that it would implement a programme of 'a hundred measures in a hundred days', aimed at structural reform of the public sector and stabilisation of the economy. Central to this programme was implementation of a new IMF austerity programme (Stock, 1985b, 1989b, pp. 157–61). This required a high degree of fiscal restraint in the public sector. Prime Minister Mário Soares promised that in 1984 the social costs of the austerity policy would be compensated by redistributive policies. This promise was not kept and the structural reforms failed to materialise (Ferreira, 1985, pp. 727–30; Cravinho, 1986a, pp. 586–90). In addition, divisions inside the PPD/PSD made it difficult to pursue consistent policies, and the atmosphere within the coalition as a whole was soured by disagreements over public appointments. Moreover Soares' intention to run for the presidency in 1986 had a negative impact on all governmental work.

Growing discontent of the PSD basis with the coalition was expressed during the eleventh and twelfth party congresses, in 1984 and 1985 respectively. The Socialist Party's announcement of the presidential candidature of Mário Soares was contrary to the coalition agreement, which stated that neither side would put up a candidate that had not been agreed by the other. As a consequence a new party leader was elected during the twelfth party congress in May 1985: Anibal Cavaco Silva, an economics professor in the Faculty of Economics at Lisbon's Technical University and finance minister in the first AD government under Sá Carneiro in 1980–1 (Opello, 1991, pp. 114–16). The new leader withdraw the PSD ministers from the Central Bloc government in June 1985 and President Ramalho Eanes had to call for early elections.

In the elections of October 1985 the Socialist Party's share of the votes fell by nearly 16 per cent. The winner was the PPD/PSD with 29.87 per cent of the votes and 88 seats. The other parties lost in terms of both votes and seats. The PS secured 20.77 per cent of the votes and 57 of the seats, the communist coalition (APU) 17.92 per cent and 38 seats, and the CDS 9.96 per cent and 22 seats. The surprising factor in these elections was the relative success of the Party of Democratic Renewal (*Partido Renovador Democratico* – PRD), which was tacitly supported by President Ramalho Eanes. The PRD intended to challenge the existing political forces and bring about a renewal of the political system. Ideologically it was on the centre of the political spectrum, between the socialists and the social democrats. It won almost 18 per cent of the votes and 45 seats. A new minority government was formed under the leadership of Anibal Cavaco Silva, who counted on the parliamentary support of the PRD.

The economic situation improved substantially towards the end of 1985, bolstered by pre-accession EC aid. Portugal's accession to the European Community on 1 January 1986 rapidly restored international confidence in the Portuguese market. Cavaco Silva's emphasis on economic and political stability related to the fact that stability was needed for Portugal's successful integration into the EC. The flow of structural funds during 1986 and 1987 contributed substantially to the further stabilisation of both the economic and the political systems. While in 1981–5 GDP had grown by just 0.8 per cent per year an average (the EC average was 1.6 per cent), in 1986–90 it rose to an average of 4.6 per cent (EC average 3 per cent).

In the meantime the opposition had become quite split. The PS had been weakened by the bad results of 1985; the socialist secretary-general, Almeida Santos, had been replaced by Jaime Gama; and in the CDS Freitas do Amaral had stepped down as leader and replaced by a university professor, Adriano Moreira (Eisfeld, 1989; Opello, 1991, pp. 120–2).

The presidential elections of 26 January/16 February 1986 led to the victory of Mário Soares. In the second round Soares won 51.3 per cent of the votes, closely followed by the conservative candidate, Freitas Amaral, with 48.7 per cent. The importance of these results was that for the first time in the young Portuguese democracy a civilian president had been elected.

The cooperation between the socialist Mário Soares and the liberal Anibal Cavaco Silva added a further dimension to the repertoire of political choices in the new democracy.

The PRD remained an ambivalent party, fluctuating between opposition to and support of the government. On the question of the budget it tended to align with the opposition parties – the PS and the PCP – despite its promise to support the government. When Cavaco Silva asked for the adoption of a supplementary budget in September 1986 he was vigorously opposed by the PRD, the PS and the PCP.

Cavaco Silva was scoring well in the opinion polls and cited the tension between the opposition and his government as a reason for the need to call early elections. Meanwhile the leader of the PRD, Hermínio Martins, was replaced by General Ramalho Eanes during the party's national convention in October 1986. The polarisation of the PRD and the government led to the 1985 agreement being broken (Opello, 1991, pp. 122–6; Gallagher, 1988).

By the end 1986 Cavaco Silva had no parliamentary support. Now leading a very fragile government, he tried to hold on for as long as he could, so that in the event of early elections he could blame the opposition for undermining the work of the government. After a motion of censure by the PRD, because of the permanent impasse between the Assembly of the Republic and the government, Cavaco Silva's cabinet collapsed. President Mário Soares called for early elections to take place on 19 July 1987.

In the elections the PPD/PSD gained the first absolute majority of the young democracy, winning 50.22 per cent of the votes and 148 seats. The PS gained 22.24 per cent of the votes and 60 seats, the communist *Coligação Democrática Unitária* (United Democratic Coalition – CDU) 12.24 per cent and 31 seats, the CDS 4.44 per cent and four seats, and the PRD 4.91 per cent and seven seats.

Several factors had contributed to the PPD/PSD victory. First, the improved economic situation due to European integration and the restoration of international confidence in the Portuguese market had bolstered Prime Minister Cavaco Silva's standing. Second, the electorate had wanted to show its opposition to the motion of censure undertaken by the opposition. Third, Cavaco Silva's American-style electoral campaign had been successful in attracting popular support. His main slogan had been *Portugal não pode parar* (Portugal cannot stop now), suggesting the necessity to continue the economic-development policies that had been initiated by his minority government (*O Jornal*, 24 July 1987, pp. 18–19; *Expresso*, 25 July 1987, pp. 32–3; Gallagher, 1988).

Cavaco Silva's victory initiated a new phase in the young history of Portuguese democracy and his absolute majority brought stability to the political, economic and social systems. In spite of the negative features inherent in an absolute-majority government, it did herald a qualitative change towards stable political behaviour and policy formulation in the long term. Integration into Europe reinforced this and resulted in a more pragmatic style of Portuguese politics.

DEMOCRATIC CONSOLIDATION AND EUROPEAN INTEGRATION (1987–95)

Accession to the EC on 1 January 1986 was regarded as a new chance for Portugal. However the flow of structural funds in the first years after accession tended to be squandered on dubious projects. The actual coordination of funds started only in 1989, after the reform of structural funds at the EC level. In cooperation with the Commission, the Portuguese government designed several programmes that were tailored to meet the needs of economic restructuring (Eisfeld, 1989; Eaton, 1994; Corkill, 1993a).

Cavaco Silva's government attempted to achieve a higher level of professionalism during this period and the technocratic nature of his government conformed quite well with the culture of the European institutions. Portugal's accession to the EC coincided with the adoption of the Single European Act (SEA) and progress towards the Single European Market (SEM). In this sense the policies of the government were geared towards improving the competitiveness of the Portuguese economy. The short time in which they had to prepare and implement their various programmes and projects put considerable pressure on the fledgling administrative structures, but nevertheless Portugal experienced an economic boom in 1989 and 1990 and private investment grew to high levels in the early 1990s (Hudson, 1994, p. 11).

These favourable economic conditions were mirrored by the political system. The relationship between the various institutions improved and became more routine. In particular the cooperation between President Mário Soares and Anibal Cavaco Silva seemed to be working well. This was confirmed by the support given by the PSD to the reelection of Soares on 13 January 1991. He won the first round outright with an overwhelming 70.4 per cent. The conservative candidate, Basílio Horta, won 14.1 per cent of the votes, the communist candidate, Carlos Carvalhas, 12.9 per cent and Carlos Marques da Silva 2.6 per cent.

A further boost to stability was a repeat of Cavaco Silva's absolute majority in the legislative elections of 6 October 1991, although this was essentially because the opposition parties had been unable to present a suitable alternative. In addition, the fact that Portugal's forthcoming presidency of the EC would require a stable government played an important role in determining the choice of the electorate.

The programme of the new PSD government encompassed four leading principles for the further consolidation of democracy in Portugal: (1) modernisation of the state and assertion of a Portuguese identity; (2) commitment to the market economy and the need for economic and social development; (3) investing in the future of society; and (4) strengthening solidarity and improving standard of living. A very ambitious programme of modernisation was linked to these four guiding principles, as well as Europeanisation of the political system (Stock, 1992, pp. 505–11).

The great challenge for Cavaco Silva's government was the presidency of the Council of Ministers of the European Community in the first half of 1992. For the first time in its history Portugal was holding the presidency of a group of nations and influencing policy formulation and policy making at the supranational level. The most important issues during the Portuguese presidency were reform of the Common Agricultural Policy (CAP), the break-up of former Yugoslavia and the international conference on the environment, held in Rio.

In the second half of 1992 the economic situation in Portugal began to deteriorate. The forthcoming SEM was causing major difficulties for Portuguese industry, and the announcement by the Commission that the deadline of the transitional period allowed to Portuguese agriculture and fisheries (1996) would be anulled in view of the competitive law policy of the SEM was a further blow to the economy. In 1993 the fisheries and agriculture sectors and small and medium-sized industries were finding it difficult to cope with the competition arising from the SEM. This state of affairs continued until 1994 and caused a major crisis of legitimacy for the government of Cavaco Silva. Exacerbating the situation was the fact that the first common support framework (CSF) of the EC had expired and the new one was not due to commence until 1994.

The government came under increasing attack from the opposition. Moreover the cooperation between President Mário Soares and Cavaco Silva began to deteriorate. The open presidency (*presidência aberta*) of Mário Soares in autumn 1992 brought to the fore the extremely bad living conditions in the shanty towns around Lisbon. Soares also vetoed some of the government's draft laws, such as the anticorruption law and the plan to change fees in public universities (see Chapter 3).

Although the relationship between Soares and Cavaco Silva improved slightly during 1994, the popularity of the government continued to fall because of growing disatisfaction among the population and several allegations of corruption (Magone, 1994). In February 1995 Cavaco Silva announced he would step down as prime minister before the next elections, probably in October 1995. He also resigned his presidency of the party. In the party congress of February 1995, Franco Nogueira, the present foreign minister, was elected as new leader of the PSD. (It has been speculated that Cavaco Silva wants to run for the presidency in early 1996.)

To sum up, on the whole the European integration process and the process of democratic consolidation have had a positive spillover effect on each other and democracy in Portugal is well-established. The two absolute electoral majorities of the PSD made a major contribution to regularising and professionalising the political arena. Nevertheless the recent economic and social crisis shows that the economic structures are still inadequate and ill-adapted to the challenges of the SEM.

PERSPECTIVES OF DEMOCRATIC INSTITUTIONALISATION

As the consolidation phase comes to an end in the political field, a new process has already emerged: democratic institutionalisation, or the transformation of formal democracy into a qualitative one. This process emphasises the social and cultural basis of democracy. Democracy becomes internalised by the population and forms an integral part of the way they act. The most important component of the process is a strong education sector, in which the young are socialised into democratic practices. This kind of overall educational network is still very weak in Portugal, although it made considerable progress in the 1980s and early 1990s. Democratic institutionalisation also means that formal institutions abound with democratic practices and routines.

Developing a culture of democracy will be a crucial element in making Portuguese democracy sustainable, and the incorporation of socially disadvantaged groups will be one of its major tasks. Growing awareness in civil society, particularly in environmental matters, may be a sign that Portugal has already embarked on this process. Moreover the European integration process has emphasised the need to overcome the 'democratic deficit' of the supranational EC institutions – the Council and the Commission. Democratisation and increased transparency have become closely intertwined with European integration.

The process of institutionalising a democracy is a long-term, almost open-ended one and only when a democracy is able to survive in times of crisis can one assert that it has been successful.

3 Structuring the Political System

THE CHANGING NATURE OF POLITICAL INSTITUTIONS

Events following the breakdown of communism in Eastern and Central Europe have illustrated the fact that political institutional arrangements are crucial to the development of a successful democracy. The growing interdependence of nation-states and the globalisation of everyday life are putting pressure on nation-states that are still nationally oriented to change their structure, nature and culture. This aspect of institutional change became quite evident in the 1980s and early 1990s. The rapid advances in production technology, the transformation of class-based societies into knowledge-based ones and the reemergence of economic and political liberalism have led to a change of confining conditions for the development of present-day nation-states. The need to develop a more flexible state structure and culture have made it necessary to dismantle the institutional arrangements of the welfare state.

The idea of the 'competition state' emerged in the 1980s and is still in the making. It is a flexible institutional arrangement that delegates former powers of the public sector to the private sector. Public policy becomes privatised, segmented and local. The ideology that a national core of public policies should be undertaken by the state is questioned.

In this regard the political institutional system was one of the first victims of this shift at global level. In the case of Portugal the transition from an authoritarian political regime to democracy was accompanied by many problems of adjustment. The complete collapse of the authoritarian regime left an institutional vacuum that was first filled by revolutionary institutions in 1974–5 and only afterwards replaced by democratic representative ones. This structural change had to be followed by the development of a democratic cultural code inside the institutions. This was made possible by the gradual consolidation and institutionalisation of democracy in Portugal. In this process the Portuguese elites had to comply with the international *zeitgeist* of liberalism and democratisation and follow the prescriptions of international and supranational organisations (the EU, the IMF and the World Bank).

The Portuguese example tells us principally that institutional reshaping is heavily dependent on international factors. To an extent, the devising of the new Portuguese system has been conditioned by the demands of the global system. In the two decades of Portuguese democracy the constitution of 1976 has been revised three times to comply with the demands of the international system.

The original Marxist-inspired constitution included both revolutionary and representative Western-style elements. This eclectic document was highly controversial among the political elite. The right-wing CDS voted against the constitution and the PPD/PSD became the main actor in the process of constitutional revision (Lopes, 1976). Five years after the revolution the first constitutional revision led to the abolition of the Council of the Revolution, the highly controversial supervisional body of the MFA, and to the political system being handed over to civilians. In place of the Council, the Constitutional Court was set up to watch over the constitutionality of law and political decision making.

The constitutional revision was also aimed at giving greater authority to the government *vis-à-vis* the president of the republic. The post-revolutionary phase of democratic consolidation was characterised by a semipresidential system, surpassed only by the French and Finnish systems (Domingos, 1980, p. 122). This system was watered down by increasing the authority of the government and the Assembly of the Republic. The constitution still advocated 'transition to a classless society', but the revisions strengthened the model of a representative political system (Bruneau, 1984, pp. 138–9).

The second constitutional revision (1989) focused on its economic provisions. The revision adapted the constitution to the liberal international climate and Portugal's recent membership of the European Community. Above all, it was intended to change all the provisions inherited from the revolution aimed at protecting the huge public-enterprise sector. With the new constitutional arrangement, privatisation of these enterprises was regarded as the main objective of the liberal Social-Democratic Party, led by the economist Anibal Cavaco Silva. The constitution was also freed of all references to Marxism and Socialism, and it became quite West European in nature.

The third constitutional revision (1992) was undertaken because of the Treaty on the European Union (TEU). Several arrangements had to be made to cope with ratification of the treaty. The most affected institution was the Assembly of the Republic, which gained the additional power of monitoring and evaluating the process of European integration.

A fourth constitutional revision is currently being discussed by the major political parties, a major issue being regionalisation of the Portuguese political system, which is still highly centralised.

This constant changing of constitutional provisions is affecting institutional arrangements in Portugal, but the changing nature of political institutions is a general characteristic of modernity. The growth in complexity of political, economic and social structures is having a spillover effect on institutional arrangements. Political stability can be only achieved if institutions are flexible and adaptable, because the political instruments of the nation-state are increasingly affected and influenced by externalities. The Portuguese political system was able to achieve a high degree of stability at the end of the 1980s because the constitutional provisions had been made more flexible.

The impact upon the institutional setting was quite considerable, because the political system became more stable in the past two decades. This was only possible because the political elites were able to see the many frictions between the different institutions and were prepared to change it to achieve a better functioning among them. The two decades of institutional re-arrangement made it possible that consolidation and institutionalisation of democracy became more a process oriented to the future. Internationally, this adaptation was regarded as positive and this further reinforced the stabilisation of the democratic structures.

Further elements of a stabilisation of a political system are the routinisation of procedures and the professionalisation of the political elite inside the institutional setting.

The former became only possible in the second half of the 1980s when the majority government of Cavaco Silva restored the supremacy of the state as the main steering factor of society, economy and politics. The legitimacy of a government is related, too, to the ability to achieve compliance of law. A good performance of the government may be followed by dissemination to other aspects of social and economic life.

The two absolute majority governments of Anibal Cavaco Silva since 1987 led to a qualitative change of this routinisation. Hand in hand one has to see the professionalisation of politicians. A new political regime requires a political elite who adopts and internalises the logics of democratic government. This happened in the second half of the 1980s when personalism and factionalism were replaced by more moderate forms of political behaviour.

THE PRESIDENCY OF THE REPUBLIC: SYMBOL OF POLITICAL STABILITY

The Portuguese constitution of 1976 reflected the prevailing configuration of military and civilian power. As discussed earlier, the first president to be elected by universal suffrage was general António Ramalho Eanes – figure head of the newly integrated military-political system, head of the armed forces and president of the Council of the Revolution. The second pact between the MFA and the political parties assured the continuing dominance of the military in the development of the new political system.

The president played a pivotal role in preserving the stability of the new political system. This was vital because the early phase of consolidation was characterised by a very fragmented, factionalised parliament with a minority government. His interventionist role was regarded as important in preventing Portugal from falling back into the political instability of the first republic, and his almost two-thirds majority in the presidential elections gave him a high degree of legitimacy.

The failure of the socialist minority governments between 1976 and 1978 further increased Eanes' role in stabilising the political system. Instead of calling for new elections he decided to nominate independents to form a caretaker government. The three 'presidential governments' in 1978–9 made the new civilian political elite aware that the military dimension of the new political system was still very much intact. Consequently the right–centre coalition government of the Democratic Alliance made it a priority to abolish the Revolutionary Council and reduce the role of the president.

The conflict between the president and the Democratic Alliance became evident during Eanes' reelection campaign. His candidacy was opposed by the leader of the Alliance, Sá Carneiro, who supported Soares Carneiro, a right-wing military candidate. Nonetheless Eanes was reelected in 1981 and maintained his left-wing stance throughout his presidency. Relations between the presidency and the government remained tense. The president continued to dominate the political affairs of the country because governmental instability due to internal differences among the coalition partners continued to prevail.

With the constitutional revision of 1982 the military dimension of the new political system was abolished and the powers of the president in relation to those of the prime minister were restricted (Matos, 1983, pp. 254–61). Nevertheless Eanes was able to play a semipresidential role because of the instability of the successive coalition governments.

Until 1986 the political system was characterised by tension between the president and the prime minister. This was particularly the case during the time of the Central Bloc government (1983–5) under the leadership of Mário Soares, of whose austerity policies the president was very critical.

In 1985 a party supporting the president, the PRD, was founded by Herminio Martins as an alternative to existing parties. From 1986 the PRD was headed by Ramalho Eanes. The formation of the party partly related to the fact that the military wanted to continue to play an important part in the political system, even though the military aspect of the constitution had been abolished in 1983. The PRD became a very conflictual party that eventually discredited itself in the eyes of the population and caused a swing towards the PSD, which resulted in the latter's absolute majority in the 1987 elections (Cruz, 1994, pp. 252–3).

The election of Mário Soares to the presidency in 1986 marked the end of the military's importance in governmental affairs as the new socialist president further consolidated the 'civilianisation' of the political system. Soares avoided conflict with the right–liberal PSD government – his was a cooperative presidency that supported the government in achieving successful integration into the European Community. The president's support of the government was criticised by the opposition, particularly the socialists, but he was eager to foster 'institutional solidarity' in this his first presidency (Cruz, 1994, pp. 253–8). The only major critical actions that he had to undertake were dissolution of the Assembly and dismissal of the PSD minority government in 1987 after a successful motion of no confidence, initiated by the PRD. The absolute majority of the PSD in the elections of 17 July 1987 became a further factor of stability.

The first presidency of Mário Soares introduced a more popular approach towards the office. The *presidências abertas* in all parts of the country contributed to an increase of the popularity of the president and to greater solidarity between Lisbon and the less-developed regions of Portugal, as well as helping to enhance the importance of the office of the president.

The spirit of cooperation that prevailed until 1991 changed completely after the overwhelming victory of Soares in the presidential elections of late 1991, supported by the PSD government and the Socialist Party. The PSD's absolute majority in the 1991 elections led to a more critical and oppositional role on the part of the president. Because, according to the Portuguese constitution Soares could not be reelected to a third term he felt free to criticise the government. The open presidencies, the emerging civil associations, the courts and the Socialist Party at various times were all allies of the president against the government.

During the second terms of the PSD government the Portuguese political system again became rather semipresidential in nature. Presidential visits, particularly to the shanty-towns of Lisbon in autumn 1992, were designed to expose the failures of the PSD government. The new independent television channel, owned by media tycoon Francisco Balsemão, gave extensive coverage to this event.

The reemergence of semipresidentialism could also be observed in the vetoing of several governmental bills, such as the anticorruption bill, the bill for the reform of the armed forces and the highly controversial bill to introduce higher fees for higher education in 1992–3. Between 1986 and 1992 Soares sent 26 bills that had been approved by the government or the Assembly of the Republic to the Constitutional Court to determine their constitutionality – 19 of these were declared unconstitutional (Cruz, 1994, pp. 254–62; *Expresso*, 18 July 1992, pp. 26–30, 13 July 1992, p. 3, 7 July 1992, p. 3).

The climax of Soares' semipresidentialist stance was his support for a congress on 'Portugal, what Future?' (*Portugal, Que Futuro?*), held by left-wing intellectuals in March 1994, which turned into a forum in which to criticise the government's policies. The leader of the Socialist Party, Antonio Guterres, distanced himself from the president's activities, and after the congress Soares' popularity fell to an historical low.

During this period there were rumours that the president wanted to dismiss the government and call for new elections. The argument was that Portugal was experiencing a social and economic crisis and therefore the president had the authority to dismiss the government (Magone, 1996). This claim could not be supported by the constitution, which clearly states that 'The president of the republic may, after seeking the opinion of the Council of State, dismiss the government when necessary to safeguard the proper functioning of the democratic institutions' (Constitution, 1995, Article 198(2), p. 120).

Although Prime Minister Anibal Cavaco Silva attempted to exert his influence on the members of the Constitutional and Auditing Courts, and to have the constitution changed so that these would be answerable to the executive, his wishes never materialised and the counterbalancing institutions (the Assembly of the Republic and the presidency) were able to prevent such a move.

The two presidents that had been elected since 1976 were wise to use their power to dissolve the Assembly. This was very important in the early phase of consolidation, when parliament was quite fragmented and polarised after the revolution. A stable majority never emerged between 1976 and 1979, and it was solely due to the presidency of General Ramalho Eanes that the negative effects of parliamentary instability of the first republic (1910–26) and the German Weimar Republic were avoided. Mário Soares, in his second presidency, activated the democratic institutions as counterbalances to the absolute majority government of Aníbal Cavaco Silva.

On the whole, one can assert that the presidency has been a crucial pivotal institution in stabilising the new democratic political system. Indeed it has been the only stable institution throughout the twenty years of democracy.

THE GOVERNMENT: FROM MINORITY COALITION TO ABSOLUTE MAJORITY

The political system from 1987 has been described by the well-known Portuguese political scientist Adriano Moreira as the 'presidentialism of the prime minister' (*presidencialismo do Primeiro-Ministro*). He wrote that Portugal was experiencing a change of regime without constitutional revision. The trust of the electorate was not placed in the party supporting the candidate, but in the candidate himself (Moreira, 1989, pp. 36–7). This explanation of the absolute majority gained by the PSD in the legislative elections of 1987 and 1991 bears some truth, and the style of Anibal Cavaco Silva was quite presidential and suprapartisan. Nonetheless the PSD's absolute majority was regarded as a great achievement after the long and unstable consolidation period between 1976 and 1987.

Studying the past twenty years of government we can assert that it gained increasing power and autonomy in relation to the other institutions of the political system. The early PS minority governments were in office for a very short time and were characterised by inexperienced ministers that were blocked by a divided supporting party and a polarised, post-revolutionary parliament.

The centre–right AD coalition of the early 1980s found it difficult to maintain a united position on key issues. The factionalism in the PSD after the death of the charismatic leader Francisco Sá Carneiro and the demands of its coalition partner, the CDS, caused many problems for Prime Minister Francisco Pinto Balsemão. Moreover the channels of information between the prime minister's office and the other ministers did not function optimally (Portas and Valente, 1990, pp. 347–8).

The Central Bloc government of the PSD and the PS lasted only until the Portuguese economy had achieved a high degree of stability in 1985. During its term of office it suffered from factional splits within the PSD over government policies. After 1985 the minority PSD government, led by Anibal Cavaco Silva, was characterised by increased stability. The prime minister's charismatic leadership made it possible to achieve a cooperative relationship with the rest of parliament, and the PSD particularly relied on the support of the PRD, which was torn between its oppositional role and supporting the government. This dilemma led to the near collapse of the PRD in the elections of 1987 after its successful motion of censure caused the PSD government to fall. The absolute-majority governments from 1987 onwards initiated a more stable and long-term style of government. Details of the various governments are presented in Table 3.1.

As can be seen, in general, the duration of governmental terms of office increased over the years, as did the overall stability of the cabinet, resulting in an improvement of cabinet performance from a short-term, day-by-day approach to a more long-term one, particularly after 1985 with Cavaco Silva's first government. Cavaco Silva's second government was the first to survive the full four-year parliamentary term.

The life of cabinets increased in the course of the past twenty years. The first five governments did last less than two thirds of a year. In the first half of the 1980s the average duration increases to more than one year. But it is only on the turn to the 1990s that the cabinet survives a whole four-year legislature. The second absolute majority of the PSD government in 1991 confirms this development towards an increasing ability of the cabinet to survive a whole legislature period (see Table 3.2).

The composition of the government is clearly defined in the constitution and consists of ministers, secretaries of state and undersecretaries of state. The Portuguese government is quite large by international standards. The number of ministers has remained quite constant at around 18–19 members. The main group has been in secretaries of state, which can be seen as an indicator of the thrust towards specialisation within the Portuguese government. Among the secretaries of state are the very important Secretary of State for European Affairs, who plays a coordinating role in EU-related matters, and the Secretary of State for Cul-

Table 3.1   Duration, form and party composition of government, 1976–95

Prime minister	Government form and composition	Dates	Duration (No. of days)
Soares	Minority (PS)	23.7.76–9.12.77	474
Soares	Coalition (PS–CDS)	23.1.78–28.7.78	185
Nobre da Costa	Presidential (independents)	29.8.78–15.9.78	18
Mota Pinto	Presidential (independents)	22.11.78–11.6.79	189
Pintassilgo	Presidential (independents)	31.7.79–27.12.79	147
Sá Carneiro	Coalition (AD: PSD–CDS–PPM)	3.1.80–9.1.81	371
Pinto Balsemão	Coalition (AD: PSD–CDS–PPM)	9.1.81–14.8.81	217
Pinto Balsemão	Coalition (AD: PSD–CDS–PPM)	4.9.81–23.12.82	474
Soares	Coalition (Central Bloc: PS–PSD)	9.6.83–6.11.85	877
Cavaco Silva	Minority (PSD)	6.11.85–3.4.87	512
Cavaco Silva	Absolute majority (PSD)	1.9.87–6.10.91	1506
Cavaco Silva	Absolute majority (PSD)	7.10.91–1.10.95	1454

Sources: Ferreira, 1985; Administração, 1987; Stock, 1992, 1993; Stock and Magone, 1994

ture, a position that became quite important during the two absolute majorities of the PSD because it was the government's intention to project a new, more self-confident image of Portugal through cultural events (see Table 3.3).

If we class different styles of government as being predominantly party political, as in the case of the United Kingdom, or administrative, as in the case of the consociational models of Austria and Finland (Blondel, 1986, p. 7), we have to locate Portugal among the former. Although there were attempts to move towards a more consociational model of politics, the highly polarised genesis of the political system led to the predominance of a party political style of government. This could be observed during the AD government, which was quite unstable and aimed predominantly at changing the constitution. Until the mid 1980s the government was quite dependent on parliament and was not able to achieve autonomy. It could be regarded as the weakest chain in the institutional triangle. This changed after 1985 with the

Table 3.2   Duration of cabinet life, 1976–91

Cabinet	Duration	Average	Number of governments
1976–9			
Governments			
Mário Soares I	474 days		
Mário Soares II	185 days		
Nobre da Costa	18 days	204 days	5
Mota Pinto	189 days		
Pintassilgo	147 days		
1979–85			
Sá Carneiro	371 days		
Pinto Balsemão I	217 days		
Pinto Balsemão II	474 days	485 days	4
Mário Soares III	877 days		
1985–91			
Cavaco Silva I	512 days		
Cavaco Silva II	1506 days	1009 days	2
1991–5			
Cavaco Silva III	1454 days	1454 days	1

Source: Gonçalves, 1985; Stock, 1992, 1993, Stock and Magone, 1995

minority government of Prime Minister Cavaco Silva. He introduced a technocratic governmental style, which became even more evident during his two absolute-majority governments after 1987, when the autonomy of the government increased. Cavaco Silva adopted a longer-term perspective and was dedicated to structural transformation rather than short-term management. His technocratic style was ideologically related to a neo-Thatcherite approach to political and economic liberalism with a view to national modernisation.

The transformation of the government over the past two decades has reflected mainstream developments at the world level and reproduced the economic and political strategies chosen by other countries. After 1987 the office of the prime minister dominated the government and organised the cabinet agenda in an hierarchical way.

Table 3.3 Composition of government, 1976–95

Cabinet leader	Ministers	Secretaries of state	Under secretaries of state	Total
Soares (first term)	18	41	7	66
Soares (second term)	16	33	3	52
Nobre da Costa	15	28	2	45
Mota Pinto	17	31	4	52
Pintassilgo	21	33	4	58
Sá Carneiro	16	38	1	55
Pinto Balsemão (first term)	18	40	1	59
Pinto Balsemão (second term)	19	43	3	65
Soares (third term)	19	37	1	57
Cavaco Silva (first term)	19	34	–	53
Cavaco Silva (second term)	21	39	–	60
Cavaco Silva (third term)	18	40	12	70

Sources: Ferreira, 1985; Stock, 1992, 1993; Administração, 1987, p. 12; Stock and Magone, 1994, 1995; Rotário da Administração Interna (Lisbon: Secretariado para a Modernização da Administração 1993); Expresso, 31 October 1992, p. A4).

THE ASSEMBLY OF THE REPUBLIC: THE CENTRE OF DEMOCRATIC LEGITIMACY

Recent studies on democratic transition and consolidation in Eastern Europe have assigned an important role to parliament. This democratically elected body is not only the main source of legitimacy for a new political system, but also an important forum for political learning. The democratic procedures agreed in the constitutional settlement have to become part of the cultural repertoire of the new political elite. Parliament is the ideal location in which to foster new forms of democratic behaviour based on tolerance of other and peaceful conflict management. Moreover parliament can be regarded as a mirror of the democratisation process in the country concerned by looking at the routinisation of procedures, the professionalisation of political actors and the importance devoted to the democratic accountability of the political institutions (Mishler and Rose, 1994; Agh, 1994; Agh and Kurtan, 1995).

The Portuguese case can tell us much about this process. After the constitution was settled in July 1976 the legislative body was quite split and none of the parties was able to build up a stable majority. This parliamentary instability spilled over into governmental instability, causing a general political crisis. The only stable element of the institutional triangle was the presidency.

Until 1985 the parliamentary fragmentation caused problems for majority and coalition building. The AD government of the early 1980s was not only dependent on the support of the coalition partners (the PSD, the CDS and the PPM) in parliament, but also on the internal cohesion of the individual parties. However the junior coalition partner, the PSD, in particular was split into factions. This changed radically after 1985. Anibal Cavaco Silva was able to transform his minority government into an absolute majority by stating that he was willing to govern, but was always being blocked by the opposition parties in parliament. Indeed, between 1985 and 1987 the new party PRD led by former president Ramalho Eanes and other opposition parties criticised the policies of the government, leading to its downfall in early 1987. Nevertheless, the charismatic nature of Cavaco Silva seemed to appeal to the population which did not honour this position of the opposition in 1987. Governmental stability then had a spillover effect on the stability of the Assembly of the Republic. In the second half of the 1980s parliamentary work became more viable because the four-year legislative term allowed for longer-term agenda setting. Parliament lost its power over the executive, but gained in professionalism and procedural routine.

The relationship between governmental and private members' bills in the Assembly of the Republic shows clearly that the opposition became more active during the period of the PSD absolute-majority government (Table 3.4). The main pattern of behaviour was that the opposition parties tended to work together with minority governments, but adopted a more conflictual style with governments that had absolute majorities (Cruz and Antunes, 1990, p. 360). In Table 3.3 it is evident that during the Central Bloc coalition of the main parliamentary parties (the PS and the PSD, from 1983–5) the number of private members' bills went down and government bills predominated. Conversely, during the Cavaco Silva's minority government (1985–7) the opposition parties adopted a more cooperative stance and the number of private members' bills fell.

Table 3.4 Number of governmental and private members' bills, 1976–91*

Legislative sessions	Government bills	Private members' bills	Total
1976–80	4	335 (36.5)	587 (63.5)	992
1980–83	3	192 (19.6)	350 (79.4)	542
1983–85	2	391 (71.0)	159 (29.0)	550
1985–87	2	446 (91.0)	55 (9.0)	491
1987–91	4	204 (18.0)	890 (82.0)	1104
1991–92	1	35 (11.5)	276 (88.5)	311
1992–93	1	37 (13.5)	137 (86.5)	274

* The figures in brackets are percentages. Ratifications have been excluded to emphasise the proportion of private members' bills submitted.

Sources: Magone, 1996; Cruz and Antunes, 1989, p. 361, Cruz 1990, p. 172; Memória da IV Legislatura, 1988, p. 133; Memória da V Legislatura, 1992, pp. 119–23; Diário da Assembleia da República, 28 November 1992a; Diário da Assembleia da República, 28 de November 1993.

As can be seen in Table 3.5, this changed drastically after 1987. When Cavaco Silva's majority government took power the number of private members' bills – particularly of the PCP – shot up to an all-time high. During Cavaco Silva's third term of office several government bills were vetoed by President Mário Soares, who played an important 'check-and-balance' role.

Another indicator of oppositional activity are the number of interpellations made to the government. This form of intervention is used by parliamentary groups to clarify issues of national interest. It is regarded as the queen of parliamentary control methods and has been used quite often in recent years (Table 3.5).

Although most of the interpellations in the fifth legislature were quite short, their number had increased substantially in relation to the fourth legislature. The use of this instrument is a way of showing the general public that parliamentary control is being exercised (Bandeira and Magalhaes, 1993, p. 134). Other forms of parliamentary control have been used in recent years, such as committees of enquiry and questions to the government. All such instruments were used more often during the term of Cavaco Silva's two majority governments.

The relationship between government and parliament was quite tense after 1991. The absolute majority of the PSD in the Assembly of the Republic made it very difficult for the opposition to block the ratification of decree laws. Furthermore the number of ad hoc and enquiry

Table 3.5   Number of interpellations made by the opposition, 1976–91

Year	Number
1976–79	2
1979–80	4
1980–83	10
1983–85	7
1985–87	4
1987–91	22

Sources: Cruz, 1990, p. 177, Cruz, Antunes 1989, p. 367; Assembleia da República 1988; and 1992a, pp. 192, 137; Bandeira and Magalhães, 1993, p. 134.

committees has increased considerably (Table 3.6). This has been explained by Cristina Leston Bandeira and Pedro Magalhaes (1993) as the absence of a political culture that places a high value on parliament. Their study of legislative–executive relations seems to confirm that antiparliamentarianism – particularly with regard to democratic behaviour – is still widespread in São Bento. Parliament has retained the negative image it acquired in the nineteenth century and during the First Republic (1910–26) (Bandeira and Magalhaes, 1993, pp. 161–3). Cavaco Silva used this image to discredit parliament during his first absolute-majority government and even declined to take part in face-to-face television interviews with the opposition leaders during the legislative election campaign of 1991. His neo-Salazarist style was welcomed by the population, as his second victory confirms.

Nevertheless the Portuguese parliament is gaining in significance and the level of professionalism has increased. The parliamentary elite structure has become more stable, but the former ideal of representation for the people, such as prevailed in the first legislatures of the Communist parliamentary group, has slowly been replaced by a more functional cohort of parliamentary specialists. From a democratic perspective, this may be a negative feature of the present Assembly of the Republic, but it can be seen as an important development in achieving a higher degree of parliamentary stability. It remains to be seen whether new social movements – particularly environmental groups – will emerge and change the highly individualistic style of Portuguese politics.

At the moment the generation born after the revolution is entering political life and contributing to a change in the way of thinking. This new generation is quite European, issue-oriented and very concerned with national development.

Table 3.6 Permanent parliamentary committees, 1991–5

---

 1. Constitutional affairs, civil rights and liberties
 2. Health
 3. Foreign affairs, Portuguese communities and cooperation
 4. Labour, social security and family
 5. Education, science and culture
 6. Economy, finance and planning
 7. Agriculture and sea
 8. National defence
 9. Internal administration, social infrastructure, environment and local government
10. Committee of social infrastructure
11. European Affairs
12. Youth
13. Petitions
14. Regulations and Mandates

Sources: Diário da Assembleia da República, 28 November 1992, 19 November 1993.

THE COURTS: THE EMERGENCE OF DEMOCRATIC ACCOUNTABILITY

Several courts were enshrined in the constitution to pass judgement on infringements of the rule of law in different spheres of political life. Presently there are four main courts in the Portuguese political system, whose decisions are final: the Constitutional Court, the Auditing Court, the Supreme Court of Justice and the Supreme Court of Administration.

The Constitutional Court (*tribunal constitucional*) was created in 1982 and took over the powers of the abolished Council of the Revolution. Between 1976 and 1982 the Council of the Revolution – supported by its advisory body, the Constitutional Commission (*comissão constitucional*) – was in charge of the judicial review of laws. The legacy of the revolution gave the military the power to watch over the constitution. A diffused form of judicial review was adopted and shared between the Council of the Revolution, the Constitutional Commission and the courts (Mendes, 1989). This changed in 1982, when the Constitutional Court was set up to monitor all aspects relating to the constitutionality of laws, thus concentrating the political side of judicial review in its body. It resembles constitutional courts in other West European countries and is quite separate from the Supreme Court of Justice and the Supreme Court of Administration, which deal with legal aspects that are not under the jurisdiction of the Constitutional Court.

The Constitutional Court determines the constitutionality of legal diplomas, which before their enactment are sent to the court by the president, by the ministers or by one fifth of the members of parliament (Constitution 1992, 1995, Article 280). It also decides whether legal diplomas violate any superior legal bindings, national laws or the statutes of autonomous regions. In this case, the president of the Republic, the president of the Assembly of the Republic, the prime minister, the ombudsman, the attorney general or one-tenth of the deputies of the Assembly of the Republic may ask the Constitutional Court to check whether or not a law is constitutional (Constitution 1992, 1995, Article 281).

Thirdly, the Constitutional Court may declare that legislative acts are unconstitutional because of a failure to implement provisions of the constitution. Such matters can be raised by the president, the ombudsman or the president of the autonomous regional assemblies (Constitution 1992, 1995, Article 283).

The court consists of 13 judges, 10 of whom are appointed by the Assembly of the Republic and three are coopted. Six judges are coopted from the courts, the remainder are jurists.

The significance of the Constitutional Court has increased since 1987. The absolute majority of the PSD allowed President Mário Soares to request a judicial review of bills that had been unanimously approved by the Assembly of the Republic. Bills such as the anticorruption law, the 'law on incompatibilities' and the Official Secrets Act (*a lei da rolha*, the cork law) were the most famous of such cases during 1993.

The anticorruption law was designed to give greater power to the police in their fight against drug trafficking and other forms of organised crime. The 'law on incompatibilities' particularly targeted the president of the Auditing Court, who also lectured at a university in Lisbon. The opposition saw this as a pretext for the government to remove the head of a court that produced annual reports that were very critical of governmental public spending. The Official Secrets Act required civil servants to keep secret all issues related to their office. This caused a general protest by civil servants (*Expresso*, 5 April 1993, p. A14, 22 May 1993, p. A5, 24 July 1993, p. A1). By May 1993 the president had sent about 27 legislative acts to the Constitutional Court for judicial review and 20 were deemed unconstitutional (*Expresso*, 29 May 1993, p. A7).

The emergence of the Constitutional Court as an important control-ling institution naturally caused a change in legislative behaviour and a new network of relationships between the institutions.

The Auditing Court (*Tribunal de Contas*) also gained in significance during the first half of the 1990s. This was related to the work of the prestigious president of the court, Professor António Sousa Franco. The court's annual reports on the public spending of the central govern-ment and that of the autonomous regional governments of the Azores and Madeira have caused embarrassment to these institutions. In par-ticular the very negative report on public spending in Madeira under the absolute majority PSD government caused a strong protest from its charismatic president Alberto João Jardim. It is still not clear whether the government has implemented any of the measures suggested by the Auditing Court. Nevertheless the court is very efficient and well-organised (Franco, 1993; Tribunal de Contas, 1990–4, 1992, 1994), and its relationship with the government has changed substantially since 1976.

The Supreme Administrative Court (*Supremo Tribunal Administrativo* – STA) deals with disputes that relate to administrative and fiscal le-gal matters. Although the Supreme Administrative Court has been in existence since 1976, it lacks authority. Since its inception the court has exposed several administrative irregularities, but implementation of its rulings is quite uncommon. Since 1980 the court has brought 200 cases against public institutions for not complying with court rul-ings. However some of these cases were dismissed because the institu-tions had been dismantled or because a mutual agreement had been reached (*Expresso*, 9 April 1993, p. A4). This had a lot to do with the fact that the continuous remoulding of the state structure due to govern-mental instability has not been very conducive to building up a more democratic administrative culture. Before democratic accountability can be enforced, democratic rationality will need to pervade all branches of the administration. This is beginning to happen, but it will take some time for it to become the norm.

ADMINISTRATION AND DEVELOPMENT

The discontinuity of political life in twentieth-century Portugal has had an impact on the development of state administration. Effective ad-ministration can be regarded as a crucial factor in the economic, social and political development of a nation, and policy performance is related to the organisation and efficiency of administration. Administration in modern-day Portugal has had to adjust to political regimes with different objectives.

The First Republic (1910–26) was very concerned with building up modern administrative mechanisms for the more efficient implementation of socially oriented policies. This experiment failed because the administration remained a prisoner of neopatrimonial, clientelistic practices due to the fact that most of the administrative personnel of the former constitutional monarchy were taken over by the new regime, and administrative reform was hindered by permanent political instability during the First Republic.

The *Estado Novo* (1926–74), under the dictatorship of António Salazar, made a serious efforts to modernise the administration, particularly in the 1960s, when growth in complexity due to industrialisation and modernisation led to a more technocratic approach to public policy formulation and implementation.

In spite of the revolutionary turmoil of 1974–5 and the temporary purging of higher civil servants, the administrative personnel in the new democratic regime showed a higher degree of continuity in comparison with the previous regime.

A break with the former regime is more evident in the struggle to develop a more decentralised and citizen-friendly civil service. This difficult task has been considered a major objective of all governments since 1976 (DAR, 1978–87). However until 1985 governmental instability prevented radical reform of the state administration, and until 1987 there was a tendency for new institutions to appear and disappear within a very short space of time.

Major restructuring of the Portuguese administration started only after 1987 with the absolute-majority government of Anibal Cavaco Silva. This administrative reform is still in progress and will probably last until the end of the millenium. Its main objective – a more efficient and citizen-friendly civil service – will be achieved by decentralising and democratising the provision of services (Constitution 1992, Articles 266–8; SMA, 1995, 1992). Although there is still a long way to go, the administrative structures did start to become more stable and more democratic in the early 1990s.

Administration in Portugal is divided between central administration, led by the central government, and local administration by local authorities. The central government also has a network of coordinating regional commissions (*Comissões Coordenadoras Regionais*, whose main task is to oversee policy implementation across the country. At the moment these coordinating commissions are playing a major role in coordinating the allocation of structural funds in continental Portugal. There are four kinds of local government. The *freguesias* (counties) are the smallest unit of administration, followed by the *municipios* (townships) and the *regiões administrativas* (administrative regions). The latter are still in the making, so the territory continues to be divided into 18 *distritos* (districts), which were the national units of local government during the authoritarian regime. At the lower level Portugal consists of 275 townships and 3893 counties, plus 30 townships and 202 counties in the Azores and Madeira (Administração, 1987, pp. 15–16). Madeira and the Azores also have independent regional governments and assemblies, with autonomous administrations and government programmes. The autonomous regional governments are accountable to the national courts and the Assembly of the Republic (ibid., p. 67).

The process of decentralisation is still in the early stages and the central administration still makes up the largest proportion of the civil service. In 1935 all 25 588 civil servants worked for the central administration; in 1968 the ratio was 78.9 per cent central to 21.1 per cent local, with 196 755 civil servants; in 1979 the number of civil servants almost doubled to 372 295 – 84.3 per cent central and 15.7 per cent local; in 1983 82.4 per cent of the 435 795 civil servants were central and 17.6 per cent local; in 1988 the number of civil servants rose to 544 000 (85.11 per cent central and 14.79 per cent local) and in 1991 to 624 000 (87.18 per cent central and 12.82 per cent local, Table 3.6) (Administração, 1987, p. 27; OECD, 1993, p. 28).[1]

In 1983 most of the civil servants dealt with economics and finance (18.8 per cent), education (43.1 per cent), and employment and social policy (31 per cent) (Administração, 1987, p. 33). That 92.9 per cent of all civil servants worked in these sectors is an indication of the main priorities of public policy at the time. It also documents the shift of priority in the budget structure from military spending in the 1960s and 1970s to welfare sectors such as education and social policy in the early 1980s (Esping-Andersen, 1994).

The census of 1979 revealed that 37.2 per cent of civil servants had failed to complete their primary education, and that 76.1 per cent of local civil servants belonged to this category. Furthermore about 21.9 per cent of civil servants at the local level had had no schooling at all. Although no data were available for the period after 1979, it can be assumed that the situation has improved substantially. Nevertheless a continuing problem is a labour market dominated by unqualified or poorly qualified human resources.

Table 3.7 Composition and growth of government employment (thousands)

	1979	1986	1988	1991
Total Employment	372	520	544	624
Local Government	58	80	80	81
Social Security	7	21	20	21
Health	81	101	107	123
Education	131	187	210	247
Other	95	131	127	152

Source: Administração, 1987, pp. 27, 32; SMA, 1990; OECD, 1993, p. 28.

A further impediment to the decentralisation of administration is the uneven distribution of the population across the territory. Almost 70 per cent live along the coastal fringe, the other 30 per cent are scattered among the peripheral districts of inland Portugal. The emigration of younger people to the larger towns on the west coast has worsened this situation (Administração, 1987, p. 40), so it is crucial that central administrative services are transferred to the more peripheral areas to act as poles of development. This may serve as a catalyst for the modernisation of infrastructure in these districts. In the late 1980s and early 1990s there was such a trend towards decentralising services, and the new universities in Minho, Trás-Os-Montes, Beira-Alta, Évora are major actors in local development.

Although the situation is improving, the Portuguese administration is still characterised by fragmented competences scattered between different ministries, disjointed policies that lack rationale, a discontinuity between public agencies that is adversely affecting policy implementation, a mismatch between the human resources allocated and the nature of the task, and outdated departments that coexist with new ones created to respond to the demands of Europeanisation. This is accompanied by local governments that are strong on representativeness, but weak on performance. On the whole, democratisation will require further debureaucratisation and an adequate allocation of human and material services (Graham, 1982, pp. 959, pp. 968–9, 1993, p. 104; Santos, 1990).

This is the big challenge that the Portuguese government under Cavaco Silva tried to overcome. In this it was more successful than previous governments. Since the mid 1980s a new, more pragmatic 'administrative philosophy' has taken into account the particularities of the administrative unit concerned. A small *Secretariado para a Modernização da Administração* (Secretariat for Administrative Modernisation) has been set up and is directly supervised by the prime minister. Its main objective is to make administrative matters more efficient and citizen-friendly. Another priority is transforming the administration into a supportive element of the business sector. The so-called 'Enterprise–Administration Committee' can be cited as an example of an attempt to facilitate business–bureaucratic relations (Pasquino and Sotiropoulos, forthcoming; Graham, 1993, pp. 106–8).

A further element that may lead to improvement of the Portuguese administration in the long term is the *Instituto Nacional de Administração* (National Institute of Administration – INA), which has the task of building up a more rational and efficient administrative elite. Like all the institutions in post-authoritarian Portugal, the INA is a new institution and will need a couple of decades to establish its own administrative style, such as that of the École Nationale d'Administration. On the whole, the success of Portuguese administration will depend on a continuity of policies aimed at efficient and citizen-friendly administration. This will require local governments to be given financial autonomy. Much has been done in terms of modernisation and Europeanisation from above, and it is hoped that this will have a spillover effect on the quality of administration.

CONCLUSIONS

The institutional framework of the new Portuguese democracy has been shaped by its political actors during the past twenty years. The governmental and parliamentary instability of the late 1970s and early 1980s was transformed into solid and stable government in the second half of the 1980s and early 1990s. The absolute electoral majority of Anibal Cavaco Silva was crucial to stabilising relationships in the institutional triangle of government, parliament and presidency. The semipresidentialist political system slowly integrated the other political institutions into the overall framework. The Court of Justice, the Auditing Court and the Supreme Administrative Court introduced a degree of accountability into what had been a token democracy, transforming it into a more participatory one.

A vital element in sustaining this will be the ability to implement public policies efficiently. The Portuguese administration is still suffering from a lack of coordination between the policies of different ministries, a fragmented distribution of responsibilities between different institutions and excessive dominance of the central administration over the local ones. The sustainability of participatory democracy will depend very much on public policy performance in the long term. In this respect it is crucial to look at the problems local government is facing today in order to gauge the quality of participatory democracy that currently exists. This will be the topic of the next chapter.

4 The Local Political System

In the Middle Ages the independence of local communities in Portugal was slowly replaced by domination from the centre, particularly because of the centre's need to increase its revenues and this continued into the fifteenth and sixteenth centuries. The stagnation of local government and development until the twentieth century prevented economic, social and political modernisation from being diffused to the peripheral areas of continental Portugal and the Atlantic islands of Madeira and the Azores. Part of the scarce human and material resources were used to hold the vast empire together, and most of the remainder went to the coastal fringe of continental Portugal.

The political elite of the First Republic (1910–26) wanted to remedy the backwardness of the peripheral regions by improving their educational infrastructure, but the continual political and economic instability prevented the successful implementation of such a process. The authoritarian regime of Antonio Oliveira Salazar had little interest in modernisation and focused primarily on industrialisation in the 1960s and 1970s. This has been called 'industrialisation without modernisation' (Medeiros, 1994). This technocratic approach reinforced the domination of the centre over the periphery. Local development and government was controlled by loyalists with close connections with the economic and social elites of their particular communities (Makler, 1979).

The post-revolutionary constitution gives special emphasis to local government as a major factor in the democratisation of the country and the introduction of local elections has meant an improvement in the place of the regions in the political system. In terms of representativeness, the elections have enhanced the legitimacy of the new democratic regime and made local government decisions more accountable to the population. In the Portuguese context, this is crucial for the attainment of 'participatory democracy', as defined in the constitution. Nevertheless this high degree of representativeness, as Lawrence Graham (1993) rightly asserts, has not been reflected in policy performance. The social, economic and cultural gaps continue to widen between the coastal fringe of western Portugal and the eastern district bordering Spain.

One of the obstacles seems to be the low share of budget expenditure on local government. Although local governments in most

Table 4.1 Expenditure on lower levels of government (percentage of total expenditure, excluding social security)

	1980	1990
Portugal	10.8	10.0
Germany	65.6	61.4
France	25.9	22.3
Austria	42.9	38.7
Belgium	22.1	18.2
Netherlands	50.5	43.0
Spain	n/a	39.0
Sweden	50.4	49.6

Sources: OECD, National Accounts and Ministry of Finance, quoted from OECD, 1993, p. 30.

industrialised countries had to face a slight decline in their share of government expenditure from 1980 to 1990, in Portugal it not only declined but was extremely low in comparison (Table 4.1). This has made it difficult for local government to play a more important role in local development, as well as having no financial say in the areas of health, education and social security. Financial autonomy is further restricted by the very strict budgetary guidelines imposed by the central government.

The overcentralisation of expenditure, personnel and material allocation is a serious obstacle to improving the quality of life in the localities. Nevertheless events in the past twenty years have changed the mentality and perspective of local decision makers. Being made democratically accountable to the electorate has put them under pressure to improve their performance.

The emergence of 'Regional Europe' in the 1990s as a collective actor in EC/EU affairs is encouraging local and regional Portuguese decision makers to search for other strategies of economic, social and cultural development beyond the nation-state framework. *L'Europe des Regions* is still embryonic, but it has become a powerful catchword at the regional and local levels in Europe. The founding of the Assembly of the European Regions, the Four-Motors Group and the new Committee of the Regions and Local Authorities makes us aware that this tier of government may increase in significance during the next couple of decades.

In budgetary terms, regional and structural funds have substantially increased their share. Regional policy is vital to the success of the

Single European Market, which will be linked to social and economic cohesion across Europe. In this context the southern EU member-states and Ireland will be allocated the largest share of structural and regional funds until end of the millenium. These policies have already made a major contribution to development in Portugal (Harvie, 1994; European Commission, 1994a, 1994b; Ravet, 1992; Balme *et al.*, 1993; Bassot, 1993).

The emergence of regional consciousness in northern Portugal – promoted by the socialist mayor of Oporto, Fernando Gomes, who is developing regional contacts and projects with other European regions, particularly those in Spain – may represent a model for the further development of Portuguese local government. His approach can be regarded as very innovative and as showing a self-confident and open-minded search for alternative models of development.

Moreover the process of globalisation has led to a transformation of modes of production and economic advantages in the world economic system. The region has become a major site for transnational corporations (TNCs). In a recent report, conducted on behalf of the EU, it was stated that improving the flexibility of the modes of production, the velocity of technological innovation and the flexibility of the labour market will require a more flexible response by decision makers. In this sense the region is seen as a much more flexible unit of decision making than the nation-state. It is a combination of different factors – such as the skill level of workers, the accessibility of the location, the availability of regional aid packages, and the social and cultural environment – that determine whether a region is attractive to investors. The report suggests that the Portuguese regions are not very attractive for high-technology investment, only for low-technology or low-labour-cost production plants. This is a clear disadvantage that may in the short term lead to increased employment, based mainly on short-term contracts, but in the long term prevent the development of a more diversified human-capital-based economy (Netherlands Economic Institute, 1993, p. 77).

After outlining the macro conditions of local development in Portugal, this chapter will analyse the process of decentralisation over the past twenty years, the structure of the local political system, the significance of local elections and the problems of policy formulation and implementation that local government has to face at the micro level.

ORGANISATION OF THE LOCAL POLITICAL SYSTEM

The Portuguese local political system is still in the process of formation. The past twenty years have been an important time for learning to deal with the new institutions and developing a culture of local government. The Portuguese constitution, after the second revision of 1989, defines the organisation of the local political system. According to the constitution the main tiers of local government are the *freguesias* (counties), *municipios* (municipalities) and *regiões administrativas* (administrative regions), of which only the *municipios* can be traced back to the Middle Ages. Some authors seem to suggest that municipalities existed before the creation of the Portuguese nation-state in the mid-twelfth century (Coelho and Magalhaes, 1986, pp. 2–3).

The lowest local authority unit is the *freguesia*. Its main bodies are the *junta de freguesia* (parish board) and the *assembleia de freguesia* (Parish Assembly). The *assembleia de freguesia* is elected by the population of the corresponding locality and is the representative body of the *freguesia*. The representatives on *junta de freguesia* are coopted by the *assembleia da freguesia* from among its members. The *junta* is the executive body of the *freguesia*. (Constitution 1992, 1995, Articles 245–8).

Above this unit is the *municipio* (municipality), which comprises several parishes. The *assembleia municipal* (municipal assembly) and the *câmara municipal* (municipal chambers) are the main bodies of this tier of local government. The *assembleia municipal* is composed of the chairmen of the parish boards and an equal number of members elected by an electoral college of the municipality. The *câmara municipal* is the corporate executive of the municipality. It is elected by the citizens of the area. The president of the *câmara municipal* is normally the head of the party that captures the most votes (Constitution 1992, 1995, Articles 250–2).

Theoretically the highest tier of local government is occupied by the *regiões administrativas* (administrative regions), but these are yet to be established as no agreement has been reached on their delineation. Moreover there is a fear that their creation will lead to fragmentation of the country and the appearance of competing powers in the centre. From a constitutional point of view this is not the purpose of the administrative regions, which are supposed to be 'responsible for the direction of public services and for coordinating and supporting the activities of the municipalities, while respecting municipal autonomy and not limiting their powers' (Constitution 1992, 1995; Article 257).

Furthermore administrative regions should be created on an individual case-by-case basis following a favourable vote by a majority of the municipal assemblies representing the majority of the population of the region, and only later defined in terms of their economic and social viability by the central administration (Constitution 1992, 1995, Article 256).

A crucial condition for the even development of the territory is the implementation of regional plans, which should be in accord with the overall objectives of the national plan (Constitution 1992, 1995, Articles 61, 62, 258).

When introduced, the main bodies of the regional tier of government will be the *assembleia regional* (regional assembly) and the *junta regional* (regional board). The regional assembly will be composed of members directly elected by the citizens enrolled in the electoral register for the regional area and of a smaller number elected, by a system of proportional representation and the d'Hondt highest average method, by an electoral college comprising the directly elected members of the municipal assemblies in that area. The regional board will be the corporate executive organ for the region, elected in a secret ballot by the members of the regional assembly from among their number (Constitution 1992, 1995, Articles 261, 262).

Furthermore, attached to each region will be a representative of the government, appointed by the Council of Ministers, who will have authority over the other local institutions in the regional area (Constitution 1992, 1995, Article 262).

Until the revision of 1989 all these tiers of local government were to be provided with further representative bodies called parish, municipal and regional councils which was a tribute to the popular institutions created in 1974–5 during the revolution, such as the *comissões de moradores* (residents' councils). These bodies were abolished in the second revision of the constitution, although residents' committees still have the right to submit petitions on administrative matters of concern to the population, and to attend local government representative assemblies, but not to vote in them.

A provisional structure that lies above the municipality is the *distrito* (district). The main body of the distrito is the *assembleia distrital* (district assembly), consisting of representatives of the municipalities and presided by the *governador civil* (civil governor), who represents the government. The district assembly merely has consultative powers.

Another form of local government is that found in the autonomous island regions in the Atlantic – the Azores and Madeira. Both have

their own institutions, financial autonomy, legislative powers in compliance with the constitution and the general laws of the republic, and
executive powers. The main bodies of the autonomous regions are the
assembleia regional (regional assembly) and the *governo regional* (regional government). The regional assembly has legislative powers and
is directly elected by the population. The regional government is the
corporate executive body. A representative of the national government,
the *Ministro da República* (Minister of the Republic), ratifies the legislative acts of the regional assembly (Constitution 1992, 1995, Articles
227–36).

LOCAL ELECTIONS AND THE REPRESENTATIVENESS OF THE LOCAL POLITICAL ELITE (1976–93)

Local elections are a crucial factor in the legitimacy of a democracy
in that they reinforce the democratic accountability of the actors in the
political system. There is quite a large local political elite in Portugal,
and in the past twenty years they have learnt to deal with the new
institutions of the political system.

A look at Portugal's political geography reveals the main political
cleavages in the country. While the people of the northern rural districts of Minho, Trás-Os Montes and Beiras are mainly conservative
and vote for the CDS and the PSD, those in the more urban areas, the
central districts and the Algarve vote socialist. In the southern province of Alentejo the main party is the Communist Party. This distribution can be explained by the social structure of these different regions.
The rural north consists mainly of small landed estates, and during the
revolution landowners were a major hindrance to communist expansion. In the hot summer of 1975 several farmers set fire to communist
branch offices. Their conservatism arose from their fear of losing their
land. The subsistence-economy mentality that prevailed at that time is
now fading away and changing the social structure of these regions.

The Socialist Party has been able to gain several former PSD and
CDS municipalities (Tables 4.2 and 4.3). This is the case in the district of Bragança, where since 1989 the socialists have held sway. In
1976, of the twelve municipalities in this district six had a PSD mayor,
five a CDS mayor and one a PS mayor. In 1993 the new configuration
was 10 PS mayors and two PSD mayors. The conservative CDS is
disappearing from the area because its influence is being eroded by
the processes of modernisation and Europeanisation.

Table 4.2 Local election results, 1976–93

	No. of votes	(%)	Municipal chamber	No. of seats Municipal assembly	Parish assembly
1976					

No. of electorates: 304
No. of registered voters: 6 457 440
No. of votes cast: 4 170 494 (64.6%)

CDS	692 869	16.6	317	48	5 104
FEPU	737 586	17.7	267	674	2 336
GDUPS	104 629	2.5	5	–	–
PPM	7 496	0.2	3	–	–
PS	1 386 362	33.2	691	1700	8 407
PSD	1 012 251	24.3	623	1659	9 086
1979					

No. of electorates: 305
No. of registered voters: 6 761 751
No. of votes cast: 4 987 734 (73.8%)

AD	1 272 058	25.5	436	2186	10 368
APU	1 021 486	20.5	322	1786	5 086
CDS	344 902	6.9	165	862	4 267
PDC	6 616	0.1	2	–	–
PPM	6 162	0.1	6	–	–
PS	1 380 134	27.7	523	2749	10 939
PSD	733 384	14.7	480	2255	9 806
UDP	64 355	1.3	3	–	–
1982					

No. of electorates: 305
No. of registered voters: 7 191 084
No. of votes cast: 5 131 483 (71.4%)

AD	1 004 065	19.6	332	1656	7 863
APU	1 061 492	20.7	325	1781	5 086
ASDI	7 156	0.1	7	–	–
CDS	386 527	7.5	191	1019	4 532
PPM	11 293	0.2	5	–	–
PS	1 595 723	31.1	628	3203	12 848
PS/UE	37 102	0.7	14	–	–
PSD	750 296	14.6	442	2159	9 585
UD	30 941	0.6	6	–	–
UDP	31 973	0.6	3	–	–

continued on page 66

European Portugal

Table 4.2 continued

	No. of votes	(%)	Municipal chamber	No. of seats Municipal assembly	Parish assembly
1985					
No. of electorates: 305					
No. of registered voters: 7 594 753					
No. of votes cast: 4 853 529 (63.9%)					
APU	942 197	19.4	305	1062	3 675
CDS	471 838	9.7	224	1019	4 532
PDC	7 863	0.2	2	–	–
PPM	23 897	0.5	3	–	–
PRD	230 177	4.7	51	270	726
PS	1 330 388	27.4	571	1817	9 044
PSD	1 649 560	34.0	822	2539	13 117
UDP	28 701	0.6	3	–	–
1989					
No. of electorates: 305					
No. of registered voters: 8 121 045					
No. of votes cast: 4 946 196 (60.9%)					
CDS	451 163	9.1	179	698	3 434
CDS/PS	947	–	1	–	–
MDP	11 354	0.2	1	–	–
MDP/PRD	3 585	0.1	2	–	–
PCP/PRD/ PEV	22 972	0.5	5	–	–
PCP/PEV	633 682	12.8	252	848	2 929
PDC	5 662	0.1	1	–	–
PPM	2 765	0.1	1	–	–
PRD	38 452	0.8	4	–	–
PRD/MDP	170	–	1	–	–
PS	1 598 571	·32.3	728	2445	11 201
PS/PCP/ MDP/PEV	180 635	3.7	9	–	–
PS/CDS	34 899	0.7	15	–	–
PSD	1 552 846	31.4	781	2582	13 261
PSD/CDS	31 548	0.6	4	–	–
PSD/CDS/ PPM	161 420	3.3	9	–	–
UDP	16 093	0.3	4	–	–

Table 4.2 continued

	No. of votes	(%)	Municipal chamber	No. of seats Municipal assembly	Parish assembly
1993					

No. of electorates: 305
No. of registered voters: 8 121 045
No. of votes cast: 4 946 196 (60.9%)

	No. of votes	(%)	Municipal chamber	Municipal assembly	Parish assembly
CDS/PP	455 357	8.4	133	557	2 719
MDP	1 386	–	1	–	–
MPT	23 408	0.4	14	–	–
PCP/PEV	689 928	12.8	300	803	2 747
PRD	1 455	–	–	–	–
PS	1 950 133	36.1	795	2641	12 312
PS/CDS/ PP	11 482	0.2	7	–	–
PS/PCP/ PEV	95	–	2	–	–
PS/PCP/ PEV/PSR/ UDP	200 822	3.7	11	–	–
PS/PCP/ PEV/PSR/ UDP/PDA	10 221	0.2	4	–	–
PSD	1 822 925	33.7	807	2681	13 679
PSN	28 922	0.5	3	–	–

Source: Secretariado Técnico, 1994

The central and urban districts are dominated by the traditional petty bourgeoisie and the new middle classes, who mainly support the PS and the PSD. In the large urban centres – Lisbon and Porto – the socialists have been able to break the dominance of the social democrats. In Lisbon the charismatic Jorge Sampaio formed a coalition in 1989 with the communists and smaller parties and won the local elections. In 1993 the coalition was reelected for a second term of office. Sampaio's urban policies are being visibly manifest and he is slowly changing the face of the capital.

In Porto the former MEP Fernando Gomes is attempting to draw the attention of the government to this region. He has widened his contacts to include the neighbouring Spanish regions and the government in Madrid. In 1993 he too was able to repeat his victory of 1989.

European Portugal

Table 4.3 Presidents of municipal chambers, 1976–93

Parties	1976	1979	1982	1985	1989	1993
CDS	36	20	27	27	20	13
FEPU/APU/						
CDU	37	50	55	47	50	49
PS	115	60	83	79	116	126
PSD	115	101	88	149	113	116
AD	–	73	49	–	–	–
ASDI	–	–	1	–	–	–
PPM	1	1	1	–	–	–
PRD	–	–	–	3	–	–
PS/CDS	–	–	–	–	3	–
PS/PCP/MDP/						
CDE/PS/PCP/						
PEV/PSR/						
UDP	–	–	–	–	1	1
PS/UEDS	–	–	1	–	–	–
PSD/CDS	–	–	–	–	1	–
UDP	–	–	–	–	1	–
Total	304	305	305	305	305	305
Districts						
Braga	PSD 6	PSD 4	PSD 2	PSD 5	PSD 5	PSD 5
(13)	PS 3	AD 3	AD 6	PS 4	CDS 3	PS 7
	CDS 4	CDS 4	CDS 1	CDS 4	PS 5	CDS 1
		PS 2	PS 4			
Bragança	PSD 6	PSD 8	PSD 5	PSD 7	PS 6	PS 10
(12)	PS 1	AD 1	CDS 2	CDS 3	PSD 5	PSD 2
	CDS 5	CDS 2	AD 3	PS 2	CDS 1	
		PS 1	PS 2			
Aveiro	PSD 13	PSD 14	PSD 11	PSD 14	PSD 10	PSD 5
(19)	PS 3	CDS 2	CDS 2	CDS 4	CDS 6	CDS 6
	CDS 3	AD 2	PS 3	PS 1	PS 3	PS 8
		PS 1	AD 2			
			PPM 1			
Castelo						
Branco	PS 7	AD 8	AD 4	PSD 6	PS 5	PSD 7
(11)	PSD 3	PS 3	PS 4	PS 3	PSD 6	PS 4
	CDS 1		PSD 2	CDS 1		
			CDS 1	PRD 1		
Coimbra	PSD 8	PSD 9	PSD 6	PSD 11	PSD 8	PSD 8
(17)	PS 9	AD 4	PS 8	PS 6	PS 9	PS 9
		PS 4	AD 3			

Table 4.3 continued

	1976	1979	1982	1985	1989	1993
Guarda	PSD 4	PS 3	PSD 6	PSD 8	PSD 8	PSD 7
(14)	CDS 7	AD 7	AD 1	CDS 2	CDS 2	PS 7
	PS 3	PSD 2	CDS 3	PS 4	PS 4	
		CDS 2	PS 4			
Evora	FEPU 12	APU 12	APU 13	APU 10	CDU 10	CDU 10
(14)	PS 2	PS 1	PS 1	PS 3	PS 4	PS 2
		PSD 1		PSD 1		PSD 1
Beja	FEPU 9	APU 12	APU 13	APU 11	CDU 11	CDU 10
(14)	PS 4	PS 1	PS 1	PSD 2	PS 2	PS 3
	PSD 1	PSD 1		PS 1	PSD 1	PSD 1
Faro	PS 15	PS 11	PS 11	PS 10	PS 12	PS 10
(16)	PSD 1	AD 3	PSD 2	PSD 4	PSD 2	PSD 3
		PSD 1	AD 1	APU 2	CDU 2	CDU 3
		APU 1	APU 2			
Leiria	PS 7	AD 4	AD 3	PSD 9	PSD 8	PSD 9
(16)	PSD 8	PSD 8	CDS 4	CDS 2	PS 6	PS 6
	CDS 1	PS 3	PSD 3	PS 4	CDS 1	CDS 1
		APU 1	PS 5	APU 1	APU 1	
			APU 1			
Lisbon	PS 13	PS 4	PS 4	PS 5	PS 7	PS 9
(15)	FEPU 1	APU 5	APU 5	PSD 6	CDU 4	CDU 4
		AD 4	AD 5	APU 4	PSD 3	PSD 2
		PSD 1	PSD 1		PSD/	
		CDS 1			CDS 1	
Portalegre	PS 12	PS 10	PS 10	PS 8	PS 7	PS 7
(15)	FEPU 3	APU 2	APU 4	APU 3	CDU 4	PSD 5
		PSD 1	PSD 1	PSD 4	PSD 4	CDU 3
		AD 2				
Porto	PSD 5	PSD 3	PSD 2	PSD 6	PS 12	PS 9
(17)	PS 10	AD 9	AD 3	PS 8	PSD 3	PSD 7
	CDS 2	CDS 2	PS 9	CDS 3	CDS 2	CDS 1
		PS 3	CDS 3			
Santarém	PS 15	PS 9	PS 10	PS 9	PS 10	PS 11
(21)	FEPU 2	AD 6	APU 4	APU 5	PSD 5	CDU 6
	PSD 3	APU 4	PSD 1	PRD 1	CDU 6	PSD 4
	CDS 1	PSD 2	AD 5	PSD 6		
			CDS 1			
Setúbal	FEPU 10	APU 13	APU 13	APU 11	APU 12	APU 12
(13)	PS 3			PS 2	PS 1	PS 1

continued on page 70

Table 4.3 continued

	1976	1979	1982	1985	1989	1993
Viana	PSD 5	AD 7	AD 4	PSD 6	PSD 4	PSD 4
do Castelo	PS 3	PS 2	PS 3	PS 3	PS 5	PS 5
(10)	CDS 2	CDS 1	PSD 2	CDS 1	CDS 1	CDS 1
			CDS 1			
Vila Real	PS 2	AD 3	AD 6	PSD 11	PSD 9	PS 6
(14)	PSD 10	PSD 8	PSD 6	CDS 1	PS 4	PSD 7
	CDS 1	CDS 1	CDS 1	PS 2	CDS 1	CDS 1
	PPM 1	PPM 1	PS 1			
		PS 1				
Viseu	PSD 14	AD 8	PSD 10	PSD 15	PSD 14	PSD 15
(24)	PS 2	PSD 9	AD 3	PS 2	PS 7	PS 7
	CDS 8	PS 1	PS 3	PRD 1	CDS 3	CDS 2
		CDS 6	CDS 8	CDS 6		
Auto-						
nomous	PSD 18	PSD 16	PSD 17	PSD 17	PSD 9	PSD 15
Region of		PS 3	ASDI 1	PS 2	PS/	PS 4
The Azores					CDS 3	
	CDS 1		PS 1		PS 7	
(19)						
Auto-						
nomous	PSD 10	PSD 11	PSD 11	PSD 11	PSD 9	PSD 9
Region of	PS 1				PS 1	PS 2
Madeira					UDP 1	
(11)						

Source: Secretariado Técnico, 1994b, pp. 182, 184–203.

Last but not least, the industrial city of Setúbal is a PS-dominated municipality, although the district is overwhelmingly dominated by the communists. The dominance of the PCP not only reflects the fact that this is a strongly working-class area with a long history of political and social activism, but also that the party – as in the case of the Italian PCI/PDS – has a good reputation for policy performance at the local level, the only political level in the post-revolutionary period in which the PCP has been allowed to play a role. This has to do with the very polarised relationship the two main parties – the PS and the PSD – had with the communists during the revolutionary period.

The district of Guarda in east-central Portugal changed drastically between 1976 and 1993 from a PSD- and CDS-dominated area to a PSD and PS one. In 1976, of the 15 municipalities four had a PSD mayor, seven a CDS mayor and three a PS mayor. In 1993 this changed substantially in favour of the two largest parties: seven had a PSD mayor and seven a PS one.

Quite a mixed composition can be found in the district of Aveiro in the centre of coastal Portugal. In 1993 it had five PSD mayors, six CDS mayors and eight PS mayors. This contrasts with the situation in 1979, when of the 19 municipalities two were PS and the rest AD.

In the southern district of Alentejo the former dominance of the Communist Party is eroding, due to the fact that its traditional supporters – rural labourers – are slowly declining in number. The strength of the Communist Party was drawn from the agrarian collective farms, *Unidades colectivas de produçao* (collective production units – UCP), established after the revolution. The AD government and later the PSD majority government had a policy of returning the occupied estates to the former landowners. Moreover young people are leaving the countryside in search of a better life in the cities. These two factors are changing the social structure of the area, which is characterised by a high proportion of elderly people who are completely disoriented by this rapid process of social erosion. The communist dominance of the 1970s and early 1980s was challenged by the other parties in the second half of the 1980s and early 1990s. Nevertheless it continues to be the stronghold of the Communist Party.

The Algarve has long been dominated by the socialists, and some municipalities – such as Lagoa and Lagos – are PSD strongholds.

In the autonomous regions of Madeira and the Azores the PSD has been dominant since 1976. In the case of Madeira this can be explained by the strong populist leadership of the regional president, Alberto João Jardim, and his autocratic political style. In the Azores the regional president, Mota Amaral, is successfully playing the card of regional autonomy and is steadily gaining more concessions from the central government in Lisbon.

SOCIOPROFESSIONAL REPRESENTATION

One indication of the strength of a new democracy is the inclusion of representatives of all social strata. In this sense the Portuguese case may be seen as quite successful, because representatives have indeed been recruited from all segments of the population. Nevertheless it has to be recognised that cultural, educational and social status can be of advantage in gaining a political position at the municipal level. At the parish level the composition is more democratic.

Comparing two surveys undertaken by the Ministry of Home Affairs among the new members of local government after the elections of 1982 and 1989, one can recognise a major difference between the composition of municipal bodies and those in the parishes. Nationally, the majority of those elected to municipal chambers and municipal assemblies in 1982 and 1989 belonged to the higher social strata, such as 'higher and middle technical and scientific cadres' and 'landowners, directors and entrepreneurs', as well as 'administrative personnel'. In this sense the political actors in the municipalities were highly skilled and well-prepared for their position (Secretariado Técnico, 1993, pp. 44–5, 1986, p. 137).

Quite different was the composition of the parish political elite. The elected members in 1982 and 1989 were recruited fairly evenly from all social strata, a slight majority coming from the industrial and agricultural sectors. This means that at the parish level the political personnel had fewer educational qualifications but their concerns, outlook and approach were closer to those of the general population. (Secretariado Técnico, 1986, 1993, pp. 45–6).

At the party level there were slight differences in the socioprofessional composition of the CDS and the PCP compared with the national average. Although in 1989 most of the incoming presidents and members of the municipal bodies were elected from the 'higher and middle scientific cadres', the second and third major recruitment groups were 'administrative personnel' and 'industrial/agricultural workers'. At the parish level, in general the CDS followed the national pattern of being dominated by industrial and agricultural workers, but it recruited slightly more than the national average from among the 'higher and middle technical and scientific cadres' and 'landowners, directors, entrepreneurs' (Secretariado Técnico, 1993, pp. 40–53).

In 1989 the district composition of the local political elite was fairly evenly split between the socioprofessional groups. However in the districts of Leiria and Setúbal on the west coast and in the autonomous region of Madeira most of the municipal chamber presidents were in the 'administrative personnel' category. In the southern district of Portalegre the principal recruitment categories were 'higher and middle technical cadres' and 'administrative personnel'. Likewise, in the southern districts of Beja and Portalegre and the autonomous region of the Azores the majority of the members of the municipal chamber were 'administrative personnel'.

Municipal assemblies nationwide showed the same even distribution apart from Lisbon, where 43 per cent came from the 'higher and middle technical and scientific cadres' and 'administrative personnel', and the autonomous region of Madeira, where 30 per cent were from the 'higher and middle technical and scientific cadres' and 'landowners, directors and entrepreneurs'. In Beja and the autonomous region of the Azores those in the category 'higher and middle cadres' were equalled by 'agricultural workers' (27 per cent each). In the Azores, the 'higher and middle cadres' and 'agricultural workers' had an equal 33 per cent share.

At the parish level the socioprofessional composition was less uniform than in the municipalities. Although industrial and agricultural workers dominated local politics, in some districts the presidents of the parish board were recruited from other social groups, such as 'adminstrative personnel' and 'trade and services employees'. In the autonomous regions of the Azores and Madeira 'administrative personnel' dominated, with a share of 41 per cent and 33 per cent respectively. This was also the case among the members of the parish boards of the autonomous regions, with a share of 40 per cent and 38 per cent respectively.

The presidents of parish assemblies were predominantly 'industrial and agricultural labourers'. The main deviation was in Leiria, where the presidents came from almost all socioprofessional categories in equal share, and Lisbon, where 'administrative personnel' and 'industrial workers' were equal at 26 per cent. Last but not least, nationwide the majority of the members of the parish assembly were industrial and/or agricultural workers. They had the highest share in the north-eastern districts of Bragança, Vila Real and Guarda, where most of the members were small farmers, and the southern district of Evora, which had a large share of communist farm labourers (Secretariado Técnico, 1993, pp. 54–7).

The average age of the local government representatives was 43 years in the municipal chambers, 43 in the municipal assemblies, 46 in the parish boards and 44 in the parish assemblies. Among presidents it was 45 in the municipal chambers, 47 in the municipal assemblies, 48 in the parish boards and 44 in the parish assemblies. The average age of the members of the various bodies was 43 for in the municipal chambers, 43 in the municipal assemblies, 45 in the parish boards and 44 in the parish assemblies. One can see that the age average distribution was quite homogeneous among the different local bodies (Secretariado, 1993, pp. 68–70).

The share of female presidents and members was quite low at the
local level in 1989. Only 7 per cent of local representatives were women.
They were better represented in the local assemblies and less well in
the executive bodies. In the municipal assemblies their share was 11
per cent, in the parish assemblies 7 per cent, in the municipal chambers 6 per cent and in the parish boards 4 per cent. On average only 4
per cent held the presidency of a local body: 5 per cent of parish
assemblies, 4 per cent of municipal assemblies, 3 per cent of parish
boards and 2 per cent of municipal chambers. The highest percentage
of female participation in local bodies was in the autonomous region
of Madeira (16 per cent) followed by Setúbal and Lisbon (15 per cent
each). The communist coalition had the highest share of women in
their local government teams with 13 per cent, followed by the PS
with 6 per cent and the CDS and the PSD with 5 per cent each. Female participation had slightly improved since 1982, when it was around
5.1 per cent (Secretariado Técnico, 1986, pp. 227–364, 1993, pp. 21–
35). Structurally, female participation was quite similar after the two
elections.

The integration of women into the local political system is an important task for the future, because of the necessity to bring in new
issues that are related to the well-being of the majority of the population. In what is still a male-dominated society, politics is seen as the
domain of men. Moreover in Portuguese male discourse there is a tendency to believe that women need male protection in the political field,
so female politicians can be only liberated with the help of their male
colleagues (Faria, Grosso and Lopes, 1986, p. 218).

PROBLEMS OF PERFORMANCE IN LOCAL GOVERNMENT

Having analysed the representativeness of local government political
personnel, we will now turn our attention to the efficiency of policy
formulation and implementation at the local level.

The 1970s and 1980s were decades of decentralisation and deconcentration of central-state activities. However political instability until
the mid 1980s prevented a thorough reorganisation of centre–periphery
responsibilities.

The legal framework for the democratic local political system was
defined in several laws. The first (number 79/77 of 25 October 1977)
defined the activities of the new local bodies (this law was revised by
decree on 29 March 1984 – number 100/84). The first law merely

gave local government the right to administer its own properties, to act as a development agency, and to ensure the maintenance of public health, culture and assistance. The areas of health, education and teaching, leisure activities and sport, environmental control and civil protection were added later. Full details of these were not specified in the law, so much depends on the dynamism of individual local governments and how they interpret its scope.

Law number 1/79 of 2 January 1979 granted some financial autonomy to local government and introduced the *Fundo de Equilibrio Financeiro* (Fund of Financial Balancing) as an additional instrument for transfering funds from the centre to the local authorities. This was extended in decree number 98/84 of 29 March 1984 (Pessoa, 1986, pp. 515–16). In 1987 a further legislative act required local authorities to prepare municipal development plans for approval (*Plano Director Municipal – PDM*) (Syrett, 1994, pp. 169–70).

This legislation has been gradually implemented in the 1980s and 1990s, and the role of local government as a factor of development has been increasingly recognised by Portuguese scholars and the central administration alike. The main problem is that the 'grand design' outlined in the constitution is still not fully implemented. The main missing link between the lowest units of government — the parish and the municipality – is the the administrative region. This would be a far more important tier of local government then one would think, because it could enhance coordination of development strategies between the scattered municipalities and promote even development across the country. In the 1980s, several studies on local government were carried out in order to identify its problems. The main problem seems to be the restricted financial autonomy granted by the government. Local government in Portugal has strict budgetary guidelines: current expenditure must not exceed current receipts, expenditure on wages must not exceed three quarters of the receipts of the current year. Medium- and long-term borrowing is only allowed for investment purposes. Therefore local government debt is quite a low proportion of total government debt – in 1991 it amounted to just 1 per cent).

Local direct taxes are property taxes and a surcharge on business taxes (up to a maximum of 10 per cent). Indirect taxes are related to VAT receipts from tourism. On average these revenues constituted 26 per cent of local government receipts in 1991 (Table 4.4). A further 10 per cent was generated from user charges, which seem only to have covered 60 per cent of the total cost of the services provided.

Central government accounted for 35 per cent of local government

European Portugal

Table 4.4 Local government accounts (Percentage of total
receipts and outlays)

	1987	1991
Receipts		
Taxes	24.2	25.9
Charges and property income	10.2	10.2
Current transfers	28.3	21.1
Other receipts	4.0	2.2
Total current receipts	66.7	59.4
Capital transfers		
FEF*	18.8	14.1
Community funds	3.7	11.6
Other	3.5	4.5
Other capital receipts	7.2	10.5
Total capital transfers	33.2	40.6
Outlays		
Personnel	29.0	29.1
Goods and services	14.7	14.2
Interest payments	2.9	2.8
Other current expenditure	7.7	7.1
Total current expenditure	54.3	53.1
Capital expenditure		
Investment	38.9	39.1
Other capital expenditure	6.8	7.8
Total capital expenditure	45.7	46.9

* From the state budget.

Source: Ministry of Planning, quoted from OECD, 1993, p. 32.

funds in 1991. The transfer criteria are based on a formula that takes
several factors into account, such as population size, area, number of
dwellings, per capita fiscal receipts and basic needs. Local authorities
have had to face a steady and continuous decline in central government transfers since 1991, which has been only partly compensated by
funds transferred from the EC/EU (OECD, 1993, p. 31).

These financial constraints are preventing local government from
playing a more central role in the development of the country. In the
1980s several surveys seemed to confirm that local government representatives were very aware of these financial constraints and perceived them as the major impediment to their adopting a more innovative
role in local affairs. Instead the tendency was to remain within the
legally defined boundaries imposed by the centre. This was quite evi-

dent in the early 1980s, when most of the local representatives were learning to deal with central–local relations. This changed to a more diversified approach on the part of local authorities during the second half of the 1980s and the 1990s. Different, sometimes very innovative strategies were developed to change their relationship with the central government including informal approaches to the central authorities. Moreover local representatives seemed to be very worried about the strong element of bureaucracy in the relationship between centre and periphery, which was only natural in light of the very restricted financial autonomy granted to local government (Mozzicaffredo *et al.*, 1991; Ruivo, 1993).

Furthermore it seems that policy making and implementation has been a direct response to the short-term needs expressed by the population rather than taking long-term planning considerations into account. In the 1980s only a very limited number of municipalities had a Directive Municipal Plan (PDM) with long-term implications and integrated into the general national development plan (Mozzicaffredo *et al.*, 1991). On the whole it seems that the need for long-term planning is still not sufficiently appreciated at the central and local levels, and coordination between the different levels is still in the early stages. In addition the continuing disparity in service provision between the west-coast districts and the eastern ones, the shortage of human and material resources, the need to introduce modern technologies in certain policy areas, such as the environment, and above all the slowness in devolving financial autonomy are major obstacles to improving efficiency at the local level.

These problems seem not to be due to a lack of will, but rather to a culture of short-termism and the legacy of underdevelopment and centralisation inherited from previous state traditions (Graham, 1982, 1993; Gago and Pereira, 1990; Portas and Gago, 1980, pp. 236–7; Syrett, 1993). This is reinforced by the persistence of patrimonial patterns of behaviour and the practice of patronage (Silva, 1993). Nevertheless one has to acknowledge that these are gradually being eroded and replaced by democratic conduct and accountability.

The local situation improved slightly after Portugal joined the EC, and the flow of structural funds has been a major factor in local development. The European Regional Development Fund (ERDF) has contributed 50 per cent of the cost of local projects and grants from the European Social Fund have led to the creation of local agents to work in the area of vocational training.

The Europeanisation of local government is also leading to new forms of cooperation between localities. Intermunicipal cooperation is becoming a frequent strategy to overcome financial constraints when developing new projects. In central Portugal the number of local initiatives to set up new industrial plants, parks and tourist areas has increased (Syrett, 1993, pp. 57, 59–60).

In spite of all the obstacles caused by the lack of coordination between the central and local administrative structures, local representatives and administrators seem to be actively engaged in promoting the importance of local government in Portugal. Local authorities have set up a local-interest group called the *Associaçao Portuguesa de Autarcas Municipais* (Portuguese Association of Municipalities). The president of the association, Mário de Almeida, who is also president of the municipal chamber of Vila do Conde, was able to enhance the image of local authorities by criticising the cuts the central government made in budget transfers to local government in 1992–3. For example, on 11 December 1992 he united the local municipal representatives in a one-day general strike to protest against the government's plan to transfer additional responsibilities to the local authorities without providing them with extra funds – on the contrary, the central financial transfer was to be reduced. Most of the PSD municipalities boycotted this strike, but several of them did join in (*Expresso*, 12 December 1992, p. A8, 5 June 1993, p. A24).

Although regional disparities between the coastal local authorities and the peripheral eastern ones widened in the early 1990s and most of the structural funds went to the better-developed regions (Eaton, 1994, pp. 41–5), the EC/EU has been an important agent in changing attitudes and improving the quality of life in Portugal. The process of Europeanisation is a twin of democratisation. It is fostering open-mindedness, institutionalising democratic behaviour through cooperative projects, eroding authoritarian patterns of thinking, changing the quality of life of the citizens, enhancing the manoeuvrability of local governments by providing them with financial alternatives, supporting the decentralisation of government and its services, increasing the awareness of local politicians and promoting democratic accountability. All these processes are feeding each other and are crucial to the sustainability of local politics. Political learning is not an individual process, it is a social, intergenerational one. Local politics is the ideal tier of representation to build up an ethos of democratic politics.

CONCLUSIONS

At the end of July 1994 Prime Minister Cavaco Silva announced that he was against the creation of administrative regions in continental Portugal. He said that Portugal was traditionally a unitary country and the introduction of administrative regions would lead to particularism and threaten national cohesion. The opposition was surprised by this statement as the creation of administrative regions had been defined in the constitution of 1976, in 1991 a law framing the administrative regions had been unanimously approved by parliament and so far there had been interparty consensus on the importance of regionalisation for the development of the country (*O Público*, 30 July 1994, pp. 2–5).

In my view administrative regionalisation will be the crucial issue for the next couple of decades, because it will lead to a further deconcentration of the administration and bring services closer to the citizens. Moreover the regions will be legitimate, democratically accountable tiers of government and will improve the coordination of local development among municipalities, mostly because regional governments will include delegates from the municipalities and the parishes. Besides, regional and local development will make it possible for certain ministries and institutions (for example auditing institutions such as the Constitutional Court and the Court of Auditors) to be transferred to peripheral urban areas in line with the German *Land* model.

Local authorities are still facing many problems, most of which are related to the very bureaucratic central–local relationship and the restricted financial budget. Nevertheless it seems that during the past two decades local authorities have learned to cope with these difficulties and have developed strategies to overcome the more acute problems. Intermunicipal cooperation seems to be the trend for the future. This will be supported by the EU Common Support Framework 1994–9. Democratic accountability through elections will be an important factor in sustaining this inevitable process of cooperation and democratisation.

5 The Political Parties

THE PORTUGUESE PARTY SYSTEM: IMPERFECT
MULTIPARTYISM

After the Second World War most West European countries developed
more or less stable party systems as democratic channels of popular
representation, based on the principle of electoral competition. Periodic elections gave assurance of at least a hypothetical alternation of
power and ensured governmental accountability. Most of these party
systems reflected a democratic tradition that stretched back into the
late nineteenth century. Some were a continuation of the pre-war system (for example in Sweden and Britain). Others learned from the
negative outcome of their previous experiences (for example in Germany and Italy). But all of them shared a common element – a historical blueprint to refer to and adapt. Although in some cases one can
speak of a discontinuity of party systems and political regimes, all of
them were characterised by continuous political learning to improve
the ambivalent relationship between stability and conditions of opti-
mum representation, such as electoral law, universal suffrage and the
nature of party structures. This continuous political learning is crucial
to shaping democratic behaviour and removing the uncertainty that may
be inherent during the early day of a new party system.

The postwar development of party systems was further conditioned
by the transformation of the social structure and the introduction of
the welfare state. The founding principles of some parties began to
vanish in the 1960s and 1970s. Ideology was replaced by a more technocratic, issue-oriented approach aimed at maximising votes and 'catch-
all' parties began to emerge, thus changing the nature of the electoral
field. Politics based on economic principles now occupied the political
sphere, and political marketing changed the relationship between represented and representative. The political parties defined the political
choices of those they represented and defined this in view of preserving the stability of the political system (Aguiar, 1988).

The 1980s and 1990s saw a further erosion of the traditional parties. Although the newly emerged 'catch-all' parties were still quite
dominant in the 1980s, other new movements began to challenge the
monopoly of the larger traditional parties, for example the small 'green'

parties in West Germany, Austria, Italy and Scandinavia. Environmental issues and greater governmental transparency were their main concerns. Today these issues have become a common part of our vocabulary, along with such expressions as 'sustained democracy', 'decentralisation of decision making' and 'sustained development'.

In the mid 1980s there was a resurgence of nationalism, spearheaded by xenophobic and racist parties such as Le Pen's *Front Nationale*, the *Vlamse Blok* in Belgium, the *Republikaner* in West Germany and the populist Freedom Party of Joerg Haider in Austria. Their main slogans were directed against foreigners living in their countries, arguing that the incomers were taking jobs away from their fellow nationals. In general they were opposed to the European Community, which was regarded as a threat to national sovereignty. The fall of the Berlin Wall, the collapse of communism, in Eastern Europe and the Soviet Union, the erosion of national autonomy in financial and economic matters, and the growing number of people emigrating from Eastern Europe and Third World countries were major factors contributing to the emergence of these parties.

In the 1990s we are confronted with a new phenomenon: the so-called 'anti-parties' that have emerged to protest against the established party systems. The most famous of these are Berlusconi's *Forza Italia* and the *Lega del Nord* in northern Italy, which, although founded in the early 1980s, became major anti-Rome parties in the early 1990s. The nature of such parties varies from country to country, but their main thrust seems to lie in counteracting the negative effects arising from the longevity of the traditional parties. The collapse of the Italian party system after 1992 because most of the leaders of the main Italian parties were involved in a bribery scandal is the most extreme example of a general outcry against 'partyocracy' (*New Politics*, 1995).

Last but not least is the growing transnationalisation of party systems. European parliamentary elections since 1979 have led to a more cohesive, though still fragile, supranational structure of party families that is changing the nature of party politics in Western Europe. This supranational dimension will gain in significance in the future, because the representative structures at this higher level are still in their infancy. Although this supranational party system is still in the making and many aspects of it have yet to be resolved, it is important to mention it here, so that one can better understand the external environmental context in which the new Portuguese political system has emerged.

The Portuguese case cannot be included in these general trends as the new party system emerged only in 1975 during a revolutionary process. For the first time Portuguese elections were based on the principle of universal suffrage. Nobody knew which kind of party system would emerge after the elections, especially as past experiences of electoral politics had been rather negative. As discussed earlier, the political regimes of the nineteenth and twentieth centuries were based on patronage and a restrictive electoral law, and were characterised by political, economic and social instability. During the authoritarian regime of Antonio Salazar elections were held, but opposition was quashed and the results manipulated.

The new parties had to struggle to gain a popular profile during the revolution. When most of their leaders – for example the socialist Mário Soares and the communist Alvaro Cunhal – returned from exile abroad in 1974 the political space was monopolised by the revolutionary MFA, which from the beginning opposed the formation of political parties. The MFA's first programme conceded the formation of political *associations* only, a word that implied their importance should be subordinate to the objectives of the revolutionary movement. This uncertainty over the role and place of the parties in the emerging political system was not apparent at the beginning, and the provisional governments consisted of representatives of the main political forces.

The relationship between the MFA and the political parties began to deteriorate after July 1974, when one of the MFA leaders, Colonel Vasco Gonçalves, took over the second provisional government. Before his appointment nobody knew that he had been member of the Communist Party since the 1950s. Vasco Gonçalves remained the main actor of the Portuguese revolution until August 1975. During this period he contributed to a radicalisation of the revolution and the deterioration of relations between the MFA and the parties.

Shortly before the elections of 25 April 1975 Vasco Gonçalves and other members of the MFA urged the voters to cast a blank ballot in the elections because they thought the people were ill-prepared for electoral matters. (After the *coup d'état* of 11 March 1975 the MFA had pressed the parties to sign a pact that guaranteed the leadership of the MFA would not be contested by the parties after the elections.) However the electorate not only ignored this plea but also decided to vote for the more moderate parties – the PS and the PPD. The Communist Party was only able to gain around 12 per cent of the votes.

After these elections the new party system became quite well-defined. A multiparty system emerged, which had at its core the four main parties – the PS, the PPD, the CDS and the PCP – with other smaller parties to the left and the right of the spectrum.

The revolutionary process began to collapse as the newly elected parties now had a mandate to promote representative democracy at the expense of the revolution. This led to a united front of the main parties, the PS and the PPD, against the communist stream of the MFA, the Gonçalvists. The collapse of the fifth provisional government, formed during August 1975 and supported only by the Communist Party, led to the isolation of the Goncalvists inside the MFA.

During autumn 1975 the newly elected parties were able to gain control over the political field, although the number of power centres proliferated during this period. Different actors in the revolutionary movement, the MFA and the soldiers' councils attempted to reverse the progress towards normalisation of political life. However radicalisation of the revolution was abruptly stopped in November, when a countercoup against a supposed coup by the extreme left and elements of the Communist Party was crushed by Lieutenant Ramalho Eanes.

The structure of politics did not change after the revolutionary period and it remained a four-party system. If we look at the aggregate results of the legislative elections between 1975 and 1991 we can see that voters in Portugal, although volatile, were quite conservative in their choice and mainly stuck to the four main parties (Tables 5.1–5.3).

The stability of the Portuguese party system was disturbed in 1985 following the emergence of a presidentialist party, the Renewal Democratic Party (PRD), under the leadership of Herminio Martins. The party was dominated by President Ramalho Eanes and after the end of his presidency in 1986 he took over its leadership. The PRD was able to gain almost 18 per cent of the votes, without having a very strong electoral organisation.

This transfer of votes may be seen as a protest against the former governmental coalition of the PS and the PSD, called the Central Bloc, which had imposed very austere economic measures upon the population. However two years later the PRD lost more than two thirds of its votes and in 1991 took less than 1 per cent. The main reason for its decline was that its work in the Assembly of the Republic between 1985 and 1987 was not very constructive. Nonetheless it brought down the government with a motion of censure in early 1987, which was supported by the other parties.

The case of the PRD highlights the fact that although the four-party system is very stable, the electorate seems to be continuously searching for viable alternatives. A further development is that two of the four main parties, the PS and the PSD, are attracting most of the votes, their share having substantially increased since 1987 (Table 5.2).

Table 5.1 Legislative elections, 1976–91

Party	Percentage of votes	Number of seats
1976–9		
CDS	16.00	42
PPD/PSD	24.38	73
PS	34.87	107
PCP	14.35	40
UDP	1.67	1
Others	8.73	–
1979–80		
AD (PPD + CDS + PPM)	42.52	128
PS	27.33	74
APU (PCP + MDP	18.80	47
UDP	2.18	1
Others	9.17	–
1980–3		
AD (PPD + CDS + PPM)	44.91	134
FRS (PS + UEDS)	26.65	74
APU (PCP + MDP	16.75	45
UDP	1.38	1
Others	10.31	–
1983–5		
CDS	12.56	30
PPD/PSD	27.00	75
PS	36.12	101
APU	18.07	44
Others	6.25	–
1985–7		
CDS	9.96	22
PPD/PSD	29.87	88
PRD	17.92	45
PS	20.77	57
APU	15.49	38
Others	5.99	
1987–91		
CDS	4.44	4
PPD/PSD	50.22	148
PRD	4.91	7
PS	22.24	60
CDU (PCP +'Os Verdes')	12.14	31
Others	6.05	–

The Political Parties

85

Table 5.1 continued

Party	Percentage of votes	Number of seats
1991–		
CDS/PP	4.44	5
PPD/PSD	50.40	135
PS	29.30	72
CDU	8.80	17
PSN	1.70	1
Others	5.36	

*Two independents

Sources: Cruz and Antunes, 1990, pp. 163–4; Secretariado Técnico, 1992, pp. 7–11.

Table 5.2 Aggregate electoral results, PS and PSD, 1976–91 (per cent)

	Four main parties	PS	PSD	PS+PSD
1976	89.61	34.87	24.38	59.26
1983	94.56	36.12	27.24	63.36
1985	76.09	20.77	29.80	50.64
1987	89.04	22.24	50.22	72.46
1991	92.96	29.13	50.60	79.73

Source: Own calculations, based on data in Rosário and Migueis, 1992, pp. 38–9.

Table 5.3 Aggregate electoral results, APU/CDU and CDS/PP, 1976–91 (per cent)

	Four main parties	APU/CDU	CDS/PP	CDU+CDS
1976	89.61	14.35	16.00	30.35
1983	94.56	18.70	12.25	31.20
1985	76.09	15.49	9.96	25.45
1987	89.04	12.14	4.44	16.48
1991	92.96	8.83	4.43	13.26

Source: Own calculations, based on data in Rosário and Migueis, 1992, pp. 38–9.

Table 5.4   Electoral volatility and interbloc volatility in legislative
elections, 1975–91*

	Total	Vol. Interbloc swings
1975		
1976	11.3	6.6
1979	10.5	3.2
1980	4.6	1.7
1983	11.2	7.8
1985	22.5	0.5
1987	23.2	15.5
1991	9.5	1.2

*Total electoral volatility is the sum of every difference (the absolute value
of the variation in comparison with the previous election) in the percentages
of votes cast for each party participating in the elections, divided by two.
Interbloc Volatility or Area Volatility, is the sum of the difference between
the percentage of votes cast for the right, centre and the left, divided by
two.

Source: Preliminary calculations in Morlino, 1995, pp. 318, 320.

The community and the conservative CDS have suffered a decline
in votes since the mid 1980s (Table 5.3). There are several reasons for
this, but the main one seems to be that social change is eroding their
electoral base. In the case of the CDS, its traditional supporters – the
small farmers of northern Portugal – are diminishing in number, and
some may now be voting for the PSD.

The main supporters of the communists were farm labourers in the
districts of Beja and Evora. In the 1980s the AD government and later
the PSD government withdrew the financial support that had been provided to the communist-dominated collective land estates in the south,
where most of the labourers were allocated work throughout the year.
The drying up of bank loans and other forms of aid led to the closure
of these collectives and the return of the estates to their prerevolutionary
owners. As a result, since 1987 this stronghold of the Communist Party
has been partly penetrated by the social democrats.

Very interesting is the finding by Leonardo Morlino that, apart from
the exceptional election of 1987, left–right and right–left swings by
voters are less pronounced than interparty swings in general (Table 5.4).
This means that right and left are quite well-defined in Portugal.

Looking at these findings in greater depth, it appears that the Communist Party has the most stable electoral base and has been able to

retain 86–95 per cent of the voters who voted for it in the previous elections. In the early 1980s, the communists attracted a number of traditional PS voters, but in the second half of the 1980s this additional support waned. The PS voters were quite loyal until 1983, and the PS retained between 88 per cent and 95 per cent of its voters in election after election. However this changed in 1985, when the PRD attracted 24 per cent of those who had voted for the PS in 1983. In 1985 only 45 per cent of those remaining remained loyal to the party, 7 per cent having turned to the PSD. The party's fortunes recovered slightly in 1987, when it regained 11 per cent of the votes lost to the PRD in 1985, although only 62 per cent of the PS voters of 1985 voted again for the party, 14 per cent having voted for the PSD. In 1991 it increased its percentage of returning traditional voters.

The PSD's electoral fortunes have been far more propitious. Until the mid 1980s the PSD was able to retain between 75 per cent and 81 per cent of its voters, but in 1987 the party not only retained more than 90 per cent of its voters of 1985, but also won over about 30 per cent from the CDS, 23 per cent from the PRD and 14 per cent from the PS. The PSD was able to retain this voting composition in 1991.

Finally, the CDS has experienced the greatest voter volatility of all the main parties and is in danger of losing its place in the present party system. Until the elections of 1985 its traditional voting bloc represented between 72 per cent and 75 per cent of the conservative vote. This changed in 1987, when its share declined to 50 per cent and it lost about 30 per cent of its voters of 1985 to the PSD. This downward trend continued in the 1991 elections (Bruneau and Macleod, 1986; *Expresso*, 25 July 1987, pp. 32R–38R; Bacalhau, 1989; Matos, 1994, pp. 157–60). As already mentioned, this can be explained by the erosion of its power base as a result of modernisation and social change, which also explains the success of the new populist–nationalist strategy of Manuel Monteiro in winning over farmers and fishermen, the losers of the European integration process.

A notable trend over the years has been the growing number of abstentions. While in 1975 only 8.3 per cent of registered voters remained at home, in 1979 this value increased to 12.5 per cent, in 1983 to 21.4 per cent, in 1987 to 27.4 per cent and in 1991 to 32.33 per cent. This practice is widespread among small farmers in the northeastern regions of Portugal, who are disillusioned with the new political system, as well as among the population in eastern Alentejo and the petty bourgeoisie of the small and larger cities (*Diário Popular*, 20 July 1987, pp. 24–5; *Expresso*, 7 May 1983, p. 44-R, 25 July 1987,

p. 37-R; Gaspar, 1985, p. 143; André and Gaspar, 1989, pp. 259–60, 274–6).

This general review of the changing political situation since the mid 1970s brings one conclusion to the fore: social change due to modernisation is changing the social composition of the four main parties. In 1975 the PS was mainly supported by the new, urban middle classes, the industrial workers. In the late 1980s and early 1990s the PS had a very mixed electoral base that included farmers and other social groups. In this sense, it has become a 'catch-all' party. The main strongholds of the socialists are the large urban centres of Porto, Lisbon and Setúbal, the Algarve and some parts of central Portugal around Aveiro, Coimbra and Castelo Branco.

The PSD has almost the same social composition as the PSD. It too is developing into a 'catch-all' party with a more technocratic, centre-right image. The main supporters of the PSD are farmers in northern Portugal and the rural and urban petty bourgeoisie in villages and towns of 2000 inhabitants or fewer. This tendency already existed in 1975 and became even more pronounced in the 1980s and 1990s. The party also dominates the two autonomous regions of the Azores and Madeira. The 1991 election brought gains by the party in Alentejo from among the predominantly PS-supporting farmers.

The communists are supported by the farm labourers of the southern region of Alentejo and industrial workers in southern Portugal. In addition the suburbs of Lisbon and Setúbal are dominated by the Communist Party. The communists have always found it difficult to gain the votes of landowners and the middle-classes. It remains essentially a working-class party and continues to cultivate this image. In the 1987 and 1991 elections the communists experienced a decline in its traditional support due to modernisation and the depopulation of the Alentejo region.

The CDS is well-entrenched in the northern farming community and its supporters are from the higher echelons of this group. The CDS has also found strong support among entrepreneurs and managers. Nevertheless, since 1987 many of its traditional voters have transferred their allegiance to the PSD, following the logic of the useful vote. This explains the populist discourse of the party's leader, Manuel Monteiro, who is attempting to attract those who were being neglected by the PSD government.

In 1985 the PRD was able to attract a section of the new middle classes, although it found it difficult to win over farmers and farm labourers. Its geographical stronghold was the region of Ribatejo, particularly the capital of the district, Santarém, the birthplace of its leader, Herminio Martins (Lewis and Williams, 1984, pp. 132–3; Gaspar, 1985, pp. 142–3; André and Gaspar, 1989, p. 273).

All this seems to suggest that in the 1990s the Portuguese party system is developing towards an 'imperfect two-party system' (*bipartidismo imperfeito*) comprising the PS and the PSD and excluding the other two main parties, the CDS and the PCP, from governmental responsibility (Corkill, 1993b). In the late 1970s and the first half of the 1980s an 'imperfect multiparty system' (*multipartidismo imperfeito*) existed, which excluded the PCP from governmental responsibility, largely because of the ambivalent position shown by the PCP during the revolutionary period. The political influence of the PCP was confined mainly to the local level, where it was able to build up an excellent reputation in local government.

The current discussions between the two main parties about changing the electoral law from a party list system to a mixed one based on smaller single-member constituencies and a party list may have considerable repercussions on the nature of the elections. It may be, and this is presently under discussion, that the two-party system will be reinforced by the introduction of a first-past-the post system, as in Britain, and lead to abandonment of the proportional representation system that exists at the moment (Corkill, 1993b, p. 528). Currently elections are based on the D'hondt electoral system. Although this tends to favour the largest parties in terms of parliamentary seats, it nevertheless makes it possible for smaller parties to achieve representation in the unicameral Assembly of the Republic.

The danger of introducing a first-past-post system is that it could lead to a repeat of the political excesses of the past, where a two-party system led to the reinforcement of corruption, patronage and a constant change of the constitutional provisions to suit the dominant political party. A mixed system based on constituencies and proportional representation seems to be the most appropriate in the case of Portugal. Nevertheless one should be aware that any new electoral system will need a culture to sustain it. Otherwise it could degenerate into a return of past practices, whereby most of the leaders live in Lisbon and are natives of the large urban centres (Cruz and Antunes, 1990).

One particular aspect of the present party system that needed to be reformed was the law governing the financing of parties. (The corruption scandals in Italy over party financing have their echoes in Portugal.) A decree on the matter was issued in November 1974 during the revolutionary period and before the constitution had been proclaimed, but this was never formalised. It is assumed that in the 1980s and 1990s all the parties were financed illegally. The control mechanisms outlined in the law of 1974 are very vague. It stipulates that a report on financial accounting should be published annually by each party, but in reality this has never been adhered to or enforced. The possibility of private persons or organisations influencing politics is very real. The new proposals place particular emphasis on private donations, which will have to have specific legislation. The public prosecutor has been particularly worried about the very general provisions laid down in the law, and the very ambivalent formulation of clauses relating to sanctions in the case of corruption have prevented the public prosecutor from undertaking any actions (*Diário de Notícias*, 14 August 1992, p. 5; *Expresso*, 20 March 1993, pp. A4–A5).

In 1993 several cases of falsified company invoices were drawn to the attention of the Portuguese public prosecutor. As in the case of the Italian, Brazilian, Spanish and French scandals, in some instances these related to illicit party financing, which seems to be a common practice in many firms (*Expresso*, 27 November 1993, pp. A17, A24).

The new law of party functioning and financing, which was issued in December 1993 after the regional elections, defines the maximum amount of party finances that can be raised from private donors. All donations have to be accompanied by a written declaration and the parties' accounts are subject to periodic checks by the Auditing Court. (*Expresso*, 20 November 1993, p. A5).

The Portuguese party system found its format already after the elections to the Constituent Assembly in 1975. Since then, four main parties – PS, PSD, PCP and CDS – have dominated the political spectrum. On average, they aggregate about 90 per cent of the vote in every election. This indicates that the four-party format is very stable. Looking more closely we came to the conclusion, that although the party system is ultra-stable, it is at the same time very fluid, and total electoral volatility between the main parties is high. In terms of inter-bloc volatility the party system is less fluid, with the exception of the year 1987, which led to a massive transfer of voters from the left-wing PS and PRD to the right-centre PSD (see Aguiar, 1982, 1985b, 1994).

Another feature of the party system is that the share of the two main parties in relation to the smaller parties has increased by 20 per cent, which indicates that Portugal is moving towards a two-party system. In this sense, the so-called *imperfect multipartyism*, which excluded the Communist Party from governmental responsibility, is being replaced by an *'imperfect bipartyism'* (Corkill, 1993a). The present discussion of a reform of the electoral system, which implies a change towards a mixed party list and constituency-based system, will probably reinforce this tendency towards a two-party system.

THE PARTIES

The Socialist Party (Partido Socialista – PS)

The Socialist Party was founded on 19 April 1973 in Bad Muenstereiffel near Bonn and gained the support of the German Social Democrats in terms of material resources. It based itself on the idea of 'democratic socialism' rather than the real socialism of Eastern Europe.

The new party was able to refer to a tradition of socialism in Portugal that went back to 1875. The founders of socialism in nineteenth-century Portugal were José Fontana and Antero de Quental. This first Portuguese Socialist Party came to the end of its existence in 1932 during the authoritarian rule. There were several attempts to revive the party, but all failed.[1]

The rebirth of the Socialist Party in 1973 was initiated under the leadership of the lawyer and regime oppositionist Mário Soares, who, together with other socialists in exile, had formed the Acção Socialista Portuguesa (Portuguese Socialist Action – ASP) in Geneva in 1964. During the late 1960s the ASP had had increasing contact with the Socialist International, and in 1972 it had become a full member of that organisation (Nosty, 1975, pp. 79–82, 89–92). This 'internationalisation' of the ASP during the 1960s and early 1970s proved a major advantage when the PS came to play its role in the revolution in Portugal (Soares, 1976, p. 202).

Surprised by the military coup, Mário Soares returned to Portugal in late April. The new Socialist Party had no infrastructure in continental Portugal, and the group consisted of a few intellectuals returning from exile.[2] At first the party adopted a policy of cooperating with all democratic forces, including the Communist Party. However the socialists' relationship with the latter changed during the autumn of 1974 and deteriorated into overt conflict between the two parties. The socialists denounced the PCP's attempt to control the state apparatus and the media.

By the time of the second party conference, the socialist leadership had come to realise that the party was no longer one of intellectuals, but had gained mass appeal (Soares, 1975a, pp. 7–8). This gave added impetus to the socialists' struggle against the communists and the radical faction of the MFA, represented by the prime minister, Colonel Vasco Gonçalves. This conflict became evident in January 1975, when the radical faction of the MFA wanted to introduce a law that would force all trade union branches to become part of the communist-dominated *Intersindical* and thus create a single trade union organisation. This was vigorously opposed by the PS.

The so-called 'war of the demonstrations' during the first month of the year was characterised by both sides exaggerating the number of demonstrators they could mobilise for their purposes (Ferreira, 1983, pp. 108–9). The introduction of the law was postponed after the attempted coup of 11 March 1975.

The conflict between the two parties heightened during the year. The internationalisation of the Socialist Party, described earlier, had led to solidarity between the PS and the socialist parties of other countries, and after the elections of 1975 Mário Soares was able to mobilise the Socialist International against the supposed communist takeover. A 'committee of solidarity with the democracy and freedom in Portugal' was set up by Willy Brandt, Olof Palme and Bruno Kreisky. The main purpose of the committee was to increase international awareness of the situation in Portugal, and Soares became the pivotal figure in this fight against the Communist Party. The PS's determination strengthened when the building housing the Socialist Party newspaper, *A Republica*, was occupied by elements of the extreme-left Maoist party, the MRPP. Soares accused the Communist Party of being behind this action.

The tension between the socialists and the communists continued throughout the 1970s and 1980s, but the PS managed to maintain its dominant position on the left. After the party's electoral victory in 1976 Soares organised the first constitutional government. This minority government was quite inexperienced and lacked a strong base in parliament. Moreover the lack of qualified personnel was a major obstacle to policy design.

This socialist experiment was also undermined by a lack of party unity. The members of the PS had placed high hopes on the fact that the socialist government had a unique opportunity to continue the revolutionary process by constitutional means, but the government's austerity policies disappointed many of the party's left-wing militants. Factionalism on the part of the left wing of the party, led by the former minister of agriculture, Lopes Cardoso, made it difficult for the party to implement these policies and led to this group splitting from the party in December 1978 (Rother, 1985, pp. 171–9; Magone, 1995a, p. 98).

Soares went on to guide the party towards a revision of its ideological programme, which had advocated a course between social democracy and true socialism. In 1973 and 1974 the party programme had proclaimed that fulfilment of 'democratic socialism' was its main aim, to be steadily achieved by a cultural revolution that would bring about a classless society in Portugal. While Marxism was regarded as a source of inspiration for the party, it was not treated in dogmatic terms. Rather it was decreed that 'socialist democracy' should respect the pluralism of society, which should be based on the dignity of man, freedom of speech, human rights and organisation of the state of law (Nosty, 1975, pp. 97–101; Partido Socialista, 1974).

Under Soares' guidance this ideological programme changed during the 1980s towards a more liberal social-democratic position. This 'social-democratisation' of the Socialist Party was accompanied by a 'de-Marxisation' of the party programme. In its programme of 1986 the party no longer tried to distance itself from West European social democracy. On the contrary, it seems that it absolutely identified with the position held by the Socialist International, as became evident during the sixth party congress in 1986 (Partido Socialista, 1986).

Integration into the EC reinforced this position, as incorporation into the transnational structures of the European Socialist Group, and later on the European Socialist Party, had repercussions on the programme of the PS. The party came to be run by technocrats such as Vitor Constâncio, Jaime Gama and the current secretary-general, António Guterres (Lourenço, 1984, pp. 39–43, 40–1; Gallagher, 1990; Partido Socialista, 1991; Magone, 1995b).

Mário Soares and his supporters – the Soaristas – were and are still very influential inside the party. Vitor Constâncio, Jaime Gama and António Guterres have all been subject to criticism by Soares, and all three were criticised for not being confrontational enough with the PSD government.

Recently the major cleavage within the party has been between the secretary-general, António Guterres, and the president of the municipal chamber of Lisbon, Jorge Sampaio. Sampaio was regarded as a more charismatic and popular candidate for the position of secretary-general than Guterres. The Sampaistas are very close to the Soaristas and represent the left-wing factions within the party. The Guterristas have adopted a more pragmatic, centrist stance and have a tendency to

Table 5.5   Secretary-generals of the PS, 1973–95

Mário Soares	1973–85
Vítor Constâncio	1986–88
Jorge Sampaio	1989–92
António Guterres	1992–

use the same language as the British Labour Party, for example calling themselves the 'shadow government' (*governo de sombra*).

The organisational structure of the PS is still highly centralised. It has never managed to become a mass party, rather it is a party of cadres. It was very popular during the revolutionary period and attracted almost 92 000 members. It lost about 50 000 between 1976 and 1986, but later it was able to increase its membership to about 70 000 (Table 5.6). About 20–30 per cent of the members are militants, taking part in general ballots and acting as representatives at party conferences. The main problem with the membership data is that they include people who have paid no contributions for two years or more. This has to do with the fact that the more members a branch has, the more delegates it can send to the national party conference. Therefore the figures shown in Table 5.6, even after 1986, have to be treated with reservation. Activism on the part of the militants is mainly restricted to elections and no socialist subculture as such exists between the elections.

The party is dominated by the secretary-general and the national commission. Both are elected by the national party congress, the highest body of the party. The national commission is the party's legislative body. The political commission, which includes 40 elected members and *ex-officio* members, carries through the policies approved by the congress. The real power lies in the permanent commission, consisting of seven members elected from a list proposed by the secretary-general or a third of the party members (Bruneau and Macleod, 1976, p. 68; Partido Socialista, 1991).

The tendency towards centralisation grew over the years, particularly from 1981–5 with the reentry of Mário Soares and his autocratic style (Bruneau and Macleod, 1986, p. 68; Gallagher, 1990, pp. 21–6). After 1985 the party lost a substantial number of votes and the technocratic leaders came under constant attack by the Soaristas. The present leader, António Guterres, hopes to bring about a victory over the governing PSD in the 1995 elections, and used the recent regional elections and the European parliamentary elections as precampaigns for this end.

The Political Parties

95

Table 5.6 Membership of the PS, 1974–92

Total membership	
1974	35 971
1975	77 625
1976	91 562
1983	34 109
1986	46 655
1989	62 117
1991	69 351
1992	70 000

Sources: Bruneau and Macleod, 1986, p. 69; *Expresso*, 4 July 1992, pp. 20–21.

The party's results in both elections seemed to indicate an upward trend, but were an insufficient indicator of Guterres' ability to defeat the PSD. Guterres has, at least, to achieve in building up a separate identity to president Mário Soares, who tried in 1994 to push Guterres to a more conflictual stand towards prime minister Cavaco Silva.

The present leader of the PS seems to have a majority of support at district level (Diário de Notícias, 25 May 1992, p. 4; *Expresso*, 30 May 1992, p. A4; *Expresso*, 24 September 1994) and national level, although the Soaristas continue to be very strong.

The People's Democratic Party/Social-Democratic Party (Partido Popular Democrático/Partido Social Democrata – PPD/PSD)

The origins of the PSD go back to the late authoritarian regime, which after the death of Oliveira Salazar allowed a limited degree of liberalisation and democratisation of the political system. After the elections of 1968 several liberal candidates – such as Francisco Sá Carneiro, Francisco Balsemão and Joaquim Magalhães Mota – became members of the National Assembly, a mock parliament dominated by regime-loyal MPs. The leader of this group was Sá Carneiro, the highly charismatic figure of the opposition. This liberal group was not able to bring any influence to bear on policy making, so in 1972 they gave up their seats and continued their oppositional activities outside the political system. Sá Carneiro and others were integrated into a study group called the *Sociedade para os Estudos de Desenvolvimento Economico e Social* (Society for the Study of Social and Economic Development – SEDES). SEDES became a forum in which to discuss problems related to national social and economic development. Ideologically, these liberals were concerned with the modernisation and democratisation of Portugal. Their approach was both pragmatic and technocratic.

The PPD was founded by Francisco Sá Carneiro on 6 May 1974 and its ideology was quite flexible and pragmatic. During the revolutionary period the party presented itself as social-democratic and its political language was greatly influenced by the circumstances. In the electoral programme of 1975 it defined itself as a party constructing 'socialism by democratic means'. It opposed both capitalism and totalitarian socialism, and advocated a three-dimensional democracy: politically, civil rights and freedoms should be granted to all citizens; economically, the fruits of production and national wealth should be put at the disposal of everyone; socially and culturally, welfare and culture shoulld be available to all (Eleiçoes, 1975, pp. 244–7).

The PPD attempted to join the Socialist International, but this was blocked by Mário Soares, who argued that the Socialist Party, because of its special relationship with the Socialist International, was the only legitimate Portuguese representative. This exclusion of the PPD from the predominantly social-democratic Socialist International made it difficult for the party to develop an identity of its own.

In the elections of 25 April 1975 it became the second largest party after the Socialist Party. It opposed the steadily colonisation of the state apparatus and the media by the PCP and the extreme left. It became a close ally of the Socialist Party in reversing the revolutionary process during the summer and autumn of 1975.

After the revolution the party became more moderate and began to define itself as a liberal social-democratic party that was interested in promoting the economic, social, political and cultural development of Portugal. It was technocratically liberal, and a policy of modernising structures and culture lay at the core of its ideology. It changed its name from the People's Democratic Party to the Social Democratic Party (Partido Social Democrata – PSD).

This move towards a more liberal, pragmatic approach to the modernisation of Portugal marked a return to the objectives set up in SEDES in the early 1970s. This ideology of modernisation became quite evident under the leadership of Anibal Cavaco Silva from 1985–95, when a large flow of structural funds was made available for the purpose.

The PSD has played an innovative role in Portuguese politics. The formation of the coalition *Aliança Democrática* (Democratic Alliance – AD) with the conservative CDS and the *Partido Popular Monárquico*

Table 5.7 Presidents of the PSD, 1974–95

Francisco Sá Carneiro (with interruptions)	1974–80
Francisco Balsemão	1980–83
Carlos Mota Pinto	1983–85
Anibal Cavaco Silva	1985–95
Fernando Nogueira	1995–96

(Monarchic People's Party – PPM) led to a polarisation of the political field between right and left. At the same time the AD spoke of new possibilities of building up a government based on a strong parliamentary majority. After Sá Carneiro's death in a plane crash on 4 December 1980, during the presidential campaign tussle between his candidate, Soares Carneiro, and Ramalho Eanes, the party became divided and factions began to play a major role within the party.

Francisco Balsemão, owner of the weekly newspaper *Expresso*, became the new leader (Table 5.7). He was not able to fill the gap left by the charismatic Sá Carneiro and was not regarded as a uniting figure inside the party. Under his leadership factionalism and problems with the coalition partners were quite prevalent. In late 1983 he resigned both as prime minister and as leader of the party.

He was replaced by Carlos Mota Pinto, who became deputy prime minister in the coalition government with the Socialist Party, the so-called 'Central Bloc', between 1983 and 1985. In early 1985 Mota Pinto died and was replaced by Anibal Cavaco Silva, Professor of the National Economy at the Higher Institute of Economy, University of Lisbon.

Cavaco Silva's election came as a surprise to most commentators, although he was known for his criticism of the government and his participation in the first AD cabinet under the leadership of Sá Carneiro. Since then he has become the undisputed leader of the party and can be regarded as an ideal replacement for the first charismatic leader of the PSD, Sá Carneiro.

The highly divided party was efficiently controlled by Cavaco Silva for ten years, but in February 1995 he decided to step down. After a fierce contest between Minister of Defence Fernando Nogueira and Foreign Minister Durao Barroso, the party congress elected Nogueira as the new leader. Before his election Nogueira had been characterised as an 'eternal number two' with no charisma. Nogueira was not able to control the warning factions and keep the party united after the October 1995 legislative elections (*Guardian*, 18 February 1995, p. 14).

The PSD is a highly decentralised party dominated by local barons. These so-called *baronatos* are the main cause of the dissent and factionalism within the party (Stock, 1989a; Corkill, 1995a). Powerful local leaders such as João Alberto Jardim, president of the autonomous region of Madeira, Isaltino Morais, president of the Municipal Chamber of Oeiras near Lisbon, and Eurico Melo are examples of such *baronatos* and seem to wield their local power to influence the party. Such factionalism is inherent in the PSD, and this may explain the frequency of party conferences, which are normally scheduled for every second year but in practice take place almost annually.

The question of regionalisation, fiercely opposed by Prime Minister Cavaco Silva, is but one example of the divisions within the party, particularly in 1992 during the sixteenth party congress in Oporto. There Isaltino Morais and Mendes Bota came out in support of regionalisation, while Cavaco Silva and the leader of the PSD in Oporto argued strongly against it. This split continues to dominate discussions within the PSD (*Expresso*, 25 July 1992, p. A5, 14 November 1992, p. A4).

During his ten years as leader of the party Anibal Cavaco Silva was not able fully to resolve the persistent problem of personalism and factionalism, although his strong leadership was crucial in keeping the party reasonably united. While the party has become more modern and is probably the largest in Portugal, it may be that Cavaco Silva's stepping down will lead to an upsurge of these inherent features of the PSD.

The highest body of the PSD is the congress. The lesser bodies were changed in the 1980s after the death of Sá Carneiro. At present the congress elects a national council, which is responsible for the implementation of the party programme. The national council consists of 55 members (plus 10 substitutes) and a national political committee of 17 members. It meets every 15 days and is the executive body of the PSD. Below these national structures are district organisations composed of local sections organised at the municipal level (Jacobs, 1989, p. 291; Bruneau and Macleod, 1986, pp. 81–7).

The party has a very active membership and it keeps very strict records of its members (Table 5.8), about 29.2 per cent of whom are less than 30 years old. It is the best organised party of the Portuguese political system and about 20–25 per cent of its members regularly take part in party affairs. Every weekend about 200 meetings take place throughout the country. The militancy of the party increases during electoral campaign periods. Internal elections have a high percentage, because only the delegates of the districts take part in it but not all the members (*Expresso*, 4 July 1992, pp. 20R–21R).

Table 5.8 Membership of the PSD, 1974–92

	Total membership
1974	10 875
1975	20 445
1976	25 011
1979	32 687
1984	67 324
1986	89 899
1987	101 454
1990	125 386
1991	139 253
1992	143 075

Source: Bruneau and Macleod, 1986; *Expresso*, 4 July 1992, pp. 20R–21R.

The PSD has been in power since 1979 and has become the 'party of government', in the way that the *Uniao Nacional/Acçao Nacional Popular* – UN/ANP (National Union/People's National Action) was during the authoritarian regime. The 'Mexicanisation' of the Portuguese political system (so called because of the continuing dominance of a single party, as happened with the *Partido Revolucionario Institucional* in Mexico), made it questionable whether the PSD was willing to relinquish its hold on the state apparatus. The *Estado laranja* ('orange state', a reference to the party's colour) has been a main topic among the opposition and the population during the past eight years, and the PSD has been accused of dominating the state apparatus and using patronage to ensure its control. Whatever the outcome of this discontent, the 'most Portuguese party in Portugal' has time and again displayed an incredible ability to recover in the political field, in spite of all the negative features attributed to it (*Expresso*, 16 April 1994, pp. 27–30).

The Communist Party (Partido Comunista Português – PCP)

The PCP is now the fourth largest party in Portugal and the oldest existing party in the present political system. Its history goes back to 1921, when the party was founded and decided to follow the 21 points of the third international. During the time of the First Republic it had between 500 and 3000 members, predominantly workers living in Lisbon and Porto (Pereira, 1983, pp. 4–8). After the military coup of 28 May 1926 the party was declared illegal and was repressed by the authoritarian regime.

The PCP started to become more successful after 1929, but in the 1930s Salazar's 'new state' attempted to destroy all vestiges of opposition. A major setback was on 18 January 1934, when several communist and anarcho-syndicalist organisations were targeted and destroyed by the authoritarian regime because they had taken part in a general strike that had been called in protest at the introduction of the corporatist National Statute of Labour (*Estatuto de Trabalho Nacional*) (Sertório, 1984).

Until the early 1940s the party was affected by factionalism and lack of coordination between the policies of the different factions (Cunhal, 1985, pp. 74–5). This crisis was overcome in 1943. At that time Alvaro Cunhal was acting as intermediary, but he subsequently became the *de facto* leader of the party.

The policy of the party after the war was to build up an antifascist front against the regime, and accordingly it aligned itself with the monarchist, socialist and republican opposition. This strategy failed because of the heterogeneity of the different groups and the repression exerted by the authoritarian regime. Nevertheless the Communist Party became the 'party of resistance' *par excellence* and was involved in all electoral campaigns against the regime, supporting monarchist and republican candidates such as Cunha Leal and Humberto Delgado in presidential elections (Raby, 1988, pp. 166–73). In March 1961 Alvaro Cunhal finally became the *de jure* secretary-general of the party, after escaping with his companions from the high-security prison Peniche (Raby, 1988, pp. 121–33).

In 1965, during the sixth party congress, Cunhal introduced the party's programme for the development of Portugal. The programme is very interesting in that it called for a 'democratic and national revolution'. This was defined as the armed fight of the people and the revolutionary military to destroy the military and repressive fascist apparatus (Cunhal, 1974, p. 167). This was an amazing prediction of the revolution that was to come. The programme further advocated that the main aims of the 'Democratic and National Revolution' should be: (1) to destroy the power of the monopolies; (2) to bring about agrarian reform; (3) to free Portugal from imperialist domination; (4) to acknowledge the right of self-determination and independence of the Portuguese colonies; (5) to improve the living standards of the population; (6) to establish a policy of peace and cooperation with all countries; and (7) to bring about the complete destruction of the fascist state and establish a democratic order. This programme was to remain the guiding light of the PCP (Cunhal, 1974, pp. 137–8).

In the second half of the 1960s the party was able to become more active and penetrate the state apparatus. The short period of liberalisation under Salazar's successor, Marcelo Caetano, led to the opening up of the trade unions to the opposition, and in the 1969 trade-union elections some communist candidates were elected. In 1970 18 *sindicatos* were dominated by the Communist Party, which wanted to establish a separate trade union organisation: the *Intersindical*. They asked for the rights of strike and assembly, and the free election of its leader. This led to repression by Marcelo Caetano, who was under pressure from hardliners in the authoritarian regime. The communist leaders were purged from the state trade unions (Barreto, 1990).

During the revolution the party became a central actor. The strategy of the PCP was slowly to colonise the state apparatus and the media. The original tactic was one of caution as the party wanted to determine the rhythm of the 'democratic and national revolution'. Its hopes were shattered when the MFA, under the leadership of Colonel Vasco Gonçalves, began to speed up the pace of the revolution. This led to a proliferation of power centres that the PCP could not control (Cunhal, 1976, pp. 146–81). At the end of the revolution the party was confronted with a highly antagonistic political climate that led to the complete isolation of the PCP by the other parties in the summer of 1975.

After the revolution the PCP was systematically excluded from national politics as it was regarded by the other parties as being responsible for the radicalisation of the revolutionary process. Although it was later able to gain electoral support and steadily increased its strength at the local level, particularly in the south, its permanent exclusion from national politics contributed to its decline in the late 1980s and early 1990s.

After the AD's electoral victory in 1979 the PCP tried to persuade the PS to take part in a left-wing coalition. Its electoral programmes of 1979, 1980 and 1983 were dominated by this strategic tactic against the parties of the right (*Avante*, 5 May 1983), but when the PS decided to form a coalition with the PSD, the so-called 'Central Bloc', the PCP dropped the idea of a coalition and declared the PS a right-wing party. Its new tactic was to form a 'democratic government of national salvation', in which the communists would have a leading role. This policy was followed in the elections of 1985.

In spite of its lack of success with the PS, the Communist Party did manage to form coalitions with some of the smaller groups. In 1979 it formed the People's United Front of the Left (*Frente de Esquerda Popular Unitária* – FEPU) with the Democratic People's Movement/ Electoral Democratic Coalition (*Movimento Democratico Popular/*

Coligação Democrática Eleitoral – MDP/CDE). In subsequent elections the FEPU changed its name to the United People's Alliance (*Aliança Povo Unido* – APU). When the MDP/CDE left the coalition on the eve of the 1987 elections the PCP formed an alliance with the greens, and the APU became the United Democratic Coalition (*Coligação Democrática Unitária* – CDU).

One particular reason behind the PCP's desire to form a coalition was that in the past the party's name had attracted opposition and violent attacks by people in the northern districts, and it hoped that a change of name would increase its electoral chances.

Ideologically the party continues to be committed to Leninism, which it defines as third way between Stalinism and Eurocommunism. The PCP follows an anti-EC policy, which has become less dogmatic and rigid over time, and presents itself as the defender of their 'April revolution achievements', such as the socialised sector, the extension of the welfare state, the constitution of 1976 and the agricultural collectives in Alentejo.

The party sees itself as the centre of a subculture permeated by the notion of 'communist morals' as opposed to 'bourgeois morals'. It continues to have a radical programme, but has abandoned the idea of establishing a 'dictatorship of the proletariat', as defined during the revolution.

It now acts within the legal framework of the Portuguese constitution. Indeed it has been the fiercest defender of the constitution and has voted against all revisions since 1982, agreed mainly by the PSD, the CDS and the PS.

The party structure continues to be highly centralised. The dominance of secretary-general Alvaro Cunhal has never ceased to exist. Even though a new leader, Carlos Carvalhas, was elected in 1992, Alvaro Cunhal's influence is still present because he is member of the central committee and the political commission. Cunhal is seen as an important symbol of unity. This can be observed at the party congresses, of which Cunhal's speech is seen as the climax (*Expresso*, 12 December 1992, pp. 12R–23R).

As discussed above the party has faced a steady decline since the mid 1980s (Table 5.9). The membership is stagnating, most of the members are quite old, having been militants before the revolution, and the party is finding it extremely difficult to attract young members. The number of registered members under the age of 30 has declined in comparison with those aged 50 or over. Furthermore the number

Table 5.9   Membership of the PCP, 1974–92

Total Membership	
1974	29 140
1975	100 000[1]
1976	115 000
1979	154 713
1983	200 753
1988	199 275
1992	143 075[2]

Notes
1. Approximate number.
2. Estimated number.

Sources: Cunhal, 1985, p. 175; *Expresso*, 4 July 1992, p. 21R.

of party cells declined from 9014 in 1979 to 2812 in 1992. Last but not least, the number of party functionaries has decreased by 50 per cent since the 1970s and most of these have very low educational qualifications (*Expresso*, 12 December 1992, pp. 22R–23R; Costa e Sousa, 1983).

The party will have to reformulate its approach if it wants to continue to play a major role in the Portuguese political system. However, the new leader will find it difficult to change the culture within the party, which is still dominated by a Leninist identity and defensive mentality that dates back to the days of antifascist resistance and opposition to the anticommunist policies of the AD, the Central Bloc and the PSD governments.

The Social-Democratic Centre Party/People's Party (Partido do Centro Democrático/Social Partido Popular – CDS/PP)

The ideological basis of the CDS is Christian democracy. Many of its leaders were members of the legal political opposition within the authoritarian regime and they had much in common with the PSD. However while leaders of the PSD such as Sá Carneiro, Francisco Balsemão, Magalhaes Mota and Mota Amaral originated from the liberal wing of the authoritarian legislature (the National Assembly), the CDS leadership was well integrated into the techno-bureaucratic structures and institutions of the Caetano administration.[3] At the local level it became a refuge for 'notables' of the former regime (Pinto, 1989, p. 202).

The party was founded on 24 July 1974 by Freitas Amaral, Amaro da Costa and Basilio Horta. During the revolution it was a major victim of violent acts by small parties. The first party congress on 1 January 1975 was interrupted and in the end had to be abandoned. In spite of left-wing attacks and the banning of several other right-wing parties, the CDS was able to gain a place in the new party system (Thomashausen, 1981b, p. 501).

The party had its strongholds in the conservative northern districts of Portugal. After the elections of April 1975, in which it became the fourth largest party, the CDS joined the anticommunist front, led by the Socialist Party, and supported this resistance against the steady colonisation of the state apparatus and the media by the PCP, the MFA and the extreme left (Pinto, 1989, p. 203).

The leader of the party, Freitas Amaral, distanced himself from radical right-wing parties such as the ideologically ambiguous Party of Christian Democracy (*Partido da Democracia Cristã* – PDC) and the fascist Independent Movement for National Reconstruction (*Movimento Independente para reconstrução nacional* – MIRN). It also condemned the right-wing terrorist groups, the Democratic Movement for the Liberation of Portugal (*Movimento Democrático para a Libertação de Portugal* – MDLP) and the Army for the Liberation of Portugal (*Exercito para a Libertação de Portugal* – ELP).

After the revolution the CDS was the only party to vote against the constitution of 1976, arguing that it was a 'patronising document'. Nevertheless the party accepted the democratic will of the majority in parliament (Lopes, 1976).

Between 1976 and 1979 the grass roots of the party became discontent with the tactical policies of the new leader, Adelino Amaro da Costa (Table 5.10). The coalition government with the PS in 1978 led to a massive exodus of members from the party. The failed attempt to force the PS to change its agrarian policies led to the withdrawal of the CDS minister from the coalition government.

Between 1979 and 1983 the CDS was in a coalition with the PSD and the PPM. Freitas do Amaral became deputy prime minister and Amaro da Costa defence minister. The central objective of the alliance was to revise the constitution by demilitarising it. After the tragic death of Amaro da Costa and other leaders of the CDS and the PSD, Freitas Amaral returned as leader of the party. Under the Balsemão governments the CDS felt that the senior partner was not consulting them in a proper manner, and were aggrieved that the new prime minister had been chosen by the social democrats without seeking the opinion of the christian democratic leaders.

Table 5.10 Presents of the CDS, 1974–92

Freitas do Amaral	1974–76
Amaro da Costa	1976–80
Freitas do Amaral	1980–83
Lucas Pires	1983–85
Adriano Moreira	1985–88
Freitas do Amaral	1988–92
Manuel Monteiro	1992–

After 1983 the party became less important as a governing partner and support for the CDS declined steadily. Moreover it became split over strategies. Between 1983 and 1985 the charismatic new leader, Lucas Pires, attempted to reform the party and pursued an anti-Central Bloc policy. However Pires was not able to reverse the party's decline. At the 1985 party congress the leadership was taken over by the conservative Adriano Moreira. Adriano Moreira's style was quite aggressive and he tried to regain conservative voters from the PSD. Nevertheless in the elections of 1987 the electoral support of the party more than halved. Adriano Moreira stepped down as party leader and was replaced by Freitas do Amaral, who had been narrowly defeated by Mário Soares in his bid for the presidency of the republic in 1985–6 (Jacobs, 1989, pp. 300–1).

Freitas do Amaral was able to stabilise the party, but the CDS failed to recognise that its supporters were either switching to the PSD or were being alienated by the policies of modernisation. Freitas do Amaral was replaced by 29-year-old Manuel Monteiro in 1992. The present leader is quite dynamic and highly controversial both inside and outside the party. He initiated some party reforms and made changes to part of its ideological foundations.

His most controversial act was his anti-Maastricht stand, arising from his view that the Treaty on the European Union would substantially reduce the national sovereignty of Portugal. Monteiro was very active in the pro-referendum movement in 1992 (*Diário de Notícias*, 20 May 1992, p. 4). He was supported by the party, which held an internal referendum in autumn 1992.

Freitas do Amaral decided to leave the CDS because he himself was a supporter of Christian democracy and all aspects of European integration. He split from the party in 1992 and became an independent MP (*Diário de Notícias*, 4 November 1992, p. 4). On 8 December 1992 he gave a highly acclaimed speech during the Maastricht debate, in which he declared himself a federalist and said he yearned for a federalist Europe (*Expresso*, 12 December 1992, p. A5).

The change of policies of the CDS was defined during a party congress in the the northern town of Povoa de Varzim on 23–4 January 1993, when the 700 delegates came out in favour of a more social market economy model and against regionalisation. The European question continued to be dominated by an anti-Maastricht position (*Expresso*, 23 January 1993, p. A3, 30 January 1993).

Subsequently, due to this nationalist discourse and the ideological changes introduced by Monteiro, the party was excluded from the European People's Party (*Partido Popular Europeu* – PPE) of the European Parliament, whose members had been strong supporters of the CDS since its foundation. Later the party joined the Alliance of European Democrats – RDE (*Expresso*, 3 April 1993, p. A3). During the European parliamentary elections on 12 June 1994 Monteiro's discourse focused on the loss of national sovereignty, and this had a spillover effect on the position of certain persons around the main candidate of the PSD, Eurico de Melo. The PSD's position was summarised in its main slogan: 'Europe, Yes; Portugal, Forever'. Monteiro was a very active campaigner among those who were losing most as a result of European integration, such as fishermen and farmers (Magone, 1995c).

The party structure is still highly centralised. It is a party of 'notables' and very personalistic in style. It has a weak local base. The lowest units are nuclei with at least 15 members. Above these are the communal councils and district groups.

Every second year there is a party congress. The interim body is the national political committee, consisting of 40–50 members partly elected by the party congress. The executive body is the party committee, which comprises 11 members. The party committee is led by the party president, presently Manuel Monteiro, and he is seconded by a secretary-general, who is mainly in charge of administrative tasks.

The party's membership is quite small and stable (Table 5.11). At the grassroots level militant activism does not exist and the members are fairly old in comparison with the quite young membership of the main parties. More than 60 per cent of the members are older than 45 years and 30 per cent are older than 60 (*Expresso*, 4 July 1992, p. 23R).

On the whole the CDS/PP has become more populist in the 1990s, but Monteiro's nationalist discourse has still not produced impressive elections results. On the contrary, the already small electoral support of the party is stagnating and Monteiro has not been able to penetrate other social groups.

Table 5.11   Membership of the CDS, 1979–92

	Total membership
1979	30 000
1980	10 875
1982	15 479
1984	20 789
1986	24 841
1988	25 696
1991	26 801
1992	27 062

Sources: Bruneau and Macleod, 1986; Thomashausen, 1981b; Stock, 1985a, p. 110; *Expresso*, 4 July 1992, pp. 20R–21R.

The Small Parties

A few small parties continue to play a part in the present political system. Most of them have been able to maintain their electoral support throughout the 1980s and 1990s without achieving representation in the Assembly of the Republic. Most of these parties are left wing and play a role in trade unions such as the MRPP, the UDP and the PSR. They take part in elections, sometimes in coalition with senior partners such as the Green Party in the communist coalition, sometimes as independent candidates in the party lists of the major parties, such as the leader of the UDP, Mário Tomé. In this section we will deal with the more relevant small parties.

The Democratic Renewal Party (*Partido Renovador Democratico* – PRD) is by far the most influential of the small parties. It won about 18 per cent of the votes in the legislative elections of 1985, but afterwards declined into relative insignificance. The PRD was the creation of President Ramalho Eanes, who wanted to form a party that would regenerate political life. Instead it became even more conflictual and less cooperative than the other parties between 1985 and 1987. This was the reason for the decline of the party.

The Green Party (*Partido Ecologista 'Os Verdes'* – PEV) is a small party that is trying to bring environmental issues into politics. It was founded in 1982 and has formed a coalition with the Communist Party. It is quite left wing in its ideology and advocates a decentralised, participatory democracy.

The People's Monarchic Party (*Partido Popular Monárquico* – PPM) was fairly important during the 1970s and early 1980s. It gained representation in the Assembly of the Republic and became a partner in the AD coalition. Its importance declined after 1983. The former leader was Gonçalo Ribeiro Telles, who directed the party's ideology towards environmentalism. He was minister of the environment in five of the six provisional governments. The party remained quite small, even after the replacement of Ribeiro Telles by Augusto Ferreira do Amaral in 1988 (Jacobs, 1989, p. 308). In the last European elections the party returned to its original ideological preference – the idea of a Lusitanian Commonwealth with the former colonies led by a Portuguese monarchy as an alternative to European integration (Magone, 1996a).

The People's Democratic Union (*Uniao Democrática Popular* – UDP) is the strongest party of the extreme left. It is based on a Maoist–Albanist approach towards Marxism–Leninism. In 1976 it played a major role in organising the electoral campaign of the military MFA leader, Otelo Saraiva de Carvalho, who won more than 16 per cent of the votes. Until the elections of 1980 the party always managed to win a parliamentary seat by securing 1–1.5 per cent of the votes, but afterwards it drcpped below 1 per cent at the national level. Electoral support for the party was strongest in Lisbon, Setubal and the island of Madeira (Jacobs, 1989, pp. 310–11). The UDP plays a major role in the communist-dominated trade union, the CGTP-In (Castanheira, 1985, p. 805). At the local level it takes part in the coalition led by the socialists and the communists in Lisbon – its leader, Mário Tomé, has been an independent MP on the communist list since 1991. The party is presently discussing a reform of its programme and is experimenting with a more up-to-date version of socialism.

The Socialist Revolutionary Party (*Partido Socialista Revolucionário* – PSR), led by Francisco Louça, has never managed to win a seat in the Assembly of the Republic, although it came close to it in the legislative elections of 1991. Its ideological background is Trotskyism and it is influenced by Ernest Mandel. Its electoral campaigns are quite innovative in bringing new issues into the political debate (Jacobs, 1989, p. 311; Ferreira, 1985, p. 2).

The Communist Party of Portuguese Workers/Movement for the Reorganisation of the Party of the Proletariat (*Partido Communista dos Trabalhadores Portugueses/Movimento Reorganizativo do Partido do Proletariado* – PCTP/MRPP) is a tiny party that played a very active role in the Portuguese revolution by destabilising the political field. It was involved in the occupation of media premises and was in conflict with the PCP, which was regarded as a traitor to the proletariat. After the revolution the party was unable to gain a profile at the national level. It remained an esoteric Maoist party, denouncing the events after Mao's death.

The Portuguese Democratic Movement/Electoral Democratic Coalition (*Movimento Democratico Português/Democratic Electoral Coalition* – MDP/CDE) was founded in 1969 for the authoritarian National Assembly elections. It was important during the revolution as a supporter of the PCP, and after the revolution became a coalition partner of the PCP. In 1987 it decided to leave the coalition and since then it has not been represented in the Assembly of the Republic.

On the whole the minor parties are too small to influence the current political format. At the moment it seems that a two-party system will be the likely outcome of two decades of party politics in Portugal.

CONCLUSIONS

The Portuguese party system had a four-party format until 1975, but since then it has developed towards a two-party system, making it possible for the PSD to win an absolute majority of the votes and stabilise the political arena. Nevertheless, a high degree of volatility was experienced in the 1980s. This was centered around the new middle classes, who tended to swing between the left–centre parties (the PRD, the PS) and the PSD, but this decreased over time.

The supporters of the PS and the PSD are quite heterogeneous and both parties can be considered as catch-all parties that are able to build up governmental majorities. However backing for the PCP and the CDS is restricted to certain categories of people, and this can be regarded as the main reason for their decline in importance. The modernisation of the country is eroding the social subcultures that these two parties are trying to address.

While the PCP is the only traditional party of mass membership, in the 1980s the PSD was able to build up a considerable membership to become the largest party. Nevertheless political activism in the PSD seems to be confined to a limited number of party militants, who mobilise the other party members during electoral campaigns. Another interesting feature is that all the main parties have been characterised by personalism and charismatic figures, such as Mário Soares of the PS, Cavaco Silva of the PSD, Alvaro Cunhal of the PCP and Freitas do Amaral and Manuel Monteiro of the CDS.

On the whole, one can say that the Portuguese party system and the parties themselves are well consolidated. Ironically, what seems to be missing is fulfilment of the main function of political parties, which is to act as intermediaries between the electorate and the state. Democratisation is not complete and the level of participation is still quite low. The current move towards a two-party system seems to be reinforcing these negative features of the Portuguese party and political system, even though the constitution was designed to bring about a participatory democracy.

6 Interest Groups

NEOCORPORATISM AND DEMOCRATISATION

State traditions do matter in relation to industrial relations (Crouch, 1993). The Portuguese state in the twentieth century was not able to integrate the working masses. On the contrary, the state was quite inimical to the working class. In the First Republic the small number of workers and the large, rather lethargic rural population made it possible for the state not to attempt to integrate the working class into the political system. By contrast, it was hostile to working-class organisations such as the anarcho-syndicalist movement and the Communist Party (Oliveira, 1974; Schwartzman, 1989, pp. 181–4).

The authoritarian dictatorship defined itself as anticommunist and fought against Marxist ideology and the class struggle. The new regime was based on corporatism, which emphasised class harmony in the workplace, and in family and political life. So-called *corporatisme d'état* served as an instrument to control potential social conflict. The corporatist system was rigidly adhered to during the 1930s, but its importance declined after the war because it was no longer supported by an ideological *zeitgeist*. Most of the countries with fascist regimes in the 1930s and 1940s became democracies or people's democracies after the war.

The vertical corporatist structure included trade unions called *sindicatos*, and the basic unit was the entrerprise, which comprised both workers and entrepreneurs. Further elements were the *Casas de Pescadores* (fishermen's associations) and *Casas do Povo* (people's associations) in rural villages.

The organisation and control of these basic units was quite well developed in Alentejo, which was regarded as a major zone of potential social dissent. On the employers' side there were *gremios* (employers' associations), from which workers were excluded.

The corporatist structure was never fully implemented, and even after 1969, when Caetano called for a major revitalisation of corporatism, it never took full root in Portuguese society.

Labour organisations were crushed in the 1930s. An important date was 18 January 1934, when an attempted general strike led to a complete crackdown on the workers' movement. The sole organisation to survive police repression was the Communist Party, which continued to play a crucial role as the uniting symbol of the working classes. As previously stated, revitalisation of the corporatist system by Salazar's successor, Marcelo Caetano, included liberalisation of trade-union elections at the shopfloor level by allowing alternative lists to the official one.

In 1969 the Communist Party won control of 18 *sindicatos*, but in 1972 the regime purged them from the trade union structure because they attempted to build up a separate organisation called the *Intersindical*. The *Intersindical* survived the authoritarian regime and became a major actor during the revolution (Barreto, 1990).

The situation in the revolutionary period was the antithesis of that which prevailed during authoritarian rule. The sudden collapse of the authoritarian regime had led to a power vacuum and the new political order was still in disarray. Between April 1974 and November 1975 several social movements emerged to try to change the configuration of forces that had been imposed on them during authoritarian rule. Three main movements built up separate structures: the *comissoes de moradores* (residents' committees – CM), the *comissoes de trabalhadores* (workers' committees – CT) and the movement of land labourers in the Southern province of Alentejo. These grassroots social movements further destabilised the embryonic political order.

The most interesting conflict was between the CTs and the communist *Intersindical*. CTs mushroomed in several larger and medium-sized firms after entrepreneurs fled in fear to other countries or were purged (*saneamentos*) as fascists. Occupation of the factories by the CTs led to a general withdrawal of orders from the international community. The communist *Intersindical* tried desperately to control the CTs – most of whom were infiltrated by extreme left-wingers – and incorporate them into the new communist trade union (Ferreira, 1982). However, this attempt failed and the CTs started to build up their own local, regional and national structures. Productivity fell to a very low level, worker militancy increased substantially in 1974–5, and most of the firms were close to bankruptcy in early 1975. The fourth provisional government of Prime Minister Gonçalves decreed that most of these firms be incorporated into the state sector, and the land that had been occupied by land labourers in Alentejo was made legally theirs. These measures changed the social configuration of Portugal. Suddenly the working class had reversed the relationship between capital and labour.

The state, which became the major employer after the revolutionary period, was unable to prevent the economy from breaking down. Only after the implementation of two IMF austerity programmes in 1978–9 and 1983–4 did it recover again. The relationship between capital and labour continued to be highly conflictual in the first decade after the revolution. The state was too weak to act as a broker between the trade unions and the employers' organisations.

The rebuilding of the economy in Portugal was overshadowed by a major transformation of industrial systems at the global level, and the state became more vulnerable to external economic influences than ever before. The globalisation of financial markets, the increase in transnational corporations (TNCs) and the creation of a heterogeneous, flexible labour force with different contractual arrangements (permanent, temporary, part-time) led to a substantial decrease of trade-union influence. The neocorporatist arrangements of the late 1960s and 1970s began to collapse because enterprises were changing their mode of production to a post-Fordist system that was more decentralised and flexible, less national and subject to rapid technological change.

The thrust towards globalisation put other pressures on state structures. The 'changing architecture of the state' led to the transformation of the welfare state, which was based on redistributive Keynesian principles, into the competition state, based on free-market economic criteria (Cerny, 1990).

These trends in turn led to the reconstruction of political structures at the continental level. The emergence of regional blocs such as the European Community, the North American Free Trade Association (NAFTA) and its extension to Southern Europe changed the whole political–economic geography of the northern hemisphere.

The new neocorporatist arrangement in Portugal was considerably affected by these external pressures, and the catastrophic situation after the revolution allowed little room for neocorporatist arrangements (Barreto, 1992, p. 461). On the contrary, both labour and capital were too polarised to enter into dialogue, so between 1977 and 1984 no effort was made to develop neocorporatist structures. This happened only ten years after the revolution with the institutionalisation of the *Conselho Permanente para a Concertação Social* (Permanent Council for Social Harmonisation – CPCS) in 1984 (Table 6.1).

Nevertheless it was still very difficult to bring all the social partners together, and employers only reluctantly joined the new institution. The same could be said about the communist *Intersindical*. Nonetheless, under Cavaco Silva's government intermediation became an accepted process. According to Barreto:

Table 6.1 Organisations represented in the Permanent Council for Social Harmonisation (each with three representatives)

Trade unions
  Confederação Geral dos Trabalhadores Portugueses (CGTP)
  União Geral dos Trabalhadores (UGT)
Business associations
  Confederação Industrial Portuguesa (CIP) (industry)
  Camâra do Comércio Portuguesa (CCP) (trade)
Farmers' associations
  Confederação de Agricultores Portugueses (CAP)
  Government representatives

In 1989 nearly two million wage and salary earners – 98.5 per cent of those in legal employment in private and public enterprises – were covered by industry agreements, government extensions of industry agreements, company agreements and statutory regulations in individual industries or occupations.

Taking all wage and salary earners (over three million in 1989), 61 per cent were covered by collective agreements or government extensions, 3 per cent by direct statutory regulations in private industries, 17.5 per cent by civil service statutory regulations and 18.5 per cent were not covered by any collective regulation or were workers in the black economy. Only 5 per cent of all wage earners were covered by company agreements, mostly in public enterprises (Barreto, 1992, pp. 469–70).

In 1989 the new institution became an integral part of the revised constitution of 1989 (Constituição, 1989, Article 95). The excellent economic situation between 1987 and 1992 served to improve relations between labour and capital, and because the political situation had stabilised too the government was able to launch an ambitious programme to privatise public enterprises that had been nationalised during the Portuguese revolution. All this contributed to the modernisation, increased flexibility and decentralisation of the Portuguese economy.

This privatisation of public-sector enterprises, which was made possible by the second revision of the constitution in 1989 (Corkill, 1993b, pp. 141–7), substantially weakened the already weak position of the labour organisations. It followed the general global trend, but was also designed to prepare the economy to meet the challenges of the European market, to be introduced in early 1992.

Tripartite agreements between the state, the unions and the employers' associations were reached in 1986 and 1987 – the largest union,

Table 6.2   Strikes in Portugal, 1986–91

	Number	Number of Workers involved	Days lost
1986	363	231 535	381 917
1988	181	155 535	197 902
1989	307	296 116	357 377
1990	296	128 884	146 532
1991*	152	69 334	60 513

Source: Stoleroff, 1992, p. 138.
* First six months only.

Intersindical, declined to take part. In 1988 and 1989 the introduction of the *pacote laboral* (several laws to increase the flexibility of the labour market) made it easier for enterprises to dismiss workers. This led to an upsurge in strike action against the *pacote laboral* organised by both trade unions (Table 6.2.)

A more comprehensive *Acordo Económico e Social* (Economic and Social Accord – AES) was agreed in 1990, when changes to labour legislation were negotiated between the unions and the employers' organisations. The AES covered dismissals, a reduction of the working week from 48 to 44 hours (with a further gradual reduction to 40 hours by 1995), the introduction of flexitime, vocational training, unemployment benefits, child labour (the minimum age was raised from 14 to 15), health and safety at the workplace, supplementary social security in cases of industrial restructuring, and collective bargaining (removing restrictions on the scope of bargaining and the establishment of a compulsory arbitration system). In addition a recommendation on pay policy for 1991 was approved (leading to interunion conflict, led by the UGT and some of its affiliated unions in the public sector), and annual revision of the minimum wage became subject to tripartite negotiation (Barreto, 1992, pp. 479–80).

In 1992 the CPCS entered into crisis. Both the UGT and the CGTP-In protested against the intention of the government to introduce a very restrictive revision of the law governing strikes, and both unions threatened to leave the CPCS. This was reinforced by a rigid position adopted by the finance minister, Jorge Braga de Macedo, in respect to a tripartite agreement on the nominal annual wage rise. The negotiations in the CPCS collapsed because the UGT and the CGTP-In refused to take part (*Diário de Notícias*, 8 July 1992, p. 3, 14 July 1992, p. 3, 17 July 1992, p. 3, 30 July 1992, p. 3).

The growing economic crisis in 1992 worsened during 1993 and 1994. The implementation of the SEM in 1993 led to the collapse of several small, antiquated enterprises and in several firms the salaries of workers were already some months in arrears.

Nevertheless during 1993 Jorge Braga Macedo continued to boast that Portugal was the 'economic oasis' of the European Community, with a strong escudo and a lower unemployment figure than even Luxembourg (Stock and Magone, 1994). This attitude of the government was a serious obstacle to the intermediation of interests. The same happened in autumn 1994, when Cavaco Silva said that the demands of the trade unions in relation to an increase of the nominal wage ceiling for the public sector was too high and would completely jeopardise the government's convergence plan to meet the Maastricht criteria (Stock and Magone, 1995).

The intermediation process has remained very conflictual and the polarisation of interests is preventing common agreements from being reached. The agreements of 1986, 1987 and 1990 can be regarded as exceptions to the rule as they arose from the improved economic situation of the time. In times of economic crisis, which is normally linked to a social crisis, the preparedness to negotiate a 'tripartite' agreement seems to diminish substantially. Moreover the increasing Europeanisation of the Portuguese political, economic and social systems is restricting the manoeuvrability of the Portuguese government in terms of public expenditure. In this sense Cavaco Silva's reference to the convergence plan points to the fact that the Portuguese government is under considerable pressure to meet the Maastricht criteria if it is to continue to be eligible to receive structural funds after the Intergovernmental Conference of 1996.

Europeanisation of national industrial relations systems has become a major trend across the EU member states. Although intermediation at the European level is still very fragmented, the increase of Euro-companies across the European Union is requiring both a more flexible intermediation process and better control of enterprises at the supranational level (Hall, 1992).

The internal market project initiated by Lord Cockfield in 1985 was a response to competition from the United States and Japan (Cockfield, 1994). Its main objective was to build up economies of scale that would enable European firms to compete with US and Japanese TNCs. However, the proposed SEM spilled over into other policy areas, as it was acknowledged that achieving a more competitive European economy must be accompanied by a convergence of social and regional policies. The notion of 'social Europe' became a widespread catchphrase to accompany the SEM project.

Supranational interest groups began to appear after 1958. The main intermediation body is the Economic and Social Committee. It ensures that different social and economic interest groups, including those representing workers and employers, remain in permanent dialogue. It is a consultative body, and brief the Commission on matters related to industrial relations.

On the side of the employers, the main supranational representative group is the CEEP (European Centre of Public Enterprises) and the UNICE (Union of the Industries of the European Community); on the workers' side is the CES (European Confederation of Trade Unions). The largest employers' association is the UNICE, which was founded in 1958 and has 33 branches in 22 European countries. The CES was founded in 1973 and comprises about 40 confederations and about 50 millions workers. Both sides were closely involved in defining the social dimension of the internal market in 1986 and 1987.

The 'Social Charter on the Fundamental Rights of Workers' in 1989 further consolidated the social dimension of the SEM (Lima, 1993, pp. 843–6; Sidjanski and Ayrbeck, 1990). The Maastricht Treaty introduced the concept of social and economic cohesion, and particularly addressed the regional imbalance in economic and social welfare across the EU. A special social and economic cohesion fund was agreed in the treaty, to be distributed to countries whose per capita gross national product was below 80 per cent of the EU average. The four peripheral countries of Portugal, Spain, Greece and Ireland were entitled to a share of this fund, as well as a doubling of their share of the European Regional Development Fund (ERDF) and the European Social Fund (ESF), in comparison with the last tranche between 1989 and 1993 (Lange, 1993; Hall, 1994).

This dimension of European integration was an important factor in relaunching neocorporatist intermediation in Portugal. European socialisation has been described as a crucial factor in changing attitudes at the national level, and the knowledge acquired by transnational interest organisations has led to a change in bargaining behaviour at the national level (Marques, 1990, pp. 184–6).

Before 1986 the CPCS provided the participating interest groups with funds to set up permanent representations in Brussels, the largest of which was set up by the Portuguese Chamber of Commerce (*Câmara de Comercio Portuguesa* – CCP). All the interest groups are quite committed to European integration. The Confederation of Portuguese Industry

(*Confederação da Industria Portuguesa* – CIP) is probably the most critical of the government's policies, mainly its convergence policies, which are jeopardising the existence of many industries (Lima, 1993, pp. 849–50). But on the whole one may say that the European integration process is having a positive effect on the Portuguese interest groups by fostering a culture of cooperation, which until 1986 had been undermined by personalism and individualism (Marques, 1990, pp. 190–1).

Although 'concerted corporativism'· is a very new phenomenon in Portuguese politics, it seems that is also being established in other policy making organisations, such as the National Council of Education (*Conselho Nacional de Educação*), the National Committee of Apprenticeship (*Comissão Nacional de Aprendizagem*), the National Youth Institute (*Instituto Nacional da Juventude*), the National Institute for Consumer Protection (*Instituto Nacional para a Defesa do Consumidor*), the Monitoring Commission for the Development of the Peninsula of Setúbal (*Comissão de Alom Pannamento da Operaläd Integrada de Desenvolvimento da Peninsula de Setúbal*) and the Society of Regional Development in Setúbal (*Sociedade de Desenvolvimento Regional de Setúbal*) (Lima, 1993, p. 860).

The expansion of neocorporatist interest intermediation is serving to reinforce and enhance the new Portuguese democracy, and Tripartite dialogue is creating a participatory democracy at the elite level. Although 'social harmonisation' in Portugal is still at an early stage and not yet universal, at least it formally increased the level of representativeness of interest groups at the national level after 1984 and at the supranational level after 1986. This can be regarded as the first step towards complete social harmonisation in the course of time (Kirchner, 1986, pp. 63–5; Lima, 1993, pp. 853–4).

The introduction of neocorporatist structures after 1984 made a major contribution to the democratisation of the political system, which some authors characterise as post-Salazarist in nature. This principally means that the representatives of the state are governed by both authoritarian and democratic codes of behaviour. Neocorporatist arrangements and bodies are crucial to the reinforcement of the growing democratic identity of the state by fostering a strong social dialogue (Lucena, 1989; Aguiar, 1986). Nevertheless the present situation seems to indicate that labour organisations have been substantially weakened since 1984, due to the introduction of labour flexibility and liberalisation measures. The general measures taken by the trade unions to prevent the erosion of workers' rights have not been enough to change the attitude of the government (Stoleroff, 1992, p. 138).

THE TRADE UNIONS

The monopoly of the communist-dominated *Intersindical* was contested after the revolution. The 30 April 1975 law on the unification of trade unions was soon replaced by decree no. 773/76 of 27 October 1976, which guaranteed pluralism in the trade, union sector. In 1979, a second socialist-social-democratic trade union General Union of Workers (*Uniao Geral de Trabalhadores* – UGT) was founded. In 1976 and 1977 several decrees limited the activities of the workers' committees to economic matters and eliminated almost all the workers' rights to self-administration (decrees 841/76 and 57/77).

This is accompanied by a substantial reduction of the basis movements in this post-revolutionary transition. As already mentioned, during the revolution the workers' committee movement attempted to build up alternatives to the trade unions, but after the revolution these were steadily incorporated into the unions (Eisfeld, 1984, p. 162). Another reason for the decline of the workers' committees was that the deterioration of the economic situation had forced them to adopt a purely defensive position in the enterprises, particularly after the introduction of the two IMF austerity plans in 1978–9 and 1983–4, which particularly affected workers in the public enterprises, the most militant sector of the working class.

The UGT originated from the 'Open Letter'-Movement (*Carta Aberta*) within the *Intersindical*. They constituted themselves in 1976, and presented themselves as a faction in the second extraordinary congress of the *Intersindical* in January 1977 (Lima, 1986, pp. 541–4). In the course of 1976 the 'Open Letter'-Movement lost the majority of its members. At the end of the year the number of members had declined from 59 to 10.

During the second extraordinary congress of the *Intersindical* in January 1977 part of what remained of the movement rejoined the majority in the congress. About 250 trade unions joined the newly named *Confederação Geral de Trabalhadores Portugueses* (General Confederation of Portuguese Workers – CGTP-In) (Eisfeld, 1984, p. 176; Cunhal, 1976, p. 340).

In spring 1978 the socialists and social-democrats founded an alternative trade union. The new *União Geral de Trabalhadores* (General Union of Workers – UGT) was able to gain a foothold in sectors such as textiles, chemicals and the strategically important transport industry. It was decided that there should be an equal number of PSD and PS representatives in the leading bodies of the UGT. Ideologically the union did not focus on the plight of the working class, but was more inclined towards a reformist–pluralist policy that aimed at modernising Portuguese industry (Cristovam, 1985, pp. 171–2; Optenhogel and Stoleroff, 1985, p. 187).

In the years following the formation of the CPCS in 1984 the UGT took a very active part, in contrast with the CGTP-In. However in the late 1980s the UGT's position changed substantially and it became more class-oriented. As already mentioned, the UGT's attitude became more conflictual and its representatives even walked out from the CPCS during the discussions on lay-off legislation in 1988 and 1989 and the strike law in 1992. It adopted a very uncompromising position on the public sector wage-increase ceilings proposed by the government after 1992. It is currently the only Portuguese representative in the Confederation of European Trade Unions, because the CGTP-In's application was turned down (Castanheira, 1985, pp. 814–17). (It seems that the German Trade Union Federation (DGB) had been vehemently opposed to the entry of the CGTP-In into the European Federation of Trade Unions, and that the founding of the UGT had been made possible by massive international help, particularly on the part of the Federal Republic of Germany, see Eisfeld, 1984, pp. 173–5.)

The CGTP-In is still the largest union, with almost one million members. In its early days its conflictual stance meant it was unable to influence the process of interest intermediation. Until 1987 it mobilised its members to fight against legislation aimed at making of the labour market more flexible. This was the case in 1982, when a proposal to release the lay-off legislation led to a call for a 24-hour general strike by the CGTP-In. This policy was continued throughout 1983 (Lecher, 1994, p. 78; *A Tarde*, 28 April 1983, p. 5; *Tempo*, 18 August 1983, p. 14; *O Jornal*, 19 August 1983, pp. 2–3). As a consequence it declined to occupy the seats reserved for it in the tripartite CPCS in 1983. The party changed its policies in 1987, but it continued to be a vociferous opponent in labour legislation matters and pay policies.

From the late 1980s there was a convergence of interests and policies between these two main federations, which together accounted for 210 of the 350 unions (Barreto, 1992, p. 466). In the early 1990s a unification proposal was tabled by the leader of the UGT, José Torres Couto, and taken up by one of the critical voices inside the CGTP-In, José Luis Judas. His thesis on the renovation of the Communist Party included the necessity to achieve a unified, democratic trade union federation, but the leadership of the CGTP-In described this as a propagandist act (*Semanário*, 21 April 1990, pp. 11–12; *Sábado*, 5 May 1990, pp. 21–3).

Judas left the Communist Party and the CGTP-In in March 1993 and later became a member of the Socialist Party. He was a socialist candidate in the local elections of December 1993 and became the mayor of the seaside town of Cascais, near Lisbon. He followed the example of other excellent leaders such as the present independent MEP, José Barros Moura, and the CGTP-In leader, Rosa Maria Marques.

Judas' case say much about the present structure of the CGTP-In. It is still dominated by the Communist Party, and most of the representatives on the leading bodies are also members of the Communist Party. From 1983 there was a steady communist infiltration of the top and intermediate positions in the CGTP-In, which explains the growing orthodoxy within the federation. Leaders from other tendencies, such as the socialist leader Ruben Rolo, who died in 1992, were not replaced (*Expresso, Sabado*, 6 March 1993, pp. 28R–31R).

Leader Carvalho da Silva is in control of the directing bodies of the CGTP-In. While the UGT seems to favour European integration and uses it to legitimise its critique of the liberal policies of the government, from the beginning the CGTP-In was against the European Community, calling it a 'Europe of the Monopolies'. Integration into the bodies of the European Union, such as the Economic and Social Committee, has substantially changed its position. Its anti-European declarations remain radical, but in practice it tries to secure the best deal it can for Portuguese workers by referring to the still incipient notion of 'social Europe'. The CGTP-In is very critical of the Maastricht Treaty (Lima, 1993, pp. 846–52).

An interesting phenomenon is the growing number of independent trade unions. These generally represent middle-class professionals such as judges and air traffic controllers.

Trade union membership has never been strong in Portugal, and declined even more in the late 1980s due to the introduction of greater flexibility in the labour market. An unpublished Ministry of Labour survey in 1990–1 estimated that only 42 per cent of official workers belonged to a union. It also estimated that 57 per cent of unionised workers were in the CGTP–In, 33 per cent in the UGT and 10 per cent in independent unions. Most members the UGT are white-collar workers, while the CGTP-In continues to be widely supported by blue-collar workers (Lecher, 1994, pp. 219–21).

Divisions between the unions and the low proportion of unionised workers have been major obstacles to achieving a favourable bargaining position in the tripartite negotiations in the CPCS. Recently, however, the unions have been forced to adapt rapidly to the changing institutional circumstances. Integration into the European Community in 1986 and the transformation of industrial relations due to globalisation and Europeanisation processes have brought the two main federations closer together, in spite of the many ideological differences they had in the past.

EMPLOYERS' ASSOCIATIONS

Many businessmen left the country after the revolution in 1974–5. This was partly because of the increase in worker militancy in the enterprises, and partly because of the animosity expressed by workers against their employers, which included purging the management (*saneamento*). The main justification given for the latter was that the managers had been severely compromised by the former authoritarian regime. Although many of these businessmen eventually returned to Portugal and contributed to the reconstruction of national industry, the period between 1974 and 1983 was characterised by polarisation and lack of rapprochement between workers and employers.

As already mentioned, the coalition government between PS/PSD led to a change of attitudes towards each other. When the CPCS was formed it was regarded with a certain contempt by the employers' organisations and they adopted an uncompromising stance. This gradually changed from the second half of the 1980s onwards.

The main employers' organisation to act on behalf of Portuguese industry is the Confederation of Portuguese Industry (*Confederação de Industria Portuguesa* – CIP). It was founded in June 1974 and adopted an apolitical position in order to avoid being identified with the previous authoritarian regime. The CIP pledged the institutionalisation of tripartite harmonisation so that industrial action would be rendered unnecessary. Although it strongly advocated the idea of 'industrial democracy', its central offices were attacked on 11 March 1975, one of the turning dates of the revolution, because it represented entrepreneurs (Roseta, 1985, p. 789).

After the revolution the CIP became a very fierce opponent of state intervention in the economy and called for the liberalisation of and greater flexibility in the industrial sector. It became an intermediary for those entrepreneurs who vehemently condemned the new configuration of industrial relations, which had substantially shifted in favour of the workers. In addition it was critical of the economic provisions of the constitution of 1976, the legislation on dismissals, the growing budget deficit and the inadequacy of public enterprises.

It began to intervene in politics in the early 1980s during the AD coalition government, strongly criticising the inefficiency of state monopolies in the industrial sector. From 1983 it took part in the new tripartite CPCS, and although it initially remained quite maximalist in its demands it became more willing to compromise in the late 1980s and early 1990s (Roseta, 1985, p. 794; Barreto, 1992, pp. 460–1).

The CIP is by far the largest employers' organisation and claims to represent about 75 per cent of the enterprises that belong to a confederation (roughly 35 000 private enterprises comprising almost one million employees and workers in the 1980s). Some refute this claim and estimate that no more than 60 per cent of private enterprises are members of an industrial confederation, and not all of the CIP. The unions give an even lower figures: less than 30 per cent (Barreto, 1992, p. 461; Pinto, 1991, p. 254).

The CIP is not the sole representative of employers in the industrial sector – *Associação Industrial Portuense* (Industrial Association of Oporto – AIP) is very strong in the north. Although there is competition between the two, they do work together and have been negotiating a merger for almost two decades. The proposed merger has two objectives: to gain strength in the CPCS in relation to the state and the trade unions, and to isolate their main national competitor, the *Associação Industrial Portuguesa* (Portuguese Industrial Association – AIP), which has a membership of about 3000 enterprises, mainly in the public sector, branches of the TNCs and other private enterprises (Barreto, 1992, p. 461; Lucena, 1989, pp. 521–5). Another association is the *Movimento dos Pequenos e Médios Comerciantes e Industriais* (Movement of Small and Medium-Sized Trading and Industrial Firms – MPMCI), which is closely aligned to the Communist Party.

The main trade employers' association is the *Confederaçao de Comércio Portuguesa* (Portuguese Commerce Confederation – CCP) which was founded in November 1976. The CCP is the best-organised association and has built up a complete network of branches across the land (Roseta, 1985, p. 790). Although the CCP is in solidarity with the other employers' organisations, it has displayed a greater willingness to compromise in order to achieve solutions (Lucena, 1989, p. 521), and has established better relations with the government and the trade unions. The tripartite dialogue in the CPCS is regarded as an important forum for solving industrial relations problems.

At the European level the CCP is the most active of the employers' interest groups and it set up a permanent bureau in Brussels as early as 1986. European socialisation has made considerable progress and aspects of the European arena are used to influence policies at the national level (Marques, 1990, pp. 195–8; Lima, 1993, p. 852). In the early 1990s the CCP comprised 137 affiliated associations with 125 000 member firms (this represents half of Portuguese commercial businesses) (Pinto, 1991, p. 254).

There are several agricultural associations, but only the Confederation of Portuguese Farmers (*Confederação de Agricultores Portugueses* – CAP) is represented in the CPCS. The CAP was founded on 24 November 1975, and on 25 November its prominent leader, José Manuel Casqueiro, mobilised the farmers against a possible *coup d'état* by the extreme left. Farmers closed all the roads leading to the north, thus contributing to the failure of the coup. The CAP aims particularly at improving the quality of life of Portuguese farmers. It also protects the interests of family farms and promotes the democratic right of association (*Directory*, 1984, pp. 466–7). The confederation opposes collective agricultural estates and tends to promote the interests of small and medium-sized farmers. From the outset the confederation was strongly anticommunist and condemned the constitution of 1976 as too Marxist. The member associations of the CAP represent more than 100 000 farmers (Pinto, 1991, p. 253).

The CAP has recently been involved in a corruption scandal over the allocation of agricultural funds from the public Financial Institute for the Support and Development of Agriculture and Fisheries (*Instituto Financeiro de Apoio ao Desenvolvimento da Agricultura e Pescas* – IFADAP). The CAP was deeply enmeshed in a scheme to ensure that the agricultural funds went to member enterprises. Furthermore it built up a *tráfico de influências* (traffic of influences) in the Ministry of Agriculture in order to secure grants for its members from an EC programme designed to give financial support to agricultural associations and cooperatives (*Programa para o Apoio Financeiro às associaçoes e às cooperativas agrárias* – PROAGRI) (Magone, 1994, p. 757).

Another agricultural organisation is the communist-dominated National Confederation of Farmers (*Confederação Nacional de Agricultores* – CNA). It was founded on 26 February 1978, is not represented in the CPCS and is relatively excluded from other tripartite bodies and negotiating fora of the political system. Nevertheless it is working to improve the living conditions of Portuguese workers and calls for a more interventionist state role. The CNA has been very critical of European integration because of its negative effects upon Portuguese farmers. This confederation claimed to represent 600 associations in the late 1980s (*Directory*, 1984, pp. 471–5; Lucena, 1989, p. 527).

On the whole one may conclude that the employers' organisations are too fragmented and have too low a membership to negotiate tripartite arrangements for more than a minority of firms. It seems, then, that the lack of a historical tradition of association membership is preventing a more thorough neocorporatist intermediation of interests.

PERSPECTIVES OF SOCIAL HARMONISATION IN PORTUGAL

Democratic neocorporatist arrangements are a very recent phenomenon in Portuguese politics. The prerevolution authoritarian state did not foster a culture of interest intermediation, rather all conflicts of interest were decided in favour of the entrepreneurs. This changed during the revolution and the early consolidation period, and the state played a major role in establishing a more democratic relationship between labour and capital, especially when the PS–PSD coalition government set up the CPCS in 1983. In the beginning the new institution was reluctantly accepted by both employers' organisations and labour organisations, but it began to work quite well in the early 1990s. Nevertheless the interest groups represented in the CPCS remained opposed to the liberal policies of the Cavaco Silva governments elected in 1987 and 1991. The Europeanisation of Portuguese public policy was frowned on by the interest groups, who felt the government was acting in an authoritarian manner when it set a ceiling on wages in order to meet the convergence criteria for monetary union laid down in the Maastricht Treaty. In spite of all this the new neocorporatist institutions in Portugal are crucial to democratisation and may gain in importance in the long run.

Privatisation is progressing well and the banking sector has become more pluralist. Neocorporatist arrangements are strengthening the democratic dialogue between the representatives of different interest groups, as well as fostering new cultural patterns of behaviour and a strong informal tier of meso-government. Moreover the transition to neocorporatist-oriented public policy formulation and implementation will probably help Portugal to rid itself of its to tradition of short-termism, and this could lead to a more rational approach to policy-making.

A recent study suggests that neocorporatism is a better arrangement than pluralism in fostering political learning and information gathering, encouraging effective methods of inquiry and producing pragmatic rather than ideological policy (Stewart, 1994, pp. 252–4). However, the present attempt to make state structures more flexible, and the changing economic and social conditions at the national European and global level, seem to be making neocorporatist arrangements obsolete, due to the fact that they are causing discontinuity in longstanding arrangements in Western European countries. Nonetheless, for Portugal the present transformation at different levels is a unique opportunity to create a flexible neocorporatist arrangement that will foster a new culture of policy formulation and cooperation at the national level, as well as establish a new economic and social structure that is able to respond quickly and firmly to changes at all levels and achieve a greater degree of autonomy. Continuity and democratisation of policy formulation are the crucial factors to build up a strong self-sustainable democracy.

7 The Implementation of Public Policies

PUBLIC POLICY AND DEMOCRATISATION

Recent democratisation studies have been concerned with aspects of formal democracy, and until now policy studies that relate to the democratisation process have been quite rare. This is astonishing because long-term policies are an important device with which to build up the social and economic conditions for a strong and sustainable democracy. This can be only achieved in a stable institutional setting that stresses continuity and the incremental application of policies.

Citizens and their well-being are central to public policy in a democracy. Human development, then, is the crucial variable when determining whether a new democracy has advanced towards a qualitatively sustainable political arrangement (Lane and Ersson, 1994, pp. 98–9). The outcome may be an equilibrium between the three elements of the battlecry of the French Revolution: *liberté, egalité, fraternité*. It is dangerous for a new democratic order to favour one of these to the detriment of the others – all three are interconnected and feed each other.

Public policy should be concerned with building up greater legitimacy and acceptance for the government by establishing equality of opportunity and of access to public goods, by redistributing national income to less privileged social strata and regulating the free market to avoid distortion or abuse of the rules of competition. This is closely linked to what has been referred to as territorial politics, which is concerned with the even social and economic development of the nation-state and its ability to exert control over its own territory (Tarrow, 1978, p. 1). Territorial politics does not only mean covering the country with national structures, but in the long run it requires the emergence of a democratic political systemic culture, based on the rule of law and a citizen-friendly, people-oriented administration.

The new political systemic structures and the emerging culture can be regarded as socialisation agencies for the population (Magone, 1996b). All this is related to the capitalist world economy, which imposes constraints on the policy choices of a country. Internal political instability and discontinuity of policies may lead to the breakdown of democracy and its stronger dependency on the world economy.

Previous chapters have referred to the problems that national and local administrations have had in articulating and coordinating their policies. Moreover the doubling of institutional structures, the under developed methods of information gathering and the culture of short-termism have been major impediments to the establishment of a more efficient policy implementation culture. The scarcity of human and material resources has reinforced these obstacles to efficient rational planning. Furthermore, as asserted in the previous chapter, the neo-corporatist institutions are still very new, and although they are crucial to the democratisation of the political system as a whole, as yet they lack continuity and are sometimes very polarised. Therefore neocorporatism has not yet become an efficient and rational mechanism to influence policies. Nevertheless one cannot deny that since 1985 the Portuguese state has made a big effort to overcome its past obstacles.

Quality of service to the citizen has become one of the priorities of the 1990s, and regular assessment of quality in different sectors of the state is contributing to a substantial improvement of public administration. Comparing some social and economic indicators between 1973 and 1993, there is no doubt that the Portuguese people have experienced a considerable improvement in their living conditions. The rate of urbanisation almost doubled over two decades – while in 1973 only 26.4 per cent of the population lived in urban centres, in 1993 the figure was about 47 per cent. In the housing sector the number of houses without an inside lavatory declined from 40 per cent to 22 per cent and without a water supply from 31 per cent to 26.5 per cent. There was a threefold increase of telephones and televisions. Broadcast time per week expanded from 98 to 447 hours. The number of libraries rose from 301 to 1287 and illiteracy declined from 29 per cent to 15 per cent. There is now one doctor per 327 inhabitants – two decades ago the ratio was 1 to 968. The number of families with a cooker increased substantially, from 67.6 per cent to 98.9 per cent, and with a refrigerator from 57.1 per cent to 94.3 per cent. The working population rose substantially from 36.6 per cent to 48.2 per cent, particularly because of a rise in the number of women entering the labour market since the 1960s (*Expresso, Revista*, 23 April 1994, pp. 114–15).

These data document a considerable improvement in living conditions in Portugal, which is a major point in favour of the new democratic order. Nevertheless it tells us little about the extent of public participation in national affairs, which can be regarded as the next step after provision of basic needs. This involves citizens taking part in public policy making and influencing policy design at the local, regional and national levels. In the case of Portugal, it seems that since integration into the EC/EU both processes have acted together to change the country.

The expanding public policy agenda of the EU is helping to sustain the trend towards longer-term public policies, and the Europeanisation of national public policy has been a major feature of the 1990s (Pollack, 1994; Andersen and Eliassen, 1992; Peterson, 1995). In the Portuguese case this has provided an opportunity to adopt more rational methods of public policy formulation and implementation. Indeed Portugal has profited quite substantially from the Europeanisation process. It has been a crucial factor in the consolidation of democracy, and may be quite important in sustaining the process towards qualitative democracy.

On the whole, the integration into the EC/EU produced a spillover effect on national policy formulation and implementation in European rationale terms. Policies are now formulated in European rather than national terms, combined with the increasing importance of trans-European policy objectives, may eventually lead to problems with national cohesion. This phenomenon has already arisen in the north of Portugal, where the mayor of Oporto has tried to establish an interregional cooperation arrangement with northern Spain in order to achieve economic and social development in the northern region of Minho. Another example is the increasing discontent among the population of Alentejo. There a small group of unemployed people decided symbolically to join Spain, because the Portuguese government seemed to be neglecting this part of Portugal and failed to send help during a long-lasting drought (*Expresso*, 23 April 1994, p. A4).

The following pages will evaluate several policy areas that are crucial to the improvement of living conditions and, in a way, to a better integration of citizens into the political system.

SOCIAL POLICY: THE WEAK WELFARE STATE

Development of the welfare state started very late in Portugal. Social security only began to play a major role in the 1960s and 1970s. Before that the state had no social provision system for the working population. Although most of the legal framework was defined during the First Republic and the *Estado Novo*, social security remained a very fragmented system consisting of partial regimes regulating the social insurance of certain social groups.

After the revolution the main objective was to integrate these systems of providence and social assistance into a single social security system. This objective was defined in the MFA's programme in April 1974, enshrined in the constitution of 1976 and further rationalised in the revised version of 1982. But it took until 1984, ten years after the revolution, for the new framework law on social security (no. 28/84, 14 August 1984) to be approved by parliament. It is based on the principles of universality, equality and judicial guarantee. The law allows private institutions such as charities to operate separate social welfare programmes, but provides the state with a monitoring role and overall supremacy in the provision of social security (Maia, 1986, pp. 169–77).

This new responsibility of the state was steadily institutionalised during the second half of the 1980s and the 1990s. Providing a sufficient number of regional and local social service offices throughout the land was a major aspect in ensuring the universal fulfilment of its new function. Nevertheless, parallel, private social security systems continued to be tolerated and the state system distributed low benefits in comparison with other West European countries.

This late implementation of the system was further conditioned by institutional fragmentation of areas of responsibility and indecision about which main agency would be in charge of coordinating the system. The continual creation and closure of institutions between 1970 and 1985 was yet another obstacle. This was due to political instability and the weight that different governments assigned to social policy. This fragmentation and indecision continued after 1985, but more moderately and a more stable institutional environment has begun to emerge. However, as one author has pointed out, in the same time it should have been possible to establish a national health service and a national social security system (Leal, 1985, pp. 928–35).

Nevertheless, in governmental discourses since 1974 the social security system has been regarded as a necessary precondition for a strong democracy based on social justice. Political discourse was not accompanied by academic or technical discourse. On the contrary, most of the discussions on social security were related to its juridical place in the new democratic framework. Although the importance of including a larger number of social groups in the system was recognised, the consequences of this on the quality and financing of the social security system were never studied.

This changed considerably after 1986, when Portugal joined the EC and the European institutions required more accurate information on the nature of the Portuguese social security system. Empirical studies are becoming more abundant in Portugal and this may have a spillover effect on the quality of the system (Guibentif, 1985; Santos, 1984, 1990).

The inclusion of additional social groups, the extension of social security rights to all the working population and their families and the increase in the number of categories of social transfer placed a substantial financial burden on the state. Presently the main areas covered by the social security system are pensions, family allowance, maternity benefit, sickness benefit and unemployment benefit.

More than three quarters of the social security budget is allocated to pensions. This is related to the fact that the number of elderly in the population is growing faster than the birth rate. In this sense the demographic trends in Portugal are coming closer to those of the other West European countries. In the 1980s family allowance represented about 6.6 per cent of the total budget and sickness benefit 8 per cent. The share of maternity benefit is quite low (0.9 per cent) and unemployment benefit only accounts for 4.4 per cent of social expenditure. As Manuela Silva points out, extension of the right to social security to the whole population was not accompanied by a rise in the average value of the benefits. Although there has been a steady improvement since 1985, the average old-age pension was below 20 000 escudos (approximately £85) per month in 1988. Similar values have been assigned to the other allowances and benefits. The reasons for this are that the contribution rates are low, considerable contribution evasion is practiced (particularly by employers), a large number of contributors are in arrears and some employers have been exempted from paying contributions as an incentive to create new jobs (Silva, 1993, pp. 217–18).

The inadequacy of the benefits is one of the reasons why social exclusion and poverty seem to be permanent features of Portuguese society. The increase in the number of social exclusion and poverty studies indicates that this has become a major issue in Portuguese politics in the 1990s. Poverty has to be analysed multidimensionally and should include all the structural and conjunctural factors that prevent people from becoming integrated into the political system, such as lack of education, low income, unemployment, or employment in the exploitative informal economy.

Poverty is not only a question of receiving an income that is far lower than the national average, it is embedded in a culture of deprivation. In this sense poverty and social exclusion go hand in hand and are severe impediments to the exercising of civil rights.

Speaking in broad terms, it seems that more than half of the population lives below the poverty line, or 40 per cent of the average income in the European Union (Pereirinha, 1993, pp. 225–6).

The shanty towns around Lisbon, Setubal and Oporto are sites where poverty has its own repertoire of deprivation. Urban poverty is generally regarded as more extreme than rural poverty. Although poverty and social exclusion is often related to poorly paid work or no work at all, in rural areas it can arise from the low productivity of small parcels of land (Costa, Pereirinha and Matos, 1985).

The level of poverty has increased since Portugal joined the EC because the modernisation efforts encouraged by the European development programmes have resulted in a widening of the gap between rich and poor (Almeida *et al.*, 1992). Therefore the Portuguese government has set up the High Authority Against Poverty (*Alta Autoridade contra a Pobreza*) which is designed to fight against all forms of poverty. This is a long-term, multidimensional project that embraces educational, housing, employment and vocational measures, but already some success can be observed in the urban areas of Portugal.

EDUCATION POLICY: THE KEY TO MODERNISATION

The new democratic order inherited a very weak education system with an incomplete primary school network at the national level. This was completed in the mid 1980s but the provision of secondary education continues to be a problem (Emidio, 1986, p. 90; Stoer, 1986). Portugal experienced a boom in private-sector higher education in the late 1980s and 1990s, but this could not compensate for the deficiencies of the public sector.

Education studies has become a major field in Portuguese academia and this is influencing the quality of teaching in Portugal. In addition, since 1986 several EU programmes have provided teachers with the opportunity to further their own education at schools in the main towns and cities. Most of these courses take place at weekends or in the evening and are designed to upgrade their qualifications and bring them into contact with other teachers and teaching methods. This development at the teacher-education level is being diffused to their own institutions.[1]

Nevertheless good education is still a scarce commodity in democratic Portugal. In particular the poorer segments of the population can barely afford to send their children to school, especially in rural areas (Iturra, 1990). The high drop-out level seems to indicate that the quality of schooling has still not achieved its optimal level (Benavente, 1990; Iturra, 1990).

After 1986 the education sector had to be reorganised to meet the requirements of a democratic political system. Until then the general planning of educational policy had been non-existent, including during the time of the authoritarian regime, which in its early phase also tried to prevent the lower classes from being educated lest it gave rise to social conflict. In the latter days of the regime education was introduced because the market required better-educated human resources. Quite crucial was the attempt by Education Minister Veiga Simão to reform the education system during the Caetano era.

The revolution was the turning point for serious education policy, although attempts to reorganise the education system were quite chaotic until 1986. Governmental instability contributed massively to this situation. Integration into the EC provided an impetus for better education, and the education minister between 1987 and 1992, Roberto Carneiro, saw this as the key to the development of the country (Carneiro, 1988). Therefore a general discussion with different groups was organised to discuss the reform of the Portuguese education system. Several documents were produced, which were taken into consideration at the planning stage.

Between 1989 and 1992 Portugal implemented a very ambitious project, financed partly by the EC, called the Programme for the Development of Education in Portugal (*Programa para o Desenvolvimento da Educação em Portugal* – PRODEP). The programme targeted all aspects of education but failed to set priorities, which eventually resulted in the funds being scattered among many different areas instead of being directed at those where they would serve most purpose. The programme was also designed in a rush, because the government had to respond quickly to the inflow of EC funds. Prior to 1989 a lot of money was lost to phantom education enterprises that applied to the European Social Fund for capital to set up vocational training courses that never materialised (Eisfeld, 1989; Magone, 1991).

This general *ad hoc* approach changed slowly for the better in the 1990s, although in 1992–3 the Ministry of Education, under the leadership of Couto dos Santos, was subjected to the criticism of students and teachers because of its proposed reforms.

After two decades of democracy the Portuguese education system has become diverse and complex. While the actors in this system are playing a major role in improving the quality of education, 15 per cent of the population, mostly the elderly in peripheral rural areas, are still illiterate. Moreover the Portuguese population is divided into different educational cultures. Although the 'culture of literacy', in both its functional and structural sense, applies to the majority of the population, the 'culture of illiteracy' persists, particularly in its structural form, for example an inability to understand official documents. A third culture is now emerging that could be called the 'culture of information' which relates to knowledge of how to deal with and benefit from the new information technologies. Although this tripartite division is now widespread in the United States and Europe due the social exclusion of large segments of the populations, one has to acknowledge that in the Portuguese case this phenomenon is not new, it has merely shifted to a new stage. Therefore Stephen Stoer describes Portugal as a semiperipheral country in terms of education (Stoer, 1986).

From an employment point of view one has to regard this as a considerable obstacle to improving the very low qualifications of the working population, of whom more than half have no qualifications at all or only primary school education. Therefore education will continue to be a major target area of the Portuguese government. The main task for the future will be to ensure that the entire population has access to education and that mechanisms are devised to help the less advantaged children of poor parents to attend classes. Otherwise education will continue to be a symbolic capital (Bourdieu, 1984) that guarantees a privileged starting position for those who can afford it and the permanent exclusion from the official labour market of those who can not.

EMPLOYMENT POLICY: THE CRISIS OF THE LABOUR MARKET

Education and employment are closely intertwined, both seem today to feed each other in the development of a country's prospects. The technological change requires adaptability to new challenges coming from the international economic system.

Portugal has a very segmented labour market, and the division between the formal and informal labour markets is a critical aspect of this segmentation (Lobo, 1985; Rodrigues, 1985, 1988). In the nineteenth and early twentieth centuries Portugal was divided into different subeconomies, each with a different rational and none of them interacting with one another (Schwartzman, 1985, pp. 42–5). To some extent this is still evident today and overlaps with the division between the formal and informal markets. To complicate matters some workers work in both economies, so one has to be aware of different working conditions and statuses in the Portuguese case (Reis, 1985). Even taking this into consideration, the inaction of the state is the main cause of the segmentation of the labour market. The state has been too weak to intervene in the market and its formal regulatory framework has never been backed up by concrete measures to make the labour market uniform and gain control over the informal economy.

On the contrary, before 1974 the state made no substantial attempts to regulate the labour market and labour legislation followed no particular guidelines. Only in 1980 did decree no. 444/80 define global employment policy objectives and assign an active role to the state. Among its new responsibilities were developing activities in the fields of job allocation, information provision and professional orientation, professional rehabilitation and promotion of employment.

In November 1980 the Portuguese Council of Ministers issued Resolution 380/80, which created a new interministerial coordinating structure called the Interministerial Commission for Employment (*Comissão Interministerial para o Emprego* – CIME), whose main function was to develop and structure a global employment policy (Soares, 1986, pp. 131–2). The principal coordinator of this policy is the Ministry of Labour and Social Affairs, an agency of which, the Institute of Employment and Vocational Training (*Instituto de Emprego e Formação Profissional* – IEFP), regulates and promotes employment in Portugal. The latter has become the driving force behind employment creation and improving the qualifications of the unemployed (ibid., pp. 136–7).

Although unemployment was quite high in the first half of the 1980s due to the recession and the austerity measures imposed by the IMF in 1983–4 (*Tempo*, 18 August 1983, p. 14; *Financial Times*, 14 September 1983, p. 1; *O Jornal*, 19 August 1983), it fell considerably after accession to the EC in 1986 (from 8.6 per cent in 1986 to 4.1 per cent in 1991) (Ribeiro, 1993, p. 197). This led to former finance minister Jorge Braga de Macedo's boast that Portugal was an 'oasis' in Europe, because after Luxembourg it had the lowest unemployment rate among the EC members.

But in 1992, on the eve of realisation of the single market, the economy began to slide back into recession. The crisis became quite severe during

1993 and 1994 and particularly hit labour-intensive small and medium-sized firms. From 1992 entrepreneurs become more critical of the government's economic policies, which seemed to be geared towards promoting a strong escudo. This considerably constrained the competitiveness of Portuguese industrial exports. Criticism of the government's economic policies increased during 1993 and 1994 (*Expresso*, 3 April 1993, p. 1, C8; *Expresso*, 5 June 1993, p. C9).

Nevertheless, in his 'state of the nation' speech on 1 July 1993 in the Assembly of the Republic, Cavaco Silva stressed that the Portuguese economy was resisting the recession more effectively than those of other European countries. He referred to the fact that Portugal had already surpassed Greece in economic terms (*Expresso*, 3 July 1993, p. A5, 10 July 1993, p. A11). The crisis also seemed to be ignored by the Ministry of Labour and Social Affairs, which closed the employment agencies for three months between April and June 1993 to update the unemployment figures, which turned out to be lower than had been expected by experts (*Diário de Notícias*, 20 July 1993, p. 2).

The crisis can be better measured by the increasing number of firms that were in arrears with their workers' salaries due to financial difficulties. In 1992 about 16.4 per cent of workers' salaries were in arrears (about 18 824 people), which was a considerable increase of 82 per cent in comparison with 1991. About 70.9 per cent was related to arrears in social security contributions and 21.3 per cent to monthly salary payments. About 233 firms were in this situation and they were concentrated in the districts of Braga, Oporto and Lisbon. About 17 per cent of the firms and 42 per cent of the workers were in the textiles industry, which was mostly affected by competition in the internal EC market and the new GATT Treaty negotiated by the EC, 27.5 per cent of enterprises and 15 per cent of workers in the clothing industry, and 3.5 per cent of firms and 7.2 per cent of workers in the shoe industry (*Expresso*, 13 March 1993, p. A20).

This repeat of the crisis of 1983–4 shows that structurally the small and medium-sized enterprises were still not able to compete with the other European countries and that the industrial policies incorporated into the 1993–9 Regional Development Plan (*Plano de Desenvolvimento Regional* – PDR) will have to target this sector more intensively. The government estimated that the 1993–9 PDR would create 100 000 new jobs (*Expresso*, 10 July 1993, p. C3).

On the whole the employment situation in Portugal improved considerably after it joined the EC. Nevertheless removing the structural impediments to a more secure employment situation and improving the qualifications of the workforce are the only ways to strengthen the weak employment market, which tends to become even more informal in times of crisis.

ENVIRONMENTAL POLICY: TOWARDS SUSTAINABLE DEVELOPMENT?

In 1992 the Portuguese people seemed to become more aware of and concerned about the quality of the environment. Environmental issues were ranked as a major concern after the cost of living (93 per cent), health care (93 per cent), hunger and housing (89.6 per cent) and crime and violence (87.5 per cent). This is quite interesting because it indicates that Portuguese citizens have become more demanding when it comes to quality of life. Although economic growth at all costs was regarded as the principal objective in the 1970s and 1980s, in the 1990s – at least in political discourse – environmental concerns are more often taken into consideration.

The European integration process has been a major catalyst in introducing a new way of thinking about economic and social planning. 'Sustainable development', the new EC catchphrase (European Commission, 1992), became part of the vocabulary of the Cavaco Silva government (MARN, 1993a, 1993b; *Expresso*, 24 April 1993).

The turning point in the 1990s was the Portuguese presidency of the EC during which the world environment summit took place in Rio. Portugal became the voice of the Community in these matters (*Expresso*, 30 May 1992, pp. 16R–19R). This not only changed the perception of the Portuguese government on environmental issues (interview with Pedro Liberato, 7 June 1993), but made the population more aware and mobilised environmental groups to take part in a general discussion on the state of the environment in Portugal. During 1993 the government launched this discussion by soliciting the opinion of the population in different places across the land. The meetings were not well attended, but at least they represented an opportunity for the opinions of the population to be voiced and taken into account. As Teresa Fidelis Nogueira observes, environmental impact assessment of large projects has become a major field, and one in which local populations can take part. The environmental organisations are very keen to promote this form of participation by the population, and in this sense environmentalism seems to be enhancing the project of democracy that the country has embarked upon (Nogueira and Pinho 1988, Nogueira 1993).

Although interest in it has grown considerably, environmental policy has been a concern in Portugal since the UN conference in Stockholm in 1972. Already in 1971 the authoritarian government under Marcelo Caetano had set up a National Commission on the Environment (*Comissão Nacional de Ambiente* – CNA) as part of the National Junta for Scientific and Technological Investigation (JNICT). The CNA was a coordinating interministerial commission, and after the revolution it continued to exist in ministries that had a connection with environmental matters. In 1975 it became a consultative and coordinating office in the State Secretariat of the Environment. Between 1979 and 1985 the latter formed part of the ministry in charge of living standards. In the second half of the 1980s a state secretariat dealing with the environment and natural resources (*Secretaria do Estado do Ambiente e Recursos Naturais* – SEARN) was set up in the powerful Ministry of Planning and Administration of the Territory. But in 1990, following the Basic Law of the Environment of 1987, the SEARN was transformed into the Ministry of the Environment and Natural Resources (*Ministério do Ambiente e dos Recursos Naturais* – MARN). This discontinuity was further reinforced by environmental responsibilities being dispersed among different ministries (Pridham and Magone, forthcoming; Melo and Pimenta, 1992, pp. 17–19).

The most important agency inside the MARN is the Institute for the Promotion of the Environment (*Instituto para a Promoção do Ambiente* – IPAMB), which is the successor to the former National Institute of the Environment (*Instituto Nacional do Ambiente* – INAMB). The change of name highlights the government's intention to integrate and promote environmental policy. The IPAMB has a crucial relationship with the voluntary environmental associations. This linkage has proven invaluable because the latter have been able to offer expertise and advice to local governments and have acted as important catalysts in moving local development strategies towards the principle of 'sustainable growth', based on clean technologies, the recycling of waste and the promotion of human resources (interview with Fernando Ribeiro, Ipamb, 12 May 1993).

After the European Environmental Year in 1987 two laws were passed by parliament that regulate the Portuguese environmental policy and the relationship of the state with civil associations. The Basic Law of the Environment (no. 11/87) specifies quite clearly the objectives of environmental policy in Portugal. For example Article 2 decrees that environmental policy should 'optimise and guarantee continuity of the use of natural resources, quantitatively and qualitatively, its basic principle being that of sustainable development'. The Law for the Defence of the Environment (no. 10/87) defines the role of environmental associations within the global environmental policy of the government (Pridham and Magone, forthcoming).

In general terms the Portuguese government is following very closely the model of sustainable development set up by the European Commission in 1992. This model represents an integrated strategy of development, which in the Portuguese case is not restricted to specific environmental fields but goes beyond that by linking it to a general improvement of living conditions and a long-term commitment to reducing territorial assymetries in Portugal.

Although the level of industrialisation is lower than in other West European countries, Portugal incurs a high degree of environmental damage due to the lack of public awareness of ways to protect the environment, and to the underdevelopment of basic infrastructures in households and the manufacturing and tourism industries.

It is estimated that about 50 per cent of water resources are polluted, the highest pollution levels being in the most populated regions. Furthermore the water supply network reaches barely two thirds of the Portuguese population (about 94 per cent of the EC average), only 48 per cent have access to a sewage system (about 85 per cent of the EC average); and only 24 per cent are supplied by water stations.

Moreover the coastal waters are polluted by untreated household sewage, industrial waste, waste from ships and residuals from agriculture and intensive aquaculture.

Although air quality in Portugal is quite good in comparison with other countries of the EC, the air is polluted in four the main industrial areas: Lisbon, Oporto and the southern industrial zones of Barreiro-Seixal and Sines. Around three quarters of all dangerous residuals are not properly eliminated, which is presenting a severe risk of soil and water contamination. Last but not least, soil erosion and forest fires have contributed much to the picture of environmental degradation (Melo and Pimenta, 1993, pp. 77–8, 106–9; Borrego *et al.*, 1991; Pridham and Magone, forthcoming).

To sum up, the environment has become a top priority in the Portuguese agenda. The European integration process has been a crucial factor in drawing attention to the importance of environmental issues. A very positive relationship between the government and environmental associations is being established, and in the long run this may lead to a change of attitude at the local level. Portugal is facing the twin problems of underdevelopment combined with the environmental damage caused by industrialisation. It will take some decades to achieve qualitative improvements in both areas.

THE DOMESTIC POLICIES OF THE PORTUGUESE GOVERNMENT

Portuguese policy making and implementation seems to have become more integrated into an overall framework since the 1960s, and policies have become more people-oriented . This change of planning rationale is still in the making, but nevertheless it is already meeting with success in some areas. The planning deficiencies inherited from the former authoritarian regime, which tended to adhere to the development-oriented strategies of the 1960s, reinforced the assymetrical development of the coastal and peripheral regions of Portugal.

The Salazarist state's model of industrial development was based on strict *planos de fomento* (development plans), which promoted heavy industry and sought to attract foreign investment. It was hoped that the introduction of high technology into Pórtugal through the multinationals would have a spillover effect on the quality of the workforce. In this industrialisation project the peripheral eastern regions, whose economies were based on agriculture, were neglected. In the mid 1970s the project was halted by the revolution (Cravinho, 1986a, pp. 585–6). Giovanni Arrighi called this kind of economic system, based as it was on political oppression, 'market fascism' (Arrighi, 1985, p. 265), Medeiros characterised it as 'industrialisation without modernisation' (Medeiros, 1994).

After the revolution the general disarray of the economy restricted the ability of the government to develop long-term planning policies. It was further impeded by the austerity measures imposed by the IMF in 1978–9 and 1983–4. Although a national plan was enshrined in the constitution, successive governments concentrated on macroeconomic measures aimed at balancing the trade deficit and cutting expenditure in the public sector. Therefore the period leading up to accession to the EC was characterised by permanent economic and social crisis. The social costs of economic stabilisation were borne by the population, which only survived by virtue of extensive family networks (Cravinho, 1986a, pp. 588–90, 1986b, pp. 119–26; Stallings, 1981; Dauderstaedt, 1988, p. 444).

Only after accession to the EC in 1986 did long-term development planning became a major concern of the Portuguese government. The EC acted as a source of pressure on the political system, which had to prove its ability to utilise efficiently the inflowing structural funds. However until 1989 the government was unable to achieve maximum benefit from the funds. On the one hand this was because it was ill-prepared to meet the challenge. On the other, EC fund allocation was project-oriented and was not integrated into a programme. However after the reform of the structural funds in 1988 an EC dialogue on national strategies started to take place. In addition the Portuguese government prepared a regional development plan (*Plano de Desenvolvimento Regional* – PDR) in 1989, advocating a strategy of Europeanisation. The main aim was not only to reduce territorial imbalances across the country, but to come closer to the level of development of the other member states. European-oriented social and economic cohesion became a crucial aspect in the PDR, and after 1989 the development of Portugal was regarded as an integral part of the overall development of the EC (MPAT, 1989, pp. 4–5).

Portugal's main objective was to improve substantially its socio-economic basis and bring it closer to the European average. This could only be achieved in a sound macroeconomic environment where investment in productive capital goods, infrastructure and human resources was the main instrument for national development. Macroeconomic stability would guarantee that the climate of investment would be sustained in the long term. This was necessary because economic and social cohesion could only be brought about by achieving higher growth rates than the EC average. The PDR also emphasised the importance of reducing regional disparities in this period (ibid., pp. 12–15).

From 1989–93 the PDR had three main goals. First, it aimed to increase the efficiency of the productive system by improving the economic infrastructure of all sectors and promoting investment. Second, it envisaged upgrading its human resources by improving the education and vocational training systems and providing an extensive network of health and sports facilities. Third, it wished to ensure the progressive elimination of regional disparities by reconverting regional industry, particularly in regions where the industrial sector was in crisis, and by paying attention to local development and territorial planning (ibid., pp. 89–97).

Programmes such as the Specific Programme for the Development of Portuguese Industry (*Programa Específico para o Desenvolvimento da Industria Portuguesa* – PEDIP), the Specific Programme for the Development of Portuguese Agriculture (*Programa Específico para o Desenvolvimento da Agricultura Portuguesa* – PEDAP) and the Programme for the Development of Portuguese Education (*Programa para o*

Desenvolvimento da Educação Portuguesa – PRODEP) were structural elements of this ambitious development programme, which was supported by funds from the EC Common Support Framework (CSF) (Commission of the European Communities, 1990a, 1989).

A general assessment of the impact of the PDR between 1989 and 1993 reveals that while considerable progress was made in developmental terms, regional disparities continued to prevail. Although the programmes had been designed to promote economic and social development in the peripheral regions of inland Portugal, most were in fact implemented in regions on the coast. The best example is the PEDIP, where applications approved in 1990 for professional training were mostly from firms in the counties of Lisbon (62 per cent of all funding), Oporto (13 per cent) and the northern town of Braga (4 per cent). The same can be said of subprogramme six, whose targets included industrial design and quality. In this subprogramme 42 per cent of the successful applicants were situated in Lisbon and 37 per cent in Oporto. Nevertheless, in the subprogramme for innovation and modernisation 48 per cent of applicants were situated in the less-developed counties of Guarda, Castelo and Portalegre, mostly in the textiles and clothing industry. However this exception does not hide the fact that most of the financial transfers not only went to the better-developed regions of Portugal, but also to larger companies, in many cases TNCs (Eaton, 1994, pp. 43–5; *O Público*, 30 July 1994, pp. 4–5).

The Portuguese government announced the new 1994–9 PDR in 1993. The four aims of the new PDR follow the principle of sustainable growth, and special emphasis is placed on the environment and human resources. This environmental and people-oriented approach indicates a more self-confident, technocratic approach to strategic planning.

The PDR's first aim is to increase the quality of human resources and employment by improving the quality of the education sector, promoting investment in science and technology and expanding vocational training opportunities by training additional vocational training teachers.

The second aim is to strengthen the competitiveness of the economy by improving the infrastructures that support development, such as transportation, telecommunications and energy, by modernising the economic fabric of all sectors, and by implementing the community initiative, RETEX, which relates to the modernisation of the textiles industry, which has been adversely affected by the new GATT general framework.

The third aim is related to social cohesion and improving the quality of life. This involves environmental and urban revitalisation, health measures and the social integration of less privileged social groups.

The final aim is to strengthen the regional economic basis by promoting regional development. The interesting innovation here is that the PDR outlines different strategies of economic and social development for different regions, thus tailoring strategic considerations to the specific needs of each regions (MPAT, 1993, pp. 14–39).

But this PDR has even more to offer. Its designers wanted to ensure that its implementation will be more flexible and less centralised; that is, to increase the global efficacy of the system there should be a simplification of processes and decentralisation of responsibilities, and participation by economic and civil agents should be encouraged by creating monitoring bodies at the national, regional and local levels.

Since the signing of the Treaty of the European Union the Portuguese government has been able to count on a doubling of the funds that were available from 1989–93. On top of this an additional fund, the Social and Cohesion Fund has been set up to help all member states with a per capita GDP that is below 80 per cent of the EU average, and this will be a further source of infrastructural finance for Portugal.

The Portuguese government recognises that this is the last chance for the country to draw closer to the European average, because after 1999 the European Union will probably shift its interest towards Eastern Europe.

In summary, the domestic policies of the Portuguese government have changed considerably since 1974. Prior to 1974 those of the authoritarian regime were rigid and oriented towards specific targets. From 1974–86 there was a long period of crisis management, but then the domestic policies of the Portuguese state began to be more coordinated. The Europeanisation of domestic policies after 1989 due to EC/EU partnership and funding led to rationalisation and the conceptualisation and implementation of the PDR.

Coordination between national and European policy makers increased after 1989, so while the present PDR emphasises social and economic cohesion between the Portuguese regions, it is always within the European context. Very interesting is the emerging recognition that civil society must take part in the PDR if it is to be successful.

DEFENCE POLICY

After the end of the 1962–74 colonial wars the Portuguese army had to be reduced considerably, and one of the most important aspects of the new democratic regime was to assign a new role to the military. After the first and second pacts between the MFA and the political parties, the military ensured that they would continue to play a role in Portuguese politics through a monitoring institution, the Council of the Revolution. Moreover the first elected president, General Ramalho Eanes, was a military man. Demilitarisation of the political system was only achieved in 1982 with the revision of the constitution and the replacement of the Council of the Revolution by the Constitutional Court. Furthermore the election of Mário Soares as president in 1986 consolidated the civilianisation of the political system. The restructuring of the Portuguese armed forces could now take place (Bruneau and Macleod, 1986, pp. 12–16).

The AD government was able to push through a Law of National Defence on 26 November 1982, which restored civilian control over the military apparatus, in spite of a veto by Ramalho Eanes. Under the new law the defence minister became the key policy-making figure in the area national defence. The president would only take part in matters related to the deployment of troops in emergency situations. High-ranking officers would be appointed by the government in consultation with the president. A National Council of Defence integrated the other parliamentary parties into the decision-making process (Graham, 1993, pp. 48–52; Ferreira, 1989).

In the second half of the 1980s the minister of defence steadily gained control over the military and started a general modernisation programme. A long-term plan, implemented in 1987, envisaged the gradual replacement of outdated military equipment. Moreover the size of the armed forces, which consisted of around 270 000 persons on the eve of the revolution, was reduced to around 80 000 in the late 1980s.

Today, defence strategy is increasingly being incorporated into the overarching framework of the European Common Foreign and Security Policy (CFSP). Membership of the North Atlantic Treaty Organisation (NATO), and more recently of the West European Union (WEU), is central to the defence strategy of the Portuguese government. Portugal is quite involved in regional security and defence arrangements, such as the '4 + 5' talks between the southern European countries (Portugal, Spain, Italy and France) and North African ones (Morocco, Tunisia, Algeria, Libya and Mauritania) and the proposal for a conference on security and cooperation in the Mediterranean. In addition Portugal, Spain, France and Italy are to form a regional Mediterranean corps to act in the event of a regional crisis, which may come from North Africa due to growing Islamic fundamentalism. Portuguese nationals have played and are playing an advisory role in the reorganisation of the armed forces in Angola and Mozambique (Vasconcelos, 1991, pp. 113–22; Magone and Kintis, 1994, pp. 35–6; *The European*, 8 June 1995, p. 2, 15 June 1995, p. 2).

One can expect that Portuguese defence policy will become increasingly integrated into regional and European arrangements and will stress collective security rather than national defence objectives. This is probably the more realistic approach in an age of growing regional interdependence and integration.

CONCLUSIONS

The third revision of the constitution of 1989 states that Portugal's aims are 'social, economic and cultural democracy and the deepening of participatory democracy' (Constitution 1992, 1995, Article 2). Although Portugal still has to overcome many obstacles to achieve these aims, since accession to the EC/EU the country has come closer to realising them. The policy makers seem to be very sensitive to these objectives and have designed their policies according to them. The overarching domestic policies strongly emphasise the importance of integrating civil society into the process. Many problems are still to be solved, but policy formulation and implementation have become more democratic in the past decades. Further democratisation of public policy making can only be achieved by fighting against the social exclusion experienced by the majority of the population due to illiteracy, lack of information and lack of the financial means to improve their qualifications, and against the marginalisation of peripheral regions and excessive centralisation of public policy formulation.

All this is addressed in the most recent PDR, but in the end it will depend on whether the Portuguese government can prevent the better-equipped firms and the better-educated population in the coastal regions from attracting most of the PDR funds. A policy of positive discrimination is probably the most suitable way of preventing a widening of the regional disparities in Portugal. In the past two decades a storehouse of knowledge has been acquired about public policy making and implementation in Portugal and the problems related to it, and this should be used to prevent the widening of economic, social and regional disparities at the end of the millenium.

8 The Emergence of Civil Society

DEMOCRATIC INSTITUTIONALISATION: THE QUALITATIVE DIMENSION OF DEMOCRACY

Recent studies of democratisation seem to recognise that democracy not only requires institutional stability and policy continuity, but also a strong civil society to sustain the emerging democracy (Lipset, 1994; Schmitter, 1993; Perez-Diaz, 1993; Furlong, 1993). In this regard structure and culture shape each other. The structuring of a democratic culture can be only successful if institutions and policy processes are based on a democratic rationale that leads to the full participation of civil society.

Democratisation is a long-term project that requires a constant dialogue between central institutions and civil associations at all levels of the political system. The so-called participatory democracy enshrined in the Portuguese constitution is not a new idea. It corresponds to what Alexis de Tocqueville, the greatest French political scientist of the nineteenth century, saw in the young American democracy and to which he ascribed the strength of America in comparison with the European nations (Tocqueville, 1981, vol. II, pp. 147–52). Decentralisation is an essential element of diffusing democratic behaviour outwards to the local level, such as in the case of Denmark, where the democratisation process led by a continuous long-term, people-oriented public policy and decentralisation of structures, targeted at lowering the level of anomy and increasing the will to participate. In spite of some negative aspects, Danish democracy may be regarded as a good example of a civil society shaping institutions rather than just being shaped by them (Bogason, 1986; Esping-Andersen, 1985; Borish, 1991).

Although the concept of civil society has changed over time, present works seem to defined it as the ability of collective associations to play an influential part in policy making and implementation. The role of non-governmental organisations (NGOs) is strongly emphasised as a means of controlling and limiting the powers of the state (Stieffel and Wolfe, 1994, pp. 211–19).[1] Another aspect is that the retreat of the state in the 1980s, due to the crisis that resulted from expansive

Keynesian policies, led to a general decline of public expenditure in all sectors.

The vacuum left by this retreat required substitution by strong civil associations that would be prepared voluntarily to take over the new tasks. This was related to the rebirth of the fallacy of 'free market rationality', which assumed that everybody would instinctively follow market principles.

In reality the commodification of labour and nature destroys existing cultures and atomises individuals – nothing is worth preserving if no value is attached to it (Polanyi, 1944; Sternberg, 1993, pp. 105–6). What people experienced in the 1980s and 1990s was not a move towards a stronger civil society, but towards an economic concept of it, an artificial construction that was ancillary to the market and permeated by its logic. Democratisation was linked to liberalisation of the market and did not take into account the fact that a market economy needs to be planned, regulated and structured because it consists of persons competing in the market from different starting positions. Moreover institutions have to be imbued with what Silvana Malle calls 'institutional ethics', which have been absent in the Eastern European cases and this has led to the occupation of the market by mafia-like groups (Malle, 1994, pp. 11–15).

The nature of institutions and policy processes do matter in creating a sound relationship between civil society and market capitalism. The unstable situation in Russia reminds us that institutions are needed to structure the economic, social and political space by setting up the boundaries of ethical democratic behaviour and socialising the population into it.

The one-world theory of a capitalist world economy is a construct that may be attenuated by alternative solutions such as that of a social market economy (Hage and Shi, 1993). The need for a balance between the three ideals of the French Revolution – liberty, equality, fraternity – has never ceased to exist, and is behind the tense relationship between civil society and the state.

The road to modernity depends on the extent to which capitalist market rationale permeates institutions and behaviours. It seems that the Portuguese case documents a discontinuity of this process of capitalist diffusion, and a capitalist rationale coexists with premodern ones. Therefore some authors have characterised the country as 'patrimonial' or 'semiperipheral', a reference to the fact that the Portuguese state is still not very democratic and is based on relationships of clientage and patronage that favour certain privileged social groups to the detriment of others. The main reasons for the persistence of this patrimonial state are the high level of illiteracy (15 per cent), the poorly qualified workforce, the tendency to defer to educated segments of the population, the lack of dignified treatment in public offices, hospitals and social services, and the high level of social exclusion due to poverty and unemployment (Santos, 1990, 1993; Aguiar, 1984, 1985, 1990b).

All these factors condition both the development of a stronger civil society and a 'sound' reception of capitalist values. Therefore it is essential to take into consideration the development of capitalism in a particular country which is closely interlinked to the dissemination of modern rationality among the population through socialisation and participation systems (Magone, 1996b; Wallerstein, 1974, 1980, 1989).

In the case of Portugal one has to assert that the permeation of capitalist thinking and rationale is still in progress, unlike in those West European countries that have transformed their cultural values from premodern to modern, and are presently advancing towards more postmodern ones. In a way the Portuguese political culture encompasses all three. That Portugal is lagging behind in the structuring of its economic, political and social spheres means that 'institutional reflexiveness' in relation to policy making and implementation has been imported as a 'package' from more developed countries and has not been adjusted to the particularities of Portugal.[2]

In sum, civil society is being treated in economic, utilitarian terms and participatory democratic considerations are being neglected. In the past participation was regarded as the key to political emancipation (Pateman, 1970). Today it merely fulfils an ancillary function, having been discarded by the state during its retreat in the 1980s and 1990s (Cerny, 1990). In the following pages we will deal with cultural transformations that have occurred in the past twenty years.

THE EMERGENCE OF NEW VALUES IN SOCIETY

In a study of the image portrayed of youth in television advertisements between 1974 and 1984, Maria Luisa Schmidt found it had changed quite considerably. Between 1974 and 1978 TV advertisements in Portugal presented an image of 'love' and 'sociability', where confident young men were the dominant element in the advertisement. This changed substantially in the first half of the 1980s. The new representation of youth tended to give to young women a more active, assertive role (Schmidt, 1985, pp. 1054–6) and 'love' was often replaced by eroticism. Furthermore individuality rather than sociability became the main aspect of advertisements in the 1980s. The portrayal of male–female relations was reversed, and self-confident young men and insecure young women were replaced by young women with a new self-confidence and young men made insecure by this change (ibid., pp. 1062–4).[3] This reversal of roles opened the way to a wider repertoire of relationships in the 1990s.

Luisa Schmidt's study tells us that Portuguese society has changed very rapidly during the past two decades. The values of youth are becoming more instrumental, and lacking in idealistic purpose. 'Individualisation' and 'atomisation' are related to an adjustment to the market and its values. However it should be noted that this mainly applies to urban youth, and since the late 1980s to young people in rural areas as well.

In a study carried out by sociologist Eurico Figueiredo in the mid 1980s it was found that the values of youth have changed considerably from those of their parents. The values held by young people are those that relate to personal self-fulfilment, such as inner harmony, freedom, a sense of fulfilment and being in love, while their parents continue to advocate socially oriented values such as family security, world peace and equality. Young men place value on being happy, open-minded, intellectual, imaginative, ambitious and logical; their parents see greater virtue in being educated, helpful, controlled, obedient and clean. This represent a shift from premodern to modern values, where values related to familial and social solidarity are being replaced by more individualised ones in a competitive world (Figueiredo, 1988).

All this has considerably influenced politics. The 'privatisation' and 'atomisation' of social life is reflected in the participatory willingness of urban youth. Studies in the 1980s on political participation seem to suggest that this is a general trend in the population.

The process of 'atomisation' and 'individualisation' and the penetration of capitalist rationale into former islands of precapitalist thinking can be observed most clearly in the rural areas. The collapse of rural life based on a subsistence agricultural economy has been an ongoing process since the Second World War, but it has accelerated since the 1980s. The abandoning of peripheral villages and the migration of young people to the larger coastal towns is speeding up social erosion in the peripheral areas. The southern province of the Alentejo may be regarded as an extreme case in this respect. Although after the revolution of 1974–5 land labourers occupied the latifundia, with the logistical help of the Communist Party, whose main aim was to assure a stable income and permanent work for this social group, the ideological battles by the socialist and social-democrat governments in the 1970s and 1980s against these Communist-dominated collectives led to the collapse of this quite extensive network (Eisfeld, 1984, pp. 157–8; Vester, 1986, pp. 497–8).

The ideological battle between the socialists/social-democrats and the communists – stemming from the role the communists played during the revolution – ended at the end of the 1980s with the return of the landed estates to their prerevolutionary owners. The consequent lack of work, the extreme living conditions and the absence of regional development programmes led to the migration of younger men and women to Faro, Setubal and Lisbon.

In the 1990s this trend of social and economic crisis in the Alentejo has been reinforced by permanent drought, which is destroying the main economic activity – agriculture. The new Common Agricultural Policy, finalised during the Portuguese Presidency in 1992, is not very favourable to the economy of the Alentejo. On the contrary it will require major restructuring measures to make it work more efficiently (*Expresso*, 6 March 1993, p. C3). Meanwhile the Portuguese government is continuously being challenged by the desperate populations of the peripheral areas. The spectre of hunger and deprivation requires swift measures to change the face of Alentejo.

Recently the inhabitants of several villages on the border with Spain have expressed their desire, at least symbolically, to become citizens of Spain, (*Expresso*, 23 April 1994, p. 94) and the number of Portuguese crossing the border to work in Spanish agriculture under inhuman conditions is growing considerably (*Expresso*, 30 April 1994, p. 12). This complete neglect of Alentejo by the government may be corrected by the new regional development plan, but the EU Interregional Programme (Interreg) is likely to be of greater importance. About 592.83 million ecus have been made available for common transfrontier projects that will affect about six million people (2.2 million in Portugal and 3.5 million in Spain). Besides Alentejo and the other border regions of Portugal, the Spanish regions of Extremadura, Andalusia, Galicia and Castile will also benefit.

The main aims of the programme are (1) to improve the accessibility of the regions, (2) to stimulate an endogenous development process, (3) to promote intraregional trade and (4) to develop the surface water potential of the region. The main projects are related to developing the road network, agricultural and industrial development, the

promotion of tourism, crafts and local heritage, exporting hydroelec-
tricity, and encouraging innovative ideas that will further development
(European Commission, 1994b, pp. 32–3).

Social change and difficulty in adapting to the logic of capitalist
rationale can be observed in all regions of Portugal. The modernisation of the various infrastructures, the adoption of consumerism in the
urban centres and the inflluence of the images coming from imported
television programmes and films, as well as Brazilian and Portuguese
soap operas, are major factors in the erosion of premodern lifestyles.

A crucial factor of social integration is employment. Social dignity
is increasingly related to the right to work, if possible quality work
that leads to self-fulfilment. This is quite a problem in Portugal, where
the employment system is still very archaic and segmented. Young
people seem to have different strategies in relation to the working world.
The existing insecurity among young people in the interregnum between school and work is not so much related to not having work, as
to not having the financial means to gain independence and participate
in the consumer market.

Social integration is related to market participation, to participation
in the routinised ways of living between home and work. Many young
people in Portugal are stuck in a situation where the poor qualifications acquired at school or in the new private universities limit them
to jobs in the informal market while giving them the illusion of being
part of the market.

Both the working class and the new middle classes, predominantly
consisting of highly skilled technicians, are growing in number in comparison with the dwindling agrarian classes such as land labourers and
farmers, and the traditional middle classes. This indicates that Portuguese society is becoming increasingly urban. Also of interest is the
social movement of people from working class to the new middle classes,
and to a lesser extent, new middle-class persons becoming workers
(Pais, 1991, pp. 947–60, 964, 983). The new middle classes are quite
market-oriented and very flexible in outlook. Their volatility in terms
of politics, social behaviour and market behaviour can be regarded as
important qualities in adapting to the changing nature of the world
economy.

On the other hand the proletarianisation of some social groups continues, such as in the labour-intensive textiles and footwear industries,
where child labour was common and was further liberalised by the
government in 1993 (Commission of the European Communities, 1990b;
Expresso, 5 June 1993, p. A17).

In 1956 Almond stated that the reason the American political system was working so well was because the political culture was showing market behaviour (Almond, 1956). In the Portuguese case it could be concluded that values related to a large ideological design are in decline and are being replaced by short-term electoral packages whose main purpose is to attract the largest share of votes. The new middle classes may be a crucial factor in disseminating this new approach (Aguiar, 1988). This seems to be confirmed by the move from nationalist to regionalist politics. As Manuel Braga da Cruz points out:

> The transition to democracy in Portugal meant not only the transition from an authoritarian to a democratic regime, but also, and perhaps above all, the transition from overseas integration to European integration and with it the transition from a nationalism which claimed to be multi-racial and pluri-continental to a regionalizing Europeanism. Portugal, in fact, passed not only from one form of state to another – from an authoritarian, centralized state to a democratic, decentralized one – but also from one system of external references to another – from the overseas system to the European one (Cruz, 1992b, pp. 151).

The conveyors of this modernising regional Europeanism are predominantly the well-educated new middle classes, who seem to espouse the European model of development, which gives special emphasis to the regions as units of economic organisation. Modernisation is no longer an exclusively national task, but also local and regional (Cruz, 1992b, p. 850).

On the whole, one may assert that Portuguese society is in the process of complete transformation. This is leading to the emergence of new middle classes, who seem to be important conveyors of the new market behaviour. A major problem that has to be solved in the medium term is absorbing young people into the official labour market. This will require new public policy strategies and is quite crucial because young people will form the social basis of a future participatory democracy that will go beyond a market-oriented political culture.

CASE STUDY: THE ROLE OF ENVIRONMENTAL ASSOCIATIONS IN THE LOCAL AND CENTRAL DECISION-MAKING PROCESS

The seeds of 'participatory democracy' have already been sown by environmental associations across the country. Since the 1980s there has been a burgeoning of such associations and they are playing a very active role in environmental education, as well as helping local and national government by sharing their expertise. This expertise is particularly welcome because most of the local authorities are under-staffed in this area and frequently require the advice of these organisations.

After the European Year of the Environment in 1987, the Cavaco Silva government started to show a greater sensitivity to environmental issues. Codification of the Basic Law on the Environment (law 13/87) and the Law on Associations for the Protection of the Environment (12/87) defined the legal framework for the activities of these associa-tions. They acquired a privileged place in the political system and are entitled to receive the support of the national government through the latter's liaison body, the National Institute of the Environment (Inamb), now called the Institute for the Promotion of the Environment (Ipamb) (Lei de Bases, 1987, Article 39). Furthermore the Basic Law gives special emphasis to the right of citizens to a clean environment and to participate at the local level in improving the quality of life (Lei de Bases, 1987, Article 40).

Environmental associations began to increase in number in the mid 1980s, and in 1993 there were 120 of them (interview with Fernando Ribeiro, Ipamb, 12 May 1993). Most are concentrated in the coastal regions – representation in the peripheral areas is less strong. In 1993 there were 17 national associations with regional and local branches.

Environmental activism in Portugal has a short history. Before the authoritarian regime only a few individuals dared to speak out on the matter, for example the journalist Afonso Cautela (Cautela, 1977). The only association to exist before 1974 was the League for the Protec-tion of Nature (*Liga para a Protecção da Natureza* – LPN), a very academic circle, that made focused on local aspects of environmental degradation. (Baeta Neves, 1966–70). Environmental activism began to spread only after the revolution.

Several movements began to protest about projects that could have negative consequences for the environment. For example in 1978 sev-eral associations grouped together to protest about the establishment of a nuclear power station in Ferrel, and this led to the abandonment of the project. The attempt to transfer the project to another locality (Freixo de Espada à Cinta, Mira, Vila Nova de Milfontes and Mértola were mooted as possible sites) met strong local opposition. Four years later a massive protest movement against the National Energy Plan, which again considered the introduction of nuclear energy into Portu-gal, met with success when the government decided to drop the idea

Table 8.1 Environment associations at local and regional level (1992)

North	27
Centre	19
Lisbon and Vale do Tejo	47
Alentejo	11
Algarve	6
Azores	4
Madeira	1
Total	115

Source: Melo and Pimenta, 1993, pp. 181–8.

(Lemos, 1988, p. 286). Other examples of successful environmental activism, in spite of the use of force by the police, are the prevention of kaolin (china clay) mining in the northern village of Barqueiros in the 1980s (Magone, 1991) and the planting of eucalyptus trees across the country.

Three environmental organisations have been the catalysts of this type of activism. The oldest is the LPN, which was founded in 1948 and held a solitary position during the time of the authoritarian regime. It was very academic and insular in nature, but it changed after 1986 and became more open to the public.

By far the largest association is Quercus – the National Association for the Conservation of Nature, which has more than 7000 members and is presided by Professor Viriato Soromenho. It was founded in 1986. Although the association attempts to maintain a constructive dialogue with local and national authorities, it does not restrain itself from more sensationalist activities to overcome impasses and alert the public to environmental dangers.

The third of the main associations is the Study Group on Territorial Organisation and Planning (*Grupo de Estudos de Ordenamento do Território e Planeamento* – GEOTA). It was founded in 1981 and became an association in 1986. Most of its members are environmental engineers or professionals in the field of environmental science. In comparison with the other two main associations, it speaks freely about the interdependency between development and the environment (Melo and Pimenta, 1993, pp. 151–2).

In 1989 the environmental associations decided to found an overarching national confederation, which would send representatives to the council of Ipamb, the governmental body that supports environmental associations. A major meeting was held for this purpose in November 1989 in Viseu, and about 70 associations took part. The result was the founding of the Portuguese Confederation of Associations for the Protection of the Environment (*Confederação Portuguesa de Associações para a Defesa do Ambiente*) in 1991. This cooperation between the various associations is fostering new forms of behaviour that emphasise the commonalities between the associations rather than their differences (ibid., pp. 153–4).

The discussions over Agenda 21 of the Eco-92 conference in Rio de Janeiro were launched and sustained by the environmental associations during and after the event. They supported the government's commitment to implement Agenda 21 in Portugal and the dialogue that the government tried to establish with civil society. They organised several conferences, and on 15 June 1993 a major conference – on the impact of the Rio Conference on Portuguese environment, held in the Calouste Gulbenkian Foundation in Lisbon – enjoyed the participation of President Mário Soares, the president of the Assembly of the Republic, Barbosa de Melo, MEPs Carlos Pimenta and Maria Santos, the Professor of Constitutional Law Jorge Miranda and Nigel Haigh from the European Institute of Environmental Policy. This shows that the environment is becoming, at least in public declarations, a major concern of the political institutions and civil society.

In general the Portuguese environmental associations consist of young people concerned with aspects of environmental degradation. Many of them are academics with some expertise in environmental issues, and the work within the associations is done on a voluntary basis. This fact enhances their credibility *vis-à-vis* national and local governmental bodies. They offer their services to improve aspects of environmental policy in areas such as environmental education, soil and water decontamination, and the identification of pollutors, work that is highly appreciated by the local government authorities.

The technocratic discourse in the associations emphasises permanent and constructive dialogue with the governmental authorities. Nevertheless, as stated earlier, they are not afraid to resort to sensationalist activities to alert the population to specific environmental problems (interview with Conceição Martins, Geota, 30 April 1993; interview with Quercus activists, 14 April 1993).

The EU directive on the Environmental Impact Assessment (EIA) of local projects is a major area where the associations hope to mobilise the population to take part in decision-making processes related to local development. The EIA directive, approved by the Council of Ministers of the European Community in 1985, requires that public and private projects that may considerably affect the living conditions of the population have to include the latter in the consultation procedure (OJ L175, 27 June 1985, pp. 40–8). This is regarded as an opportunity to achieve greater transparency in the national decision-making process and make it more democratic. Implementation of the EIA directive is also seen as a major opportunity to bring about decentralisation and of the decision-making process, which may have a spillover effect that will enhance the efficiency and efficacy of administrative behaviour (Nogueira and Pinho, 1988, pp. 96–8).

Several problems seem to account for the lack of transparency in and the centralisation of the decision-making process, as we have already seen in Chapters 3 and 4. The increasing number of environmental associations and the pressure they are exerting on the government is changing attitudes within the administration. Some of the civil servants in Ipamb, such as its vice-president, Pedro Liberato, are well-known environmentalists who are well aware of the problems within the administration and are attempting to contribute to a closer cooperation between the government and civil society (interview with Pedro Liberato, 7 June 1993; Liberato, 1992, p. 30).

The Portuguese government's response to the EIA directive has been less than satisfactory. For a start it did not implement the directive until two years after the deadline had expired. Moreover it exempted from the EIA procedure all project proposals that had been submitted before June 1990. This led to a general protest by the environmental associations and the director-general of Directorate XI of the Commission of the European Communities, Laurens Jan Brinkhorst, during 1990 and 1991 (*Correio da Manhã*, 19 July 1987, p. 64; *Expresso*, 24 November 1990, pp. 52R, 70–1R, 4 May 1991, p. A14; *Público*, 14 April 1991, p. 24). A general reformulation of the relevant domestic legislation had to be undertaken by the government in 1992 and 1993 to meet the EC demands. A particular transgression on the part of the government is that the requirement to consult the public was not adhered to in the first enactments of the EIA directive (*Diário de Notícias*, 1 June 1992, p. 5; Nogueira, 1993, pp. 18–22). This is the part of the directive that environmental associations see as an important instrument with which to integrate the population into the decision-making process, so that greater democratisation and transparency of decision making can be achieved (Marques, 1993; Chito and Caixinhas, 1993).

To sum up this section one may assert that the environmental associations are acting as an important catalyst in improving the environment, enhancing public participation, increasing the democratisation and transparency of the decision-making process, contributing to the modernisation of administrative structures and enhancing civil society at the local and regional levels.

THE TRANSFORMATION OF POLITICAL CULTURE

The emergence of a democratic civil society is still in its beginnings. Nevertheless in the past two decades Portugal has experienced a change of political values and attitudes. Society has become more open-minded and knowledgeable about the external world. The extension of infrastructure and the spread of urbanisation and democracy are eroding premodern cultures and providing space for modern and postmodern ones. This process has been neither straightforward nor smooth. On the contrary it has often been painful, involving very deep inter-generational conflict in both urban and rural areas, economic deprivation, social exclusion, competition over public resources, the coexistence of premodern, modern and postmodern forms of behaviour in administration and society and the emergence of divisions in the areas of educational standards, income and social status (Santos, 1985, 1990, 1993; Chilcote, 1993).

Markets and society are segmented in Portugal due to a long history of underdevelopment. So too is culture, and particularly political culture. Therefore Portugal has been characterised as having a 'semiperipheral culture' (Magone, 1991, 1996b). Looking at political culture in broad terms, due to different educational levels, access to public goods, spatial distribution and social representation in the political world it is not possible to identify an homogeneous pattern of values across the country. Consequently it is probably more appropriate to speak of political cultures rather than a single one.

This characterisation of Portuguese political culture arises from the excellent studies of a team of social scientists at the Higher Institute of Labour and Business Sciences (*Instituto Superior de Ciências do Trabalho e Empresa* – ISCTE) of the Technical University of Lisbon, under the directorship of Franz Wilhelm Heimer. Although the final results are still to be published, the preliminary findings reveal that there are four distinct political cultures in Portugal.

The first is called 'meritocratic individualism'. Espousing an ideology of talent and endowment, it seems to be closely linked to neoliberal idealism and social Darwinism. It is also a social representation that is very close to a religious identity with the Catholic Church. Its proponents

oppose social solidarity and economic equality. They see social difference as a natural aspect of life, and their neoliberal attitudes are very
remote from democratic values. In addition they are vehemently
anticommunist and oppose state intervention.

The second form is 'egalitarianism,' characterised by a radical stance on
society and an intention to transform it. Its proponents are against social
inequality, but are prepared to remedy it within the framework of democracy and to trust in the work of institutions. Egalitarians are widespread
among the lower social strata and are strong defenders of democracy.

Members of the third category are described as 'collectivist and
conflictual'. Their ideology focuses on domination and they value social
conflict and collective protest to overcome it. Nevertheless they defend
state interventionism and the welfare state. The democratic values they
espouse are not as strong as the social representation of egalitarianism. They distance themselves from anticommunism and are moderately associated with antifascism.

The fourth and final category is 'fatalism' and its adherents distance
themselves from political activity. Respect for political authoritarianism and conservatism are further characteristics of this group (Vala,
1989; Heimer *et al.*, 1990b; Andrade and Viegas, 1989).

While examples of the first three groupings are found more often in
urban conurbations, fatalism is more widespread in rural areas, where
apathy seems to characterise the political behaviour of Portuguese farmers.
They tend to bow to authority and refer to the main figures of the
political system in paternalist terms, for example calling the president
of the republic the father of the national family. A top-down concep-
tion of politics, support of the status quo rather than social change and
the importance of religion as an integrative element are further characteristics of this way of thinking (Viegas and Reis, 1988, pp. 85–99).
Nevertheless this fatalistic view of the world is being challenged by
the younger generation, who normally have a higher level of education, are more influenced by mass communication and pursue the more
modern life styles of the urban centres (ibid., p. 101).

These findings help us to understand that establishing a strong and
cohesive Portuguese civil society still has a long way to go. The different
attitudes of citizens in relation to public goods and the political field
are major impediments to achieving a greater degree of participation.
They also show that future governments will need to adopt different
strategies to integrate the different groups. Such a process will take
several decades and has to be sustained by a continuity of structural
and social policies.

One major point, referred to in another work (Magone, 1996b), is that in former times the Portuguese state never managed to build up a political systemic structure that covered the whole territory. On the contrary, the lack of political structures in peripheral regions facilitated the preservation of premodern cultures of subsistence and alienation from the political system. Only since the 1960s have the premodern ways of living begun to be eroded by the penetration of a capitalist rationale in Portuguese villages. This belated 'great transformation' (Polanyi, 1944) is a painful process that needs to be accompanied by compensatory social policies and strategies of social reintegration in new communitarian projects. This is even more urgent in that those most affected are elderly.

The study conducted under the directorship of Franz Wilhelm Heimer tells us another thing. Political culture is not an individual attitude, but a social one. Therefore the team rightly states that political culture is integral part of societal culture and individuals are embedded in networks of social relations reproducing social representations of the world.

CONCLUSIONS

Democracy has to be sustained by a strong civil society that is able to extend the democratisation and decision-making processes taking place at all levels of the political system. For that, equality of access to areas relating to social and economic well-being is an important prerequisite for establishing equal access to political decision making. The ideal of participatory democracy defined in the Portuguese constitution since 1989 requires the Portuguese state to guarantee equal access to political decision making to all citizens. In this sense civil society is closely intertwined with the process of social transformation. At present the social transformation of Portuguese society consists of several parallel processes, most of them induced by the penetration of a capitalist rationale that is leading to the erosion of premodern lifestyles and political cultures and to the individualisation and subsequently economisation of relationships.

Although this chapter has drawn attention to the exclusion of youth from the labour market, the undefined boundary between the formal and informal markets, the existence of poverty and the erosion of premodern lifestyles, there was no intention to denigrate the present political system. On the contrary, the actors in the present system have achieved more for the population than any of the previous regimes. Nevertheless, due to the hegemony of imported global cultural designs, it is important to reflect on which kind of participatory democracy Portuguese society is aiming at. This chapter has higlighted an alternative civil society that already exists in Portugal and is embodied in the numerous associations for the protection of the environment. Environmental activists are daily contributing to an improvement of life in Portugal by working together with local and national authorities. They are also a symbol of the participatory democracy that may slowly emerge in this quite young democracy. The most important thing is to be patient – as the Portuguese say, *devagar se vai ao longe* ('if one goes slowly, one goes further').

9 Portugal and the European Union

THE IMPACT OF THE EUROPEAN UNION ON PORTUGAL

The previous chapters have discussed the growing influence the European institutions are having on the Portuguese political system. Here a general assessment will be made of the Europeanisation of the Portuguese political system. Recently John Peterson stated that the European Union is already a political system, comprising different levels of policy decision making and formulation at the supranational level (Peterson, 1995). This has also been emphasised by Gary Marks, who speaks of a 'multilevel governance' with different levels of decision making (Marks, 1993).

Other authors emphasise different aspects of this European political system in the making. For example Robert Ladrech sees a more differentiated sharing of governance between member states, subnational actors and the supranational institutions (Ladrech, 1993, pp. 64–7), while Emil J. Kirchner explores the concept of 'transnational democracy' and applies it to the European Union (Kirchner, 1994).

This multidimensional aspect of decision making is still not developed in Portugal. This is due to the country's long history of authoritarian rule and the absence of popular participation in the political system. Unlike in other political systems in the EU, the European institutions are not only playing a role in transnationalising the objectives of the Portuguese political system, above all they are contributing to the democratisation of the political structures and administrative culture.

Since the start the impact of the EC/EU on Portugal has been closely intertwined with the democratisation process via spillover effects on the political structures. During the pre-accession period until 1986 the prospect of integration into Europe helped to consolidate the advance towards democracy in Portugal. The discourse of the political elite emphasised EC membership as a crucial factor in economically and politically stabilising the young structures (Magone, 1995b).

However after 1986 the Portuguese political institutions found it difficult to adapt to the new rationale coming from the EC. It took several

161

years to adjust to the process and coordinate the massive amount of aid coming from the supranational institutions. The flow of structural funds has been a major factor in the development of the country, not just because of the amount involved, but because it acted as a catalyst for the relaunching of the Portuguese economy, which had been in permanent crisis until 1985. In the early 1990s the economy boomed. This was due to a considerable increase in foreign investment, the privatisation of the financial and manufacturing sector and the modernisation of Portuguese public infrastructures (Corkill, 1993b; Brassloff, 1991, pp. 27–9; Wright, 1994; *Financial Times*, 4 November 1991).

Nevertheless regional imbalances continued to widen. While Lisbon and the Tagus Valley profited from the economic boom and their share of GDP reached 75 per cent of the EC average in the early 1990s, the other planning regions of the north and Algarve made only a slight improvement and remained below the 50 per cent mark. Between 1986 and 1993 the central inland area stagnated at around 40 per cent of the EC average, and the Alentejo declined considerably from almost 50 per cent to 35 per cent (Hudson, 1994, pp. 18–19, 36). Overall, Portugal was able to improve its per capita GDP from 52.5 per cent of the EC average to 56.3 per cent, surpassing Greece, whose per capita GDP declined from 55.9 per cent in 1986 to 52.1 per cent in 1992 (Katseli, 1992, p. 29). But the European Commission calculated in 1991 that Portugal would need to maintain a growth differential over its partners of 1.25 per cent per annum for 20 years in order to reach 90 per cent of the EC average (*Financial Times*, 4 November 1991).

Of crucial importance to the economy were the EC structural funds. Before the reform of the structural funds in 1988, over a two-year period Portugal received almost 1.2 billion Ecus from the European Regional Development Fund, which was mainly used for infrastructural improvements (about 90 per cent of the funds). The sum increased substantially after the reform to a total of 7.368 billion Ecus to be used in the period 1989–93. After 1989 the distribution the funds among the different categories was more even. Including the national contribution, total public expenditure amounted to 14.026 billion Ecus. Priority was given to the development of human resources (28 per cent), the creation of economic infrastructures (24 per cent), development of the regions' growth potential and local development (15.6 per cent), and support for productive investment and its related infrastructure (13.4 per cent). On the whole the structural funds amounted to about 25 per cent of total fixed capital formation in Portugal and accounted for almost 14 per cent of GDP. Among the projects undertaken were the construction of highway networks and the huge Ford/VW car factory in Setubal (Cabral, 1993, pp. 136, 142–3; Eaton, 1994).

These financial transfers were made to prepare Portugal for the Single European Market (SEM), which was due to commence on 1 January 1993 and would remove all trading boundaries between the member states and allow the free movement of labour, capital, goods and services. The aim was to create a more competitive market and economies of scale that would enable Europe to compete more efficiently with the Asia–Pacific and North-American markets (Cockfield, 1994).

The well-known Cecchini report advocated that the SEM would create economies of scale, which would be able to compete against the American and the Pacific Market (Cecchini, 1988). Integration of Portugal and Spain into the EC required the Iberian economies to adjust to the challenge of the SEM. More than that, it seems that Lord Cockfield, who was in charge of organising and implementing the SEM, actively sought the support of these newcomers for the huge EC/EU project. He was strongly committed to achieving a doubling of the structural funds, a demand put forward by the poorer Southern European states. This was approved in the Edinburgh Council meeting in December 1992 (Cockfield, 1994, pp. 43–4). Therefore from the very start the structural funds were an integral element in the construction of the SEM.

The time allowed for implementation of the SEM directives (1986–92) was rather short. Nevertheless in early 1993 Portugal had already incorporated 95 per cent of the 282 directives into its national legislation (*Assembleia de República*, 1994, p. 34), a rate second only to that of Denmark (Table 9.1). However the appearance of the directives on the statute books does not imply that the directives were actually enforced

Even before the Treaty on the European Union (TEU) was ratified, the impact of European integration on the Portuguese economy and legal system was quite considerable. The political dimension of European integration became salient for the Portuguese government in the first half of 1992, when it took over the presidency of the Council of the European Community. It was during Portugal's presidency that the Danish population rejected the TEU, which was adopted in December 1991 in Maastricht during the Dutch presidency.

European Portugal

Table 9.1   Implementation of SEM directives by the end of 1994

Member State	Total directives	Directives implemented (No.)	(%)
Denmark	1213	1184	97.6
Portugal	1213	1171	96.5
Luxembourg	1213	1137	93.7
Netherlands	1213	1137	93.7
France	1214	1120	92.0
Ireland	1213	1115	91.2
Spain	1214	1108	91.2
Germany	1216	1107	91.0
Belgium	1213	1088	89.7
United Kingdom	1213	1084	89.4
Italy	1213	1072	88.4
Greece	1214	1053	86.7

Source: The European, 7–13 July 1995, p. 2.

THE PORTUGUESE PRESIDENCY OF THE EUROPEAN COMMUNITY (1992)

Although studies on the presidency of the Council of the Ministers of the European Union are scarce, this office constitutes an original element of the European institutional setting. Small countries seem to grasp the opportunity provided by the presidency to enhance their international profile.

The rotation of the presidency from country to country, the troika arrangement that unites the incumbent holder with the previous and following ones, and the coordinating role assigned to this office, which requires a high level of crafting between the different institutions, are some of the aspects that characterise the presidency. Nonetheless the presidency has to be regarded as a mere coordinator and implementor of the legislative agenda set up by the Commission of the EC/EU (O'Nullain, 1985).

The office of the presidency is not an easy one to manage. On the contrary, as Wallace states:

> Each presidency has simultaneously to watch over its own country's concerns and to act as temporary collective manager and mediator. Effective impartiality is only easily achieved when the government

in the chair has few key interests – more often the case for the smaller countries – or has concerns that lie close to the centre ground. Occasionally, individuals can overcome the structural handicaps of partisanship by deploying political skills and flair that push their colleagues closer towards agreement (Wallace, 1986, p. 586).

Moreover, holding the presidency has a considerable spillover effect upon the coordinating bodies dealing with European affairs in the home country. Due to the range of topics that the presidency has to deal with, efficiency of coordination becomes a crucial aspect in the six-month period (Hine, 1991, pp. 19, 30–5).

The integration of Sweden, Finland and Austria into the EU in 1995 will probably raise the question of whether the presidency should continue to last for six months, or even whether the number of countries eligible to hold this office should be reduced, as suggested by Germany and France in 1994. Both countries referred to the fact that the future integration of Eastern European countries will increase the number of members to 27, and advocated that a German–French axis should hold the presidency, so that implementation of the legislative agenda could be carried out more smoothly. This was criticised by the smaller member states as a discriminatory proposal that would reduce their importance in the European Union.

Portugal held the presidency for the first time between January and June 1992. Previously it had adopted a low profile in the process of European integration and had deliberately rejected the opportunity to take over the presidency shortly after its accession in 1986 (Matos, 1993, p. 170), mainly because of lack of knowledge and preparedness for the task (Eisfeld, 1989).

The Portuguese presidency followed the Dutch one, which had managed to bring about an agreement on the TEU in Maastricht in December 1991. The year 1992 was a very difficult one for the European Community because it coincided with the final preparations for the introduction of the SEM and the ratification process of the TEU. Moreover Portugal inherited the problem of the conflict in Bosnia-Herzegovina, to which the Dutch presidency had been unable to achieve a solution. Furthermore Prime Minister Anibal Cavaco Silva had to represent the EC in the United Nations Environmental Conference in Rio de Janeiro between 3 and 14 June.

The main objectives of the Portuguese presidency were set out in December 1991: ratification of the TEU; preparation of the Delors II package for an increase in the EC budget, which also included the doubling of the structural funds (in later presidencies the period of financing was 1994 to 1999); and creation of a new 'social and economic cohesion' fund, defined in the TEU, for countries with a national per capita GDP of less than 80 per cent of the EC average, and a European investment fund. A crucial dossier was to be reform of the Common Agricultural Policy (CAP).

Establishing solidarity with Eastern Europe and the former Soviet Union was a further objective of the presidency. Internationally, the Portuguese presidency was to focus on fostering 'renewed international solidarity' at the Rio Conference on the Environment and contribute to completion of the Uruguay round of GATT (Ministry of Foreign Affairs, 1991, pp. 9–11).

Coordination of the presidency was taken over by the Ministry of Foreign Affairs, headed by João Deus Pinheiro, a former professor of chemical engineering at the new University of Minho. The State Secretariat for European Integration (*Secretariado do Estado para a Integração Europeia*) was the specialised coordination body under Secretary of State Vitor Martins.

At the end of the presidency, the general assessment of João Deus Pinheiro was that the Portuguese presidency had avoided major mistakes by remaining in close contact with the other member states and the European institutions. There had been a general failure to handle the Bosnian crisis, which later degenerated into all-out war. Deus Pinheiro said that the EC had not been able to put enough pressure on the United Nations for it to send UN troops to Bosnia before the real conflict started (*Expresso*, 4 July 1992, p. 11R).

Several attempts to organise a peace conference in Lisbon during May failed due to the refusal of the Moslem president of Bosnia, Alija Izetbegovic, to attend. Izetbegovic was fearful of being taken prisoner by the Serbs, even though Deus Pinheiro had offered a UN escort and a safe passage in a Portuguese Air Force plane (*Expresso*, 23 May 1992, p. B1). The Portuguese presidency was reduced to pure crisis management without any hope of achieving a settlement between the Moslems, Serbs and Croats, and finally had to acknowledge that the whole conflict was more complex than had been thought (*Expresso*, 4 July 1992, p. 11R).

However the Portuguese presidency was able to conclude the major dossier on the reform of the CAP, although Agriculture Minister Arlindo Cunha found it difficult to bring the different parties to a common agreement. The reform was finally agreed after a marathon session on the last day. The reform had been proposed by Commissioner Ray

MacSharry in early 1991 and was aimed at reducing the guaranteed prices of agricultural products, particularly cereals. Moreover small farmers were no longer to be funded according to their annual production, but were to be financed directly so that they could restructure their holding towards more environmentally friendly activities, such as rural tourism. Reduction of the guaranteed prices was intended to reduce the financial commitment of the CAP to member-state farmers, and thus reduce this part of the EC budget.

A related question was the Uruguay round of the GATT negotiations, where the United States was demanding that the subsidies paid to European farmers be cut before a general settlement could be reached. In the end the deal brokered by Minister Arlindo Cunha was not completely satisfactory to the United States. Nicolas Brady, the US Treasury secretary, said on the eve of the G-7 meeting in Munich on 7–8 July that the CAP reform could only be seen as a first step in subsidy cutting and was insufficient to allow a settlement on the liberalisation of trade at the world level (*Diário de Notícias*, 19 May 1992, p. 4, 21 May 1992, p. 9, 25 May 1992, p. 7, 1 June 1992, p. 7, 2 June 1992, p. 6).

The CAP reform had a negative impact on Portuguese farmers and the price they received for their products continued to fall. Their plight worsened after the introduction of the SEM, when Spanish agricultural products very quickly penetrated the Portuguese market. One of the major advantages that Spanish producers had over the Portuguese ones was their well-developed distribution and marketing system. Moreover the ten-year preparation period the accession treaty granted to the producers of certain agricultural products, which was to last until 1996, was abolished because it contravened policy dictates that related to competition in the SEM. In the short to medium term, Portuguese agriculture suffered heavily from these changes to the European farming environment (Avillez, 1993).

Another area where the Portuguese presidency faced considerable problems was the Danish referendum on the TEU on 3 June 1992, when 50.7 per cent of the considerable turnout of 82.9 per cent voted against Denmark's participation in the treaty. The Danish vote was not against the SEM *per se*, but predominantly because of a fear that small countries would lose both their influence and their national autonomy in post-Maastricht Europe, that the achievements of Danish social policy would be lost, and that Eurocratic centralism would govern the process of European integration, as evidenced by the provisions for monetary union and a single defence policy (*Capital*, 3 June 1992, p. 3).

The first response by Deus Pinheiro was to communicate the EC's position that the TEU would be implemented even without Denmark. It would then develop towards a political union of eleven members. This position was reiterated by Anibal Cavaco Silva and the president of the Commission, Jacques Delors. At same time François Mitterrand declared that France had changed its position *vis-à-vis* ratification of the TEU and would hold a referendum rather than just seeking the approval of the French parliament (*Expresso*, 30 May 1992, p. A8; *Capital*, 3 June 1992, p. 2).

In an interview Deus Pinheiro confirmed the EC's position, saying that the Treaty of Rome and the TEU were 'marriages without the possibility of divorce or separation'. He further asserted that opting out from the Maastricht Treaty could have negative consequences for Denmark in that it would not be eligible for CAP agricultural funds. He said that the treaty would come into force on 1 January 1993 (the deadline was later postponed until 1 November 1993). This position was supported by all eleven members in a meeting in Oslo on 4 June (*Expresso*, 6 June 1992, p. A9).

Another country was in a similar situation to that of Denmark. The British Prime Minister John Major had to fight against a Eurosceptic faction within his own party to achieve support for the TEU. These Tory 'rebels' wanted Major to take a more Thatcherite position in relation to Europe. About 30 Tory rebels opened the debate in the House of Commons, and hoped to gain and hold the support of some anti-Maastricht MPs from other parties until end of the year. Therefore they were interested in prolonging the debate as long as possible (*Diário de Notícias*, 20 June 1992, p. 7).

The debate in Denmark, the United Kingdom and France gave strength to the small pro-referendum movement in Portugal, which led to some divisions within the Portuguese parliament and the ruling PSD. Although in their official statements the three main parliamentary parties – PS, the PSD and the PCP – opposed the idea of a referendum, the divisions were quite evident. The communists rejected the idea of both a referendum and Maastricht. The PS and the PSD did not want a referendum to be held and pursued a pro-Maastricht position. The CDS wanted a referendum and was extremely opposed to Maastricht. The socialists and social-democrats were quite divided. The position of the Socialist Party leader António Guterres was strongly criticised by the Soaristas Jorge Sampaio and Fernando Marques da Costa. The Guterristas were convinced that a referendum would only serve to confirm the population's support for the TEU and would complicate the whole process of ratification. In early July Guterres reached a compromise with the pro-referendum movement inside the party in that, if the constitution allowed it, a referendum would be held after ratification of the treaty in December 1992 and the regional elections due in 1993.

His position was very close to that of Anibal Cavaco Silva and Foreign Minister Deus Pinheiro. He even said that Maastricht was too complex a matter for the general population, and that only if they were given information in comic strip form would they be equipped to take part in a referendum. Cavaco Silva just said that a referendum would lead to the loss of 75 per cent of Portugal's negotiating power *vis-à-vis* the EC. President Mário Soares had been an advocate of a referendum since late May. Among the extraparliamentary opposition, the left attempted to collect enough signatures to achieve a referendum (*Diário de Notícias*, 26 May 1992, p. A2, 3 July 1992, p. 3, 5 July 1992, p. 3, 9 July 1992, p. 3; *Expresso*, 6 June 1992, pp. A2–A3, 13 June 1992, p. A2).

As well as failing to close the dossier on former Yugoslavia, the Portuguese presidency was not able to finalise the important Delors II Package, which, as stated earlier, related to the allocation of additional funds to the EC budget. Nevertheless Portugal was able to obtain an agreement from the Council of Economy and Finance Ministers (ECOFIN) that the structural funds would be doubled for the period 1993–7 (later postponed to 1994–9) (*Diário de Notícias*, 20 May 1992, p. 6). There was a sign of hope that the Delors II Package could be finalised in the European Council in Lisbon on 26–7 June. But the resistance of eight countries – the United Kingdom, Germany, France, Netherlands, Denmark, Belgium, Luxembourg and Italy – in the Council of Economy and Finance Ministers in Luxembourg on 9 June made it almost impossible for the Portuguese presidency to achieve a consensus (*Expresso*, 13 June 1992, p. A7) and in the end the dossier had to be handed over to the British presidency.

The reservations expressed by the United Kingdom during the Portuguese presidency were continued throughout its own presidency (*Diário de Notícias*, 12 June 1992, pp. 4, 6; 19 June 1992, p. 5; 2 July 1992, p. 6; *Expresso*, 20 June 1992, p. A9). During the first Council of Economy and Finance Ministers on 13 July Norman Lamont, the British chancellor of the exchequer, presented a list of 85 points on the Delors II Package that had to be responded to by the Commission before the European Council meeting in Edinburgh in December (*Diário de Notícias*, 14 July 1992, p. 28). The package was finally approved in Edinburgh after long debates and a final marathon session.

Other dossiers that were initiated or continued by the Portuguese presidency and then handed over to the British presidency included those on financial help for the Community of Independent States (CIS), which had its first meeting on 20–1 June in Lisbon, and EC representation in the conference in Rio de Janeiro. Both of these were finalised without problems. The Portuguese presidency was not successful in reactivating the Uruguay Round of the GATT negotiations, which had been on the go since 1986.

On the whole the Portuguese presidency was an important turning point for the Europeanisation of the Portuguese government. It enhanced Portugal's international image and boosted the self-confidence of its leaders. Moreover it meant that Portugal was truly an EC member because it had taken part in all institutions of the European Community. It was, in this sense, the end of a cycle. After its presidency the Portuguese government displayed greater self-confidence during European meetings and was able to negotiate strongly in favour of Portugal (for example with regard to the structural funds during the Edinburgh meeting of the European Council). This stronger involvement with and commitment to the EC had an impact on the Portuguese institutional setting.

EUROPEANISATION OF THE INSTITUTIONAL SETTING

On 10 December 1992 an overwhelming majority of 200 of Portugal's 230 MPs approved the TEU. This comfortable majority confirmed parliament's general support of the TEU. Only the conservative CDS and the communists were against the treaty.

Since 1976 the very radical socialist constitution had been brought more in line with that of other West European countries. The third constitutional revision on 25 November 1992 was specifically undertaken in response to the demands of the TEU. The third revision considerably enhanced the role of the Assembly of the Republic in monitoring the process of European integration. Article 200 stipulates that the government has 'to submit to the Assembly of the Republic, at appropriate times, information concerning the process of implementing the European Union, in accordance with article 166 (f)' (Constitution 1992, 1995, Article 200). Article 166 (f) direct the Assembly of the Republic 'to monitor and to evaluate, in accordance with the law, the participation of Portugal in the process of implementing the European Union' (ibid, Article 166 (f)).

Although it had existed before the third revision, the Parliamentary Committee on European Integration/European Affairs had had quite a low profile. After Portugal's accession to the EC the committee had the possibility of acting as a monitoring body through Law 29/87 of 29 June 1987 and Law 111/88 of 15 December 1988.

One of its general duties was to evaluate the annual report on the implementation of EC legislation that the government submitted to the Assembly of the Republic. In reality this yearly evaluation by the Committee on European Affairs never met with much cooperation from the other parliamentary committees, so that a thorough monitoring of events in the period 1986–93 was not possible. Parliament found it difficult to adjust to the new reality of European integration, particularly because the amount of legislation on EC matters increased substantially between 1986 and 1991.

Executive–legislative relations were not improved during this period. A report by the Committee on European Affairs in June 1994 concluded that Law 111/88 'was not able to establish a regular process of exchange of information and consultation between the Assembly of the Republic and the Government in these matters. . . . In this sense, it was not able to integrate more efficiently the evaluation of European affairs into the agenda of the Portuguese Parliament as it is defined by the Treaty of Maastricht' (Assembleia da República, 1994a, p. 9).

Law 20/94 of 15 June 1994 replaced Law 111/88. The new law consists of six articles and enlarges the role of the Assembly of the Republic in the European integration process. Article 1 stipulates that there must be a continuous exchange of information as well as consultation between the Assembly and the government. Other articles specify that the government must provide the Assembly of the Republic with all information that relates to agreements and conventions with other member states, binding acts of law derived from the treaties that institute the EC, acts of complementary law (decisions approved in the Council of the European Union), non-binding acts of derived law considered important for Portugal, and documents relating to general guidelines for economic, social and sectorial orientation. In the first trimester of each year the government is required to submit an annual report on the impact that implementation of EU measures has had on the Portuguese political system, and the Assembly of the Republic has the right to monitor and evaluate the impact of the structural and cohesion funds. Furthermore, after each presidency of the council by a member state a debate with members of the government should be conducted.

The Parliamentary Committee on European Affairs is the central body responsible for monitoring and evaluating the fulfilment of these requirements. A more transparent and regular contact with Portuguese MEPs and the European institutions should provide up-to-date information on the European integration process. The pivotal role of the committee in coordinating the evaluation process with the other specialised committees is emphasised in the new law (Assembleia da República, 1994a, pp. 15–19).

In 1994 the new president of the Committee on European Affairs, former Finance Minister Jorge Braga de Macedo, collected the specialised reports of the other committees and prepared the evaluation and monitoring report. On the whole the report's response to the governmental report 'Portugal and the European Union – The 8th Year' was quite positive, its main criticism being that the government report was very inconsistent. The Committee on European Affairs drew special attention to the economic and social problems that the EU would face in the near future.

The Committee's report included sections on the rights of citizens, the promotion of balanced and sustainable economic and social development, the assertiveness of the identity of the EU in international affairs, and the need to develop a closer cooperation between the member governments in the fields of justice and European affairs and in the running of the EU institutions and organs (Assembleia da Republica, 1994b, pp. 29–30, 31–74; Magone, 1995b).

Executive–legislative relations improved considerably due to the fact that Jorge Braga de Macedo had previously been in the government and was a member of the ruling PSD. The relationship with the State Secretariat for European Affairs, the main conduit between the EU institutions and the Portuguese government, was more cooperative, and the flow of information seemed to become more regular and transparent (Magone, 1995b).

On the whole institutional setting has been redefined very rapidly since 1986, and the European dimension has been a crucial factor behind the setting up of more efficient structures and the development of long-term goals for political and administrative reform.

EUROPEAN POLICY MAKING AND PORTUGAL

The globalisation thrusts of the 1980s led to a further transnationalisation of capital, manufacturing and services. They also led to a major restructuring of the mode of production, which evolved from the Taylorist–Fordist model based on assembly lines in huge factories, where workers shared the same contractual conditions, to a more flexible model in which the workforce was no longer homogeneous and new technology made some of them superfluous.

The transnationalisation of the economy also had repercussions on the structure of the state and forced the decline of the welfare state. A crucial aspect of adaptating to globalisation was the privatisation of public enterprises so that savings could be made in public expenditure in the long term, which of course meant that the use of public enterprises as the motor of the national economy was abandoned. The result was that even the strongest welfare states lost some of their national autonomy in macro- and microeconomic affairs (see Chapter 1).

The Portuguese economy was not exempt from these global changes, although when Portugal acceded to the EC in 1986 it was not predicted that this would have implications for national policy making. In the second half of the 1980s European public policy began to force a path into the countries of the EC. Until 1986–7 European public policies were almost non-existent, directives were random and did not closely follow the larger programmes of which they were a part. After 1986–7 all European public policies were geared towards the realisation of the SEM (Lavdas and Mendrinou, 1995; Pollack, 1994; Kintis and Magone, 1996). Implementation of the SEM directives became a crucial precondition for its success, and the TEU transformed what had been an economic project into a political and cultural one (Bat Smit, 1994).

The reform of the structural funds in 1988–9 completely changed the EC's approach towards the member states, and more and more states were forced to implement European public policies. The SEM was a response to the globalisation thrust of the 1980s, and the TEU is the important political means of ensuring it functions properly as the same conditions should prevail in all countries. In other words, monetary, fiscal and economic policies at the supranational level should ensure that the SEM is not jeopardised by changes of monetary, fiscal and economic conditions in the member countries. Monetary, fiscal and economic autonomy of the nation-state will be established at supranational level. It enhances so the influence of the nation-state in the international arena, by taking part in decision-making processes at supranational level.

Since Portugal's accession to the EC/EU, European policy making has been a major factor in stabilising its economy, politics and society. The Common Support Framework of 1989–93 and the new one of 1994–9 are crucial for economic, political and social development. Moreover they are having a spillover effect on administrative structures and culture. The growing concern of the EU with aspects of fraudulent behaviour in connection with the implementation of supranational policies is causing a tightening and restructuring of policy making in Portugal (Mendrinou, 1994, 1995).

The main challenge will be to meet the convergence criteria stipulated in the Maastricht Treaty[1] so that Portugal can qualify for participation in EMU at the end of the millenium. This can be only achieved by very stringent budgetary, fiscal and monetary policies.

The first years of the SEM were quite negative for Portugal – the expensive 'strong escudo' policy of the Portuguese government had to be abandoned in late 1993 and the currency devalued by 10 per cent. After that the exchange rate became more stable. Moreover in 1993 GDP growth was negative, which further undermined the prospect of meeting the convergence criteria. It recovered in 1994 and 1995 but is still lower than the OECD average. In terms of the convergence criteria, the projected deficit for 1995 was 6 per cent. This would signify an improvement in comparison with 1993, when the budget deficit soared from the 4.2 per cent of 1992 to 8.3 per cent. This was related to an inefficient tax-collection system that was very conducive to tax evasion.

Anibal Cavaco Silva was committed to improving the fiscal performance of the government by introducing reforms in the administrative sector. He has succeeded in keeping public-sector pay increases below the inflation rate by refusing to bow to the demands of the trade unions in the CPCS in 1993 and 1994. The inflation rate decreased considerably to 5.2 per cent in 1994, and a rate of 4–4.5 per cent was forecast for 1995 and 1996.

Moreover in 1994 the official unemployment figures suggested that just 6.8 per cent of those of working age were out of work, which was considerably below the OECD average of 8.2 per cent. Nevertheless it seems that the percentage of persons out of work for more than one year rose from 27 per cent in 1992 to over 34 per cent in 1994 (1993, *Financial Times Survey*, 22 February 1994, p. 12; *The Economist*, 17 June 1995, p. 138).

In the long term the 'stop–go' pattern of economic development since the 1960s may be remedied by the efficient implementation of the structural funds that have been flowing into Portugal since the 1980s, although until now the Portuguese economy has remained highly vulnerable to economic conditions in other West European countries (Gaspar, 1991; Mendes, 1994).

The new CSF (1994-9) is based on continuity and a simplication of fund allocation. The major programmes of PEDIP for industry, PEDAP for agriculture and PRODEP for the educational sector will contribute considerably to economic development. The EU programme RETEX will give special attention to the textiles industry, which plunged into crisis in the early 1990s. It is expected that 100 000 new jobs will be created by the end of the millenium (*Expresso*, 10 July 1993, p. C3). This EU support will be accompanied by further loans from the Bank for European Investment (BEI) and other programmes such as Interreg.

To summarize implementation of EU programmes designed jointly with the Portuguese government will further reinforce the Europeanisation of Portuguese public policy. EU policies may also bring about new cultural patterns of administrative behaviour in Portugal. This will be an essential element in the road towards institutionalising sustainable democratic codes of behaviour in policy making. Participation by the population will enhance the prospect of successful implementation of EU programmes.

CONCLUSIONS: THE EMERGENCE OF EUROPEAN PORTUGAL

Since Portugal's accession to the EC in 1986 the Portuguese people have strongly supported European integration.[2] In turn the EU has become a major supporter of Portuguese economic, social, political and cultural development. The structural funds have not only permitted a high level of political and economic stability, they have also provided the government and the population with a new democratic rationale.

It seems that the TEU and the referendum debate during 1992 have led to the emergence of a stronger civil society, one that wants to be well-informed and is not afraid of using democratic institutions to protest against governmental measures and policies. Democratic codes of behaviour are becoming stronger, because European socialisation is leading to a change of administrative behaviour at the central and local levels. Portugal's presidency of the Council of Ministers in 1992 was a major factor in improving the self-confidence of a country that was suffering an identity crisis after the decolonisation process (Aragão, 1985).

The institutional relationship between government and parliament is improving in relation to European affairs, and the Committee on European Affairs is being stimulated by fellow parliamentarians in other countries within the framework of the regular EU parliamentary conference.

As far as national self-identity is concerned, the Portuguese already consider themselves European Portuguese. Perhaps one day the full integration of Europe may lead them to describe themselves as Portuguese Europeans.

10 Democratisation, Political Institutionalisation and Political Culture: Some Conclusions

The growing incidence of racial attacks by skinheads on the African minority in the satellite town of Almada across the Tejo bridge and in Lisbon proper worsened considerably in June and July 1995. The murder of Alcindo Monteiro in the Bairro Alto, the popular centre of nightlife in Lisbon, on 11 June 1995 caused a wave of indignation among the political elite and the population. Several demonstrations were held in Lisbon and Oporto against racism and xenophobia. Alcindo Monteiro, who originated from Cape Verde, was only one of the eighteen victims of the assault launched by fifty skinheads in the Bairro Alto; another victim died some days later.

Throughout the months of June and July further attacks against the African minority by skinheads and other groups, and vice versa, were carried out in Almada and Lisbon. The climax was the murder of two black persons in Lisbon on 16 July by unknown killers.

Of the 170 000 foreigners living in Portugal, about 81 200 originated from the former Portuguese colonies in Africa, and it is estimated that illegal immigrants make up 1.7 per cent of the population. They live under extremely bad conditions and accept any kind of job, particularly in the construction sector. Members of the younger generation that were born in Portugal and live in the suburban outskirts of Lisbon have copied the American-style gangs, with their own subcultural language and modes of behaviour. They are victims of poor education, social exclusion and insecure family relationships. Frustration arising from failure at school and the near impossibility of entering the labour market during the so-called interregnum period reinforces this segregative, subcultural survival strategy.

Discrimination by white members of society is not overt, but it is real (*El Pais*, 23 July 1995, p. 6) and has been observed in Portugal for a long time. In the report of the Committee of Enquiry on Racism and Xenophobia (European Parliament, 1991, pp. 70–1) Maria Belo draws attention to the fact that racism and xenophobia increased in Portugal in the 1980s, and that some cases of police brutality against the black population were registered. She points out that the causes of social exclusion are related to bad social conditions such as housing problems and the lack of social security, basic trade union rights and schooling, leading immigrants to slide into criminal activities such as smuggling, drug dealing and prostitution.

Lack of social integration also gave rise to the skinhead movement in 1985. The murder of a leader of the small Socialist Revolutionary Party on 28 October 1989 shows that skinheads may attack prominent leaders of the antiracist movement as well.

Youth violence has reached football stadium too, and discontented young people are channelling their aggression into attacks on opposing supporters. This was observed in early January 1993 when Benfica supporters attacked a supporter of Belenenses, both Lisbon-based clubs. At the same game a Benfica supporter was seen with a flag bearing a swastica. All this was broadcast on television. Further incidents were registered in games between Oporto and Benfica and Oporto and Boavista (*Expresso*, 23 January 1993, pp. 6–12R).

This imported phenomenon in a country of *brandos costumes* (moderate habits) has shocked the Portuguese public and highlighted the fact that many Portuguese youths are experiencing difficulties in the interregnum between school and working life. This is not restricted to the *declassés* of Portuguese society, but can also be found among all young people who fail to pass their university entrance examinations. The *numerus clausus* in public universities is destroying the dreams of young people before they even start their working lives. The proliferation of new private universities without any facilities for students is reinforcing this frustration.

Furthermore the labour market is still very polarised. On the one hand the majority of jobs offered are low-skill ones that require no qualifications, sometimes promise the possibility of very fast money and appeal exclusively to young people. On the other, large TNCs and Portuguese firms advertise jobs in marketing and other business-oriented areas that require at least a *licenciatura* (first degree). What is missing from the market are middle-ability jobs. Here it seems that nepotism and patronage continue to persist, and recruitment is based on family membership and acquaintanship. The problem of the interregnum is therefore reinforced by a labour market structure that in times of crisis tends to become even more informal. Added to this is the growing incidence of fixed, short-term contract work of three to six months, which provides no security at all.[1]

Socially speaking, young people's first experience of the labour market may cause them to feel they have no prospect of improving their lives. Most of them have to live at home and they realise that their first job may not lead to financial security. This is not very propitious for sustainable democracy. On the contrary it is tending to reinforce the patrimonial structures that have existed since the process of democratisation started in Portugal in the early nineteenth century.

Nevertheless Portuguese society has evolved considerably since the 1970s and has become more self-critical and democratic, even though it is still far from being a qualitative democracy based on transparency and accountability.

Elements of accountability are arising from the Auditing, Constitutional and Supreme Courts and the ombudsman. Revelations of corruption have come to the fore since 1992, involving the two main parties – the social democrats and the socialists – in different scandals (Magone, 1994; *The European*, 28 July 1995, p. 2). In this sense Portugal can be seen as being on the way to a qualitative democracy as it is strong enough to remain stable in spite of corruption scandals.

Democratisation will require the political infrastructure to be adjusted to include the general population, so that participation, as defined in the constitution, can become a reality. This book does not plead for continuous, permanent participation by all citizens across the country at the same time, but before they can participate at all in policy decision making they will need to feel at ease in the political world. This means that institutions will have to become more people-oriented. Sustainable democracy is a long-term, open-ended project based on equality of opportunities, gender equality, democratic decision and policy making, and the freedom to participate.

Institutions will have to open themselves to public participation and introduce proactive policies of social inclusion. Such a project may take a number of generations, but on the way partial regimes of democratic participation will emerge. Indeed some already exist and are having a spillover effect upon other structures.

In a recent article by Barry Munslow and François Ekanga Ekogo on the relationship between democracy and sustainable development, it was concluded that there is no necessary correlation between the two (Munslow and Ekanga Ekogo, 1995). On the contrary, there are several models of democratisation that are connected with sustainable development. The main approach taken in this regard should be flexible and adjusted to the needs of the population.

The state should be proactive in the early day of democratisation in order to encourage participation and help people adjust to the new situation. This should include modernisation and reformulation of the labour market system, making it more open and less labrynthine for job seekers, a major problem in new democracies.

This study has shown that democratisation in Portugal has been closely intertwined with Europeanisation. Integration into the EC/EU initiated a process that in Portugal is called 'the regional monitoring of democratisation processes'. The huge investment made in Portugal by the EC/EU in education, industry, agriculture and other sectors can be seen as a major factor of democratisation because it has been based on democratic transparency and accountability. The policies of the EC/EU have changed considerably since 1987. They have become more biased toward promoting sustainable development and the building up of the SEM. Regional monitoring of the democratisation process is being steadily introduced into European policies and requires the participation of both policy makers and the general population. This is still not universal, but is already a growing reality in most of the member states of the European Union.

Sustainable development may be seen as an emerging paradigm that will have a different form in different countries, combined with different approaches to democratisation. At the same time, regionalisation of the global economy is leading to a different construction of the nation-state. Environmental, social and military harmony can only be achieved collectively. Sustainable development will require a change in consumption patterns, and environmental and social costs will have to be considered in economic thinking. Such changes cannot be achieved overnight, but it seems that the EU is not only interested in creating a single market, but also in encouraging a new type of consumer behaviour that takes account of the environment and the welfare of fellow inhabitants of the world. Anthropologically and social psychologically this kind of paradigm will appeal to other values inherent woman's/man's thinking which are more social than individualistic in nature.

For a small, semiperipheral country in the modern world system like Portugal such a shift of paradigms is crucial, so that a change of mentalities can be fostered.

In this work we gave a general assessment how far is Portugal from this paradigm of sustainable development.

The main aim of this book has been to assess Portugal's political and social democratisation efforts. Its findings seem to confirm that although the Portuguese political and social structures are still patrimonial in nature and patronage is rife, some progress has been made, aided considerably by membership of the EC/EU and the process of Europeanisation. In conclusion, five main observations may be made.

First, the access to political office and structures is still very patrimonial in nature. A political class in the sense of Gaetano Mosca controls the participation and socialisation structures preventing a rotation of political elites and the inclusion of other social groups such as the working class or lower classes. Participation structures are dominated by parties. Nevertheless the growing civil society seems to put forward different models of political development. These patrimonial structures include older forms of authoritarian behaviour and new democratic ones. It is normal for emerging democracies to be a *mixed compositum*. If a greater effort is not made to democratise access to political office the Portuguese political system may face the same destiny as that in Italy, where decades of privileged access to political office led to the 'implosion of clientelism and patronage' and the collapse of the Italian Republic. This problem has also been observed in Spain and Greece.

Second, the Portuguese state has been quite centralised since the sixteenth century. The emergence of local government since 1976 may be regarded as a chance to counteract this, and the process of decentralising services has progressed quite considerably in the past two decades. Local politicians are putting pressure on the central government to allow greater financial and decision-making autonomy at the local level. Until now the central government has been very reluctant to increase the share of local government in total administrative expenditure, indeed the share of local government has stagnated since the early 1980s. Although regionalisation is enshrined in the constitution, the government has made no substantial effort in this regard. The introduction of administrative regions is quite important to achieving a better coordination of municipal development and a more efficient use of material and human resources.

Third, Portuguese interest groups only reluctantly decided to take part in the neocorporatist Permanent Council of Social Harmonisation (the CPCS). The polarised relationship between workers' organisations and employers' associations was related to the plight suffered by entrepreneurs during the revolution. This situation changed in the second half of the 1980s with the introduction of the CPCS, which facilitated a process of political learning and understanding between the interest groups. The PSD government was less compromising and has resisted trade union demands related to labour law, pay ceilings and social legislation. There is still a need to strengthen the monitoring of agreed positions, but nonetheless the emergence of such as the CPCS 'meso-regimes' has been essential to the achievement of a more stable atmosphere based on dialogue and the exchange of opinions.

Fourth, one of the most interesting developments has been the Europeanisation of national policy making. Portugal has benefited greatly from European integration and the flow of structural funds since 1986 has considerably changed its social landscape. The national Regional Development Plans 1989–93 and 1994–9 are aimed at the further integration and Europeanisation of the Portuguese political system. This is supported by the EU Common Support Frameworks of 1989–93 and 1994–9. At the same, implementation of EU programmes is promoting democratic policy making based on transparency and accountability, and is probably contributing to a change of administrative culture in Portugal. Administrative learning may one day lead to a more sustainable democratic approach to national policy making.

Finally, the persistence of fragmented society in Portugal relates not only to the centre–periphery divide, but also to access to education and the social security system. The main dividing factor is education, which is crucial for the development of the country. Very roughly, the people of Portugal can be divided into three groups in this respect: the illiterate; predominantly found in rural areas and the suburbs of the larger towns, those who can read and write but are illiterate when it comes to the workings of the state and the world; and those who are both educated and have access to the new world of information technology. Clientelism and patronage, neopatrimonial structures, cultural discrimination and lack of financial support are major impediments to providing the majority of the population with quality education.

Major agents of a more cohesive and participatory society are local government and groups such as the environmental associations. As yet civil society is still very weak, but the small advances it has made is nonetheless a very important sign of hope for European Portugal.

In the summer Olympics of 1984 in Los Angeles, Carlos Lopes entered the stadium alone and won the Marathon. After him several other Portuguese runners followed his footsteps such as Rosa Mota or Manuela Machado. All these runners are showing us the way towards sustainable democracy.

Democracy cannot be established overnight. It is a long-term project that requires investment in people. Such investment may pay off only after generations, but on the way one will experience little successes. The difficult road to democracy leads to the stadium, but it needs a continuous effort towards democratic behaviour, lowering structural violence, equality of opportunities, gender equality and persistence. Many defeats and misunderstandings will reappear, past forms of behaviour are always present, but time will make democracy stronger, make democracy work. Furthermore, democracy is not only a collective effort, but a general mental attitude towards otherness. It requires a constant dialogue between the individual and society. Democratic reflexiveness is crucial to achieve a more just society. Such project does not deny the continuous tension between ideology of structures and the utopia of culture (Mannheim). A successful sustainable democracy is when older runners transmit their experience to the younger generation and give them hope and encouragement to reach the stadium.

Addendum: The Legislative Elections of 1995 and the Presidential Elections of 1996

The victory of the Socialist Party in the elections of 1 October 1995 confirms the conclusions presented in this work. The programme of the Socialist Party is tailored to follow closely the idea of a more participatory society in Portugal, but this can only be accomplished in the long term.

The elections changed the configuration of political forces. The PS won more than 43 per cent of the votes and gained 112 seats in the Assembly of the Republic; the PSD declined to 34 per cent and 88 seats (Table A1.1). The PS's comfortable majority will allow it to implement its very ambitious programme, which includes the creation of administrative regions, improvement of the education and health sectors and a strengthening of the mechanisms of social solidarity.

The PS was also able to penetrate regions where the PSD and the PCP had formerly been dominant. It won almost all the major cities of the north, which previously had tended to vote for the PSD. In Lisbon, Setúbal and their surroundings the PS was able to replace the communists as the major force.

During its first months Guterres' government has shown a commitment to its electoral manifesto. It started by abolishing the *lei das propinas* (law of fees), which had been introduced by Cavaco Silva in public higher education institutions, and announced that it will begin to introduce administrative regions by 1997. While it is too early to make an assessment of the performance of the government, the cabinet does consist of very qualified persons, such as António Vitorino, former judge of the Constitutional Court, Sousa Franco, former president of the Audit Court, and the well-known economist João Cravinho.

After October public interest shifted to the presidential elections, which took place on 14 January 1996. The PSD leadership nominated Anibal Cavaco Silva as their presidential candidate. However Fernando Nogueira felt that Cavaco Silva let him down during the campaign, and this was the general feeling in the party. From the start of the campaign the socialist candidate, Jorge Sampaio, mayor of Lisbon, led the opinion polls, and on polling day the electorate gave him a clear victory (53.83 per cent of the votes). Cavaco Silva managed to win 46.17 per cent of the votes, which shows that he still enjoyed considerable support. The results exposed a north–south divide that had not been seen since the late 1970s – the north voted predominantly for Cavaco Silva and the south for Jorge Sampaio.

This double victory of the Socialist Party put an end to the 'cohabitation period' that existed during the Cavaco Silva era and introduced a new configuration in the institutional framework.

Table A1.1   Results of the legislative elections of 1 October 1995

Party	Share (%)	Seats
PS	43.76	112
PSD	34.17	88
CDS-PP	9.08	15
PCP	8.65	15

Many elements of the socialist government's programme resemble what we presented at the beginning of this book as 'sustainable democracy', which is based on enhancing public participation in the policy-making process. The question is whether the Socialist Party will transform its rhetoric into deeds. Whatever the four years of socialist rule may bring, one can now consider that democracy in Portugal is maturing and political alternatives can be generated within a stable party system. At the least, one may confidently assert that European Portugal is moving slowly towards a strong and sustainable democracy.

Notes

1 The Rise of Democracy

1. See Huntington (1991), pp. 3–5. Since then about 30 countries have engaged in the democratisation process.
2. The difficulties of defining civil society in clear terms can be found in a recent discussion in the *Journal of Democracy* 'Rethinking Civil Society' (1994, pp. 3–56).
3. When engaging in a discussion of the alternatives to liberal democracy, one has to acknowledge that it is very difficult for a country embarking on a democratic transition and consolidation process to run against the dominant model of the *third wave of democratisation*. The experiences of past transformations further reduce the possibility of alternatives. The internationalisation of the model, and images of past failures and economic constraints during the process, reinforces the model of 'liberal democracy' as the only viable one upon which to build formal democratic structures. Nevertheless, when economic and political stabilisation in the new democracy has been achieved, one may start the democratic institutionalisation phase by deepening the democratisation process through the creation of participatory structures. This seems to be the model that one of the pioneers of democratic transition and consolidation has in mind (Whitehead, 1992).
4. Such an interpretation of civil society as ancillary to the market economy has been put forward – intentionally or unintentionally – by Matthias Stieffel and Marshall Wolfe in a publication – strangely enough – of the United Nations Research Institute for Social Development (UNRISD) based in Geneva. The authors advocate a 'democracy of diminished expectations' in which non-governmental organisations are regarded as organisers of an instrumentally oriented participation of the population (Stieffel and Wolfe, 1994, pp. 202–33).
5. Theoretically, I am very close to the approach of Goran Ahrne, who says we live in a 'society of organizations' (Ahrne, 1990, 1994). In my opinion, one should go further and ask whether the new 'organisation woman/man' contributes to a change of the condition of both insiders and outsiders when it comes to routines, work and organisational life and the increasing emptiness of everyday life as a consequence (Lipovetsky, 1983). Human dignity becomes more and more related to economic activity and an economic approach towards relationships (Garnham and Williams, 1990).
6. According to C. B. Macpherson: 'We need a revolution in democratic consciousness if we are to avoid being caught up ourselves in the backwash of the revolutions in the rest of the world. We need to give up the myth of maximisation. We need to inquire soberly whether competitive, maximising behaviour is any longer rational for us, in any ethical or expedient

sense, or whether the very high level of material productivity that we now command can be made to subserve the original liberal-democratic vision. We should be considering whether we have done, how to hold on to the liberty we have got – the liberty of possessive individualists – while moving a little towards more equality. Perhaps we should be asking, instead, whether meaningful liberty can much longer be had without a much greater measure if equality than we have hitherto thought liberty required' (Macpherson, 1973, p. 184).

7. We use 'political learning' in the sense of Nancy Bermeo. She defines it as follows: 'The concept of political learning is based on the premise that beliefs are not fixed immutably in childhood and that they can be "affected by political events" such as the replacement of one regime with another. . . . The cognitive changes involved in political learning can thus involve means or ends or both. Political learning can affect basic, ideological beliefs about political structures, or it can affect simply the means one prefers for achieving constant ends. Political learning can take ideological or tactical forms. . . . Political elites must change their evaluations of the alternatives to democratic rule; they must change their evaluations of democracy itself; they must change the ordering or nature of group goals; or they must change their perceptions of one another. . . . (A further point of clarification relates to the cumulative nature of the political learning process. Political learning occurs at an individual level, and since the stimuli in each individual's learning environment differ, the timing and nature of the learning experience may vary between individuals and between political groups. The scope of the sector of the elite that undergoes political learning is an important factor in predicting whether and when reconstruction of democracy will take place. The likelihood that democracy will be reconstructed increases with the diversity of the elite that experiences cognitive change)' (Bermeo, 1992, pp. 274–5).

8. It seems that this model of regional monitoring of democratisation processes is becoming a widespread phenomenon around the world. See the discussion on 'International Organizations and Democracy' in the *Journal of Democracy* (1993, pp. 3–69).

3 Structuring the Political System

1. Recent data, kindly supplied by the Secretariado de Modernizacao Administrativa and based on a general survey undertaken in 1988, give a different estimate of the size of the administration and the ratio between local and central government. The data were published in the *Revue Française de Administration Publique*, no. 59, 1990. The total number of employed persons is 513 770 in a ratio of 46.3 per cent in the central administration, 32.44 per cent in the central administration at the district level and 21.44 per cent in the local administration. Roughly speaking, the ratio between central and local government is 79 per cent to 21 per cent, which is a slightly different figure to that of the OECD (SMA, 1990).

5 The Political Parties

1. Such attempts were made between 1932 and 1934 with the Republican and Socialist Alliance, in 1942 with the Group for Socialist Action and Indoctrination, in 1944 with the Socialist Union, in 1950 with the Socialist Front and in 1955 with the Socialist and Republican Resistance.
2. Including Francisco Salgado Zenha, José Magalhaes Godinho, Manuel de Lucena and Sottomayor Cardia.
3. Freitas do Amaral was a member of the second chamber of the Salazarist legislature, the Corporative Chamber (*Camara Corporativa*), Adelino Amaro da Costa was active in the administration, Basilio Horta was local leader of the ANP and Adriano Moreira was minister for overseas colonies in the early 1960s under Salazar.

7 The Implementation of Public Policies

1. These observations are based on own experiences during my time as a lecturer in the Instituto Piaget in Almada near Lisbon and Arcozelo near Oporto in 1992–3, when I conducted courses on the social sciences to secondary and primary school teachers. They came at the weekends to improve their qualifications. During that time I became acquainted with the many problems that secondary schools in Portugal were facing and the desire of teachers across the country to overcome them.

8 The Emergence of Civil Society

1. The actions of Greenpeace in the last decades may be seen as an example of control of governmental and TNC policies. This kind of intervention restricts itself to denouncing environmentally or humanly damaging acts.
2. We mean here that the institutional reflexiveness carried out in other countries was adopted in Portugal without adapting it to the developmental needs of the country. Such imported institutional reflexiveness may be a major obstacle to the creation of an endogenous institutional reflexiveness that is embedded in the national culture. Institutional reflexiveness is an important long-term exercise that is based on trial and error. Such knowledge accumulates over time and structures policy style. The concept of institutional reflexiveness is taken from Anthony Giddens (Giddens, 1993, p. 20). The term 'institutional reflexiveness' is applied to the culture of dealing with social pressures through the process of reflecting and finding a solution. Over time the process becomes accumulated knowledge.
3. This interesting study by Luisa Schmidt could be followed by a study on the origins of advertisements. I would speculate that the transformation of the imagery in advertising was due to the integration of Portugal into the international marketing networks after the revolution. Thus life styles are in part exogenously generated and then nationally interpreted.

9 Portugal and the European Union

1. The criteria are as follows: (1) Price stability based on an inflation rate

that is no higher than that of the three member-states that are performing best; (2) a budget deficit that is no higher than 3 per cent of GDP; (3) exchange-rate stability within the mechanism of the European Monetary System (EMS) for at least two years without devaluating in relation to the other member states; (4) the durability of convergence achieved by the Member State and of its participation in the exchange-rate mechanism of the European Monetary System being reflected in the long-term interest-rate levels.

2. In a *Eurobarometer* survey in July 1994 about 70 per cent of Portuguese respondents answered positively to the question of whether the country had benefited from EU membership (compared with 24 per cent negative responses and 8 per cent don't knows). About 54 per cent thought the EC was a good thing, only 13 per cent that was a bad thing. On the other hand only 1 per cent of respondents felt they were very well informed about the EU, 19 per cent quite well, 46 per cent not very well, 30 per cent not at all and 4 per cent did not know (*Eurobarometer*, no. 41 (1994), pp. A22–23, A28).

10 Democratisation, Political Institutionalisation and Political Culture

1. These observations are based on field work carried out in the summer of 1992, when I was searching for a job and had the opportunity to observe and speak to many young jobseekers.

References

ADMINISTRAÇÃO (1987) *Factos e Números* (Lisbon: Centro de Informação Cientifica e Técnica da Reforma Administrativa).

AGH, ATTILA (1993) 'The "Comparative Revolution" and the Transition in Central and Southern Europe', *Journal of Theoretical Politics*, vol. 5 no. 2, pp. 231–52.

AGH, ATTILA (ed.) (1994) *The Emergence of East Central European Parliaments: The First Steps* (Budapest: Hungarian Centre for Democratisation Studies).

AGH, ATTILA and SANDOR KURTAN (eds) (1995) *Democratization and Europeanization in Hungary: The First Parliament 1990–1994* (Budapest: Hungarian Centre for Democracy Studies).

AGUIAR, JOAQUIM (1984) *A Ilusão do Poder. Análise do Sistema Partidário Português 1974–1982* (Lisbon: Dom Quixote).

AGUIAR, JOAQUIM (1985a) *O Pós-Salazarismo* (Lisbon: Dom Quixote).

AGUIAR, JOAQUIM (1985b) 'Portugal: The Hidden Fluidity in an Ultra-Stable Party System', in Walter C. Opello and Eduardo de Sousa Ferreira (eds), *Conflict and Change in Modern Portugal 1974–1984* (Lisbon: Teorema), pp. 101–26.

AGUIAR, JOAQUIM (1985c) 'Partidos, estruturas patrimonialistas e poder funcional: a crise da legitimidade, *Análise Social*, vol. XXI, nos 87–9, pp. 759–83.

AGUIAR, JOAQUIM (1986) 'A sociedade politica: o exercício do poder como acção condicionada', *Análise Social*, vol. XXII, no. 94, pp. 859–89.

AGUIAR, JOAQUIM (1987) 'Formas de dominação e sociedade: o caso do neopatrimonialismo', *Análise Social*, vol. XXIII, no. 96.

AGUIAR, JOAQUIM (1988) 'Democracia Pluralista, Partidos Politicos e Relação de Representação', *Análise Social*, vol. XXIV, no. 100, pp. 59–76.

AGUIAR, JOAQUIM (1989) 'Dinâmica do sistema partidário-condições de estabilidade', in Coelho (ed.), op. cit., pp. 295–235.

AGUIAR, JOAQUIM (1990a) 'As funções dos partidos nas sociedades modernas', *Análise Social*, vol. XXV, no. 107, pp. 287–331.

AGUIAR, JOAQUIM (1990b) 'Sociedade fragmentada e clivagens políticas', *Análise Social*, vol. XXV, nos 108–9, pp. 545–87.

AGUIAR, JOAQUIM (1994) 'Partidos, Eleicões, dinâmica politica', *Análise Social*, vol. XXIX, nos 125–6, pp. 171–236.

ÅHRNE, GÖRAN (1990) *Agency and Organization. Towards An Organizational Theory of Society* (London: Sage).

ÅHRNE, GÖRAN (1994) *Social Organizations. Interaction inside, outside and between Organizations* (London: Sage).

ALMEIDA, JOÃO FERREIRA DE, LUIS CAPUCHA, ANTONIO FIRMINO DA COSTA, FERNANDO LUIS MACHADO, ISABEL NICOLAU and ELISABETH REIS (1992) *Pobreza Urbana em Portugal* (Lisbon: Caritas).

ALMOND, GABRIEL W. (1956) 'Comparative Political Systems', *Journal of Politics*, vol. 18, no. 3, pp. 391–409.

References 191

ANDERSEN, SVEN and KJELL ELIASSEN (1982) *Making policy in Europe: the Europeification of National Policy-Making* (London: Sage).

ANDRADE, MADALENA, and SUSANA MATOS VIEGAS (1989) 'O Campo Semântico do Politico: Um Estudo Empirico em duas localidades portuguesas', paper presented to the IV International Meeting on Portugal, Durham, USA, 21–25 September 1989.

ANDRÉ, ISABEL, GASPAR, JORGE (1989) 'Portugal-geografia Eleitoral: 1975 e 1987', in Mário Baptista Coelho (ed.) *Portugal Político e Constitucional 1974–1987* (Lisboa: Instituto de Ciencias Sociais-Universidade de Lisboa) pp. 257–77.

ANTUNES, JOSÉ FREIRE (1979) *O Segredo do 25 de Novembro* (Lisbon: Europa-America).

ANTUNES, MIGUEL LOBO (1988) 'A Assembleia da República e a Consolidaçao da Democracia em Portugal', *Análise Social*, vol. XXIV, no. 100, pp. 77–95.

ARAGAO, RUI (1985) *Portugal. O Desafio Nacionalista. Psicologia e Identidade Nacionais* (Lisbon: Teorema).

ARRIGHI, GIOVANNI (1985) 'From Fascism to Democratic Socialism. Logics and Limits of Transition', in *Semiperipheral Development. The Politics of Southern Europe in the Twentieth Century* (Beverly Hills, CA: Sage), pp. 249–79.

ARTER, DAVID (1994) 'Estonia: The Case of An Anti-Party System', in Patrick Dunleavy and Jeffrey Stanyer (eds), *Contemporary Political Studies 1994. Proceedings of the Annual Conference Held at the University of Wales*, Swansea, 29–31 March 1994 (Belfast: Political Studies Association), pp. 299–313.

ASSEMBLEIA DA REPUBLICA (1988) *Memória da IV Legislatura* (Lisbon).

ASSEMBLEIA DA REPUBLICA (1992a) *Memória da V Legislatura* (Lisbon).

ASSEMBLEIA DA REPUBLICA (1992b) *A Problemática do Tratado de Maastricht. Comissão dos Negócios Estrangeiros* (Lisbon: Comunidades Portuguesas e Cooperação).

ASSEMBLEIA DA REPUBLICA (1994a) *Portugal na Uniao Europeia. Lei de Acompanhamento e Apreciação* (Lisbon: Commissão de Assuntos Europeus).

ASSEMBLEIA DA REPUBLICA (1994b) *Portugal na Uniao Europeia em 1993. Apreciação Parlamentar* (Lisbon: Comissão de Assuntos Europeus).

AVILLEZ, FRANCISCO (1993) 'Portuguese Agriculture and the Common Agricultural Policy', in José Silva Lopes (ed.), *Portugal and EC Membership Evaluated* (London: Pinter), pp. 30–50.

BACALHAU, MARIO (1989) 'Mobilidade e Transferência de voto através das sondagens', in Mário Baptista Coelho (ed.), *Portugal. O Sistema Político e Constitucional 1974–1987* (Lisbon: Instituto de Ciencias Sociais-Universidade de Lisbon) pp. 237–56.

BAETA NEVES, C. M. (1966–70) *Protecção da Natureza*, Separatas da *Gazeta das Aldeias*.

BALME, RICHARD, PHILIPPE GARRAUD, VINCENT HOFFMAN-MARTINOT and EVELYNE RITAINE (in collaboration with Lawrence Bonnet and Stéphanie LeMay) (1993) 'Les Politiques Territoriales en Europe de l'Ouest', *Revue Française de Science Politique*, vol. 43 (June), pp. 435–68.

BALOYRA, ENRIQUE A. (1987) 'Democratic Transition in Comparative

Perspective', in Enrique A. Baloyra (ed.), *Comparing New Democracies.
Transition and Consolidation in Mediterranean Europe and the Southern Cone*
(Boulder, London: Westview Press), pp. 9–52.

BANDEIRA, CRISTINA LESTON and PEDRO MAGALHÃES (1993) 'As
Relações Parlamento/Governo nas IV e V Legislaturas', unpublished manuscript, Instituto de Ciências do Trabalho e da Empresa.

BARBER, BENJAMIN R. (1984) *Strong Democracy: Participatory Politics in
a New Age* (Berkeley, CA: University of California).

BARRETO, JOSÉ (1990) 'Os primórdios da Intersindical sob Marcelo Caetano',
Análise Social, vol. XXV, nos 105–6, pp. 57–117.

BARRETO, JOSÉ (1992) 'Portugal: Industrial Relations Under Democracy', in
Anthony Fenner and Richard Hyman (eds), *Industrial Relations in the New
Europe* (Oxford: Blackwell), pp. 445–81.

BARROSO, JOSÉ DURÃO (1989) 'O Processo de Democratização: Uma
Tentativa de Interpretação a partir de uma perspectiva sistémica', in Mário
Baptista Coelho (ed.), *Portugal. O Sistema Político e Constitucional 1974–
87* (Lisbon: Instituto de Ciências Sociais, Universidade de Lisbon), pp. 29–
68.

BASSOT, ETIENNE (1993) 'Le Comité des Régions. Régions Françaises et
Laender Allemands Face à Un Nouvel Organe Communautaire', *Revue du
Marché Commun et de l'Union Européenne*, no. 371 (September–October),
pp. 729–39.

BAT SMIT, REYNAUD DE LA (1994) 'Change and Identity. Can cultural change
prompt changes in personal and social identity?', in *Insight. Newsletter of the
Centre for European Union Studies* (Hull: University of Hull), pp. 1–18.

BEETHAM, DAVID (1992) 'Liberal Democracy and the Limits of Democratization', *Prospects for Democracy* (edited by David Held), Political Studies
Special Issue, vol. XL, pp. 40–53.

BENAVENTE, ANA (1990) 'Insucesso escolar no contexto português-abordagens,
concepções e politicas', *Análise Social*, vol. XXV, nos 108–9, pp. 715–33.

BERMEO, NANCY (1992) 'Democracy and the Lessons of Dictatorship',
Comparative Politics, vol. 24, no. 3 (April), pp. 273–91.

BLONDEL, JEAN (1986) 'Introduction: Western European Cabinets in Comparative Perspective', in Jean Blondel and Ferdinand Mueller-Rommel (eds),
Cabinets in Western Europe (Basingstoke: Macmillan), pp. 1–16.

BOGASON, PETER (1986) 'Denmark', in Michael Goldsmith and Ed Page (eds),
Central and Local Government (London: Sage), pp. 46–67.

BORISH, STEVEN (1991) *The Land of the Living: The Danish Folk High
Schools and Denmark's Non-Violent Path to Modernization* (Nevada City,
California: Blue Dolphin).

BORREGO, CARLOS, F. SANTANA, F. D. SANTOS and M.M. RAMALHO
(1991) *Livro Branco do Estado de Ambiente em Portugal* (Lisbon:
MARN).

BOURDIEU, PIERRE (1984) *Distinction. A Social Critique of the Judgement
of Taste* (London: Routledge).

BRASSLOFF, AUDREY (1991) 'Portugal, 1992 and All That', *Journal of the
Association for Contemporary Iberian Studies*, vol. 4, no. 2 (Autumn), pp.
23–37.

BRAUDEL, FERNAND (1979) *Les Structures du Quotidien: Le Possible et*

L'Impossible. Vol. 3: Civilisation materielle, économie, et capitalisme (Paris: Armand Colin).

BRUNEAU, THOMAS (1984) *Politics and Nationhood. Post-revolutionary Portugal* (New York: Praeger).

BRUNEAU, THOMAS and MACLEOD, ALEX (1986) *Politics in Contemporary Portugal. Parties and the Consolidation of Democracy* (Boulder, Colo.: Lynne Rienner).

CABRAL, ANTÓNIO JOSÉ (1993) 'Community Regional Policy Towards Portugal', in José da Silva Lopes (ed.), *Portugal and EC Membership Evaluated* (London: Pinter), pp. 133–45.

CALLEO, DAVID P. (1994) 'America's Federal Nation State: A Crisis of Post-Imperial Viability?', in 'Contemporary Crisis of the Nation State?' (John Dunn, ed.), special issue of *Political Studies*, vol. 42, pp. 16–33.

CARNEIRO, ROBERTO (1988) *Educação e Emprego em Portugal. Uma Leitura de Modernização* (Lisboa: Fundacao Calouste Gulbenkian).

CARVALHO, OTELO SARAIVA DE (1986) *Alvorada em Abril* (Lisbon: Alvim).

CASTANHEIRA, JOSÉ PEDRO (1985) 'Os sindicatos e a vida politica', *Análise Social*, vol. XXI, nos 87–9, pp. 801–18.

CAUTELA, AFONSO (1977) *Ecologia e Luta de Classes em Portugal* (Lisbon: Sociultur).

CERNY, PHILIPPE (1990) *The Changing Architecture of Politics. Structure, Agency and the Future of the State* (London: Sage).

CHANUT, VERONIQUE and JANINE FLOCH-FOURNIER (1992) 'La Modernisation de l'Administration Portugaise', *Les Cahiers du Management et de l'innovation*, pp. 94–99.

CHILCOTE, RONALD H. (1993) 'Portugal: From Popular Power to Bourgeois Democracy' in James Kurth and James Petras (eds), *Mediterranean Paradoxes. The Politics and Social Structure of Southern Europe* (Providence: Berg) pp. 128–59.

CHITO, BEATRIZ and RAUL CAIXINHAS (1993) 'A Participação do Público no Processo de Avaliação Ambiental', *Revista Crítica de Ciências Sociais*, no. 36 (February), pp. 41–53.

COCKFIELD F. A. LORD (1994) *The European Union. Creating the Single Market* (Chichester: Wiley Chancery Law).

COELHO, MARIA HELENA DA CRUZ and JOAQUIM ROMERO MAGALHAES (1986) *O Poder Concelhio. Das origens às cortes constituintes* (Coimbra: Centro de Estudos e Formaçao Autárquica).

COELHO, MARÍO BAPTISTA (ed.) (1989) *Portugal. O Sistema Político e Constitucional. 1974–87* (Lisbon: Instituto de Ciências Sociais, Universidade de Lisboa).

COMMISSION OF THE EUROPEAN COMMUNITIES (1990a) *Community Support Framework, 1989–93: Portugal; for development and structural adjustment of the regions in which development is lagging behind* (Luxembourg: Office of the Official Publications of the European Communities).

COMMISSION OF THE EUROPEAN COMMUNITIES (1990b) *Program for Research and Actions on the Development of the Labour Market. Final Synthesis Report. Underground economy and irregular forms of employment (travail au noir)* (Luxembourg: Office of the Official Publications of the European Communities).

COMMISSION OF THE EUROPEAN COMMUNITIES (1990c) *PEDIP: Specific Programme for the Development of the Portuguese Industry*: progress report presented by Commission, COM (90) 205 final.

COMMISSION OF THE EUROPEAN COMMUNITIES (1992) *Towards Sustainable Development. A Programme of the European Community in matters of environmental policy and action and sustainable development*, COM (92)-23, final, 2 vols, Brussels, 26 May.

COMMISSION OF THE EUROPEAN COMMUNITIES (1993) *PEDIP: Specific Industrial Development Programme for Portugal: Final report*, presented by the Commission, Brussels, COM (93), 711 final.

COMMISSION OF THE EUROPEAN COMMUNITIES (1994) *Community Support Framework 1994–99: Portugal; Objective 1: Structural development and adjustment of regions whose development is lagging behind* (Luxembourg: Office of the Official Publications of the European Communities).

CONCEICAO, APELLES J. (1987) *Segurança Social* (Lisbon: Rei dos Livros).

CONSTITUTION OF THE PORTUGUESE REPUBLIC. Third Revision of *1992* (1995) (Lisbon: Assembleia da República).

CORKILL, DAVID (1993a) *The Portuguese Economy Since 1974* (Edinburgh: Edinburgh University Press).

CORKILL, DAVID (1993b) 'The Political Consolidation of Democracy in Portugal', *Parliamentary Affairs*, vol. 46, pp. 517–33.

CORKILL, DAVID (1995a) 'Party Factionalism and Democratization in Portugal', *Democratization*, vol. 2, no. 2, pp. 64–76.

CORKILL, DAVID (1995b) 'Portugal and the European Union: The Politics of Catching Up', in Joni Lovenduski and Jeffrey Stanyer (eds), *Contemporary Political Studies, 1995* (Belfast: Political Studies Association), pp. 808–15.

COSTA, ALFREDO BRUTO DA, SILVA, MANUELA, PEREIRINHA J. and MATOS, MADALENA (1985) *A Pobreza em Portugal* (Lisbon: Fundacao Calouste Gulbenkian).

COSTA, JANEEN ARNOLD (1992) 'The Periphery of Pleasure or Pain: Consumer Culture in the EC Mediterranean of 1992', in Thomas M. Wilson, and M. Estellie Smith (eds), *Cultural Change and the New Europe* (Boulder, Colo.: Westview Press), pp. 81–98.

COSTA E SOUSA, VINICIO ALVES DA (1983) 'O Partido Comunista Português' (Subsídios para um Estudo sobre os seus adeptos), in *Estudos Políticos e Sociais*, vol. XI, nos 3–4, pp. 497–543.

CRAVINHO, JOÃO (1986a) 'O Planeamento Necessário ao Lancamento de um modelo novo de desenvolvimento', in Manuela Silva (ed.), *Portugal Contemporâneo. Problemas e Perspectivas* (Lisbon: Instituto Nacional de Administração), pp. 573–92.

CRAVINHO, JOÃO (1986b) 'The Portuguese Economy: Constraints and Opportunities', in *Portugal in the 1980s. Dilemmas of Democratic Consolidation* (New York: Greenwood Press), pp. 111–65.

CRISTOVAM, MARIA LUISA (1985) 'A Acção Sindical em Portugal: entre mobilização por uma mudanca e compromisso social (1979–1982)', in Eduardo de Sousa Ferreira and Walter C. Opello (eds), *Conflict and Change in Portugal* (Lisbon: Teorema), pp. 171–8.

CROUCH, COLIN (1993) *Industrial Relations and European State Traditions* (Oxford: Oxford University Press).

CRUZ, MANUEL DA BRAGA (1986) 'A Evolução das instituições políticas: partidos políticos e forças armadas na transição democrática portuguesa, *Povos e Culturas*, vol. 1, pp. 205–15.

CRUZ, MANUEL DA BRAGA (1992a) 'Europeismo, Nacionalismo, Regionalismos' *Análise Social*, vol. XXVII, nos 118–19, pp. 827–53.

CRUZ, MANUEL DA BRAGA (1992b) 'National Identity in Transition', in Richard Herr (ed.), *The New Portugal: Democracy and Europe* (Berkeley, CA: University of California Press), pp. 151–62.

CRUZ, MANUEL DA BRAGA (1994) 'O Presidente da República na génese e evoluçao do sistema de governo português', *Análise Social*, vol. XXIX, nos 125–6, pp. 237–65.

CRUZ, MANUEL DA BRAGA and MIGUEL LOBO ANTUNES (1989) 'Parlamento, partidos e governo-acerca da institucionalização política, in Coelho (ed.), pp. 351–68.

CRUZ, MANUEL DA BRAGA and MIGUEL LOBO ANTUNES (1990) 'Revolutionary Transition and Problems of Parliamentary Institutionalization: the case of the Portuguese National Assembly', in Ulrike Liebert and Maurizio Cotta (eds.), *Parliament and Democratic Consolidation in Southern Europe: Greece, Italy, Portugal, Spain and Turkey* (London and New York: Pinter), pp. 154–83.

CUNHAL, ALVARO (1974) *Rumo á Vitória. As Tarefas do Partido na Revolução Democrática e Nacional* (Porto: A Opinião).

CUNHAL, ALVARO (1976) *A Revolução Portuguesa. O Passado e o Futuro. Relatório aprovado pelo CC do PCP para o VII Congresso* (Lisbon: Avante).

CUNHAL, ALVARO (1985) *O Partido Com Paredes de Vidro* (Lisbon: Avante).

DAHRENDORF, RALF (1990) *Reflections on the Revolution in Europe: In a letter intended to have been sent to a gentleman in Warsaw* (London: Chatto and Windus).

DAUDERSTAEDT, MICHAEL (1988) 'Schwacher Staat und Schwacher Markt: Portugals Wirtschaftspolitik zwischen Abhaengigkeit und Modernisierung', *Politische Vierteljahresschrift*, vol. 20, pp. 433–53.

DIAMANDOUROS, NIKIFOROS (1994) 'Transition to, and Consolidation of Democratic Politics in Greece 1974–83: A Tentative Assessment', in Pridham (1994a), pp. 50–71.

DIÁRIO DA ASSEMBLEIA DA REPUBLICA (DAR), 1990–94 (Lisbon: Casa da Moeda).

DIPALMA, GIUSEPPE (1990a) *To Craft Democracies. An Essay on Democratic Transitions* (Berkeley, CA: University of California Press).

DIPALMA, GIUSEPPE (1990b) 'Parliaments, consolidation, institutionalization: a minimalist view', in Ulrike Liebert and Maurizio Cotta (eds), *Parliament and Democratic Consolidation in Southern Europe: Greece, Italy, Portugal, Spain and Turkey* (London and New York: Pinter), pp. 31–51.

DIPALMA, GIUSEPPE (1991a) 'Totalitarismo, sociedade civil, transiçoes', *Análise Social*, vol. XXVI, no. 110, pp. 59–96.

DIPALMA, GIUSEPPE (1991b) 'After Leninism: Why Democracy Can Work in Eastern Europe', *Journal of Democracy*, vol. 2, no. 1, pp. 17–31.

Directory of European Agricultural Organizations (1984) (Luxembourg: Office of the Official Publications of the European Communities).

DOMINGOS, EMIDIO DA VEIGA (1980) *Portugal Político. Análise das Instituiçoes* (Lisbon: Ediçoes Rolim).

References

DOWNS, CHARLES (1989) *Revolution at the Grassroots in the Portuguese Revolution* (New York: State University of New York Press).

EATON, MARTIN (1990) 'Central Portugal's Textile Industry: Depression or Recovery on the Road to International Production?', *Iberian Studies*, vol. 19, nos 1–2, pp. 95–112.

EATON, MARTIN (1994) 'Regional Development Funding in Portugal', *Journal of the Association of Contemporary Iberian Studies*, vol. 7, no. 2 (Autumn), pp. 36–46.

EISFELD, RAINER (1984) *Sozialistischer Pluralismus in Europa. Ansatze und Scheitern am Beispiel Portugal* (Cologne: Verlag Wissenschaft und Politik).

EISFELD, RAINER (1989) 'Portugal in the European Community 1986–88. The Impact of the First Half of the Transition Period', *Iberian Studies*, vol. 18, no. 2, pp. 156–65.

ELEIÇOES EM ABRIL (1975) *Diário de Campanha* (Lisbon: Liber).

EMIDIO, M. TAVARES (1986) 'Educação', in Manuela Silva (ed.), *Portugal Contemporâneo* (Lisbon: Instituto Nacional de Administração) pp. 81–103.

ERICKSON, PAUL KENNETH and DANKWART A. RUSTOW (1991) 'Global Research Perspectives. Paradigms, Concepts and Data in a Changing World', in Paul Kenneth Erickson and Dankwart A. Rustow (eds), *Global Dynamics Research. Paradigms, Concepts and Data in a Changing World* (Boston: HarperCollins).

ESPING-ANDERSEN, GOSTA (1985) *Politics Against Markets* (Princeton, NJ: Princeton University Press).

ESPING-ANDERSEN, GOSTA (1993) 'Post-Industrial Class Structures: An Analytical Framework', in Gosta Esping-Andersen (ed.), *Changing Classes Stratification and Mobility in Post-Industrial Societies* (London: Sage), pp. 7–31.

ESPING-ANDERSEN, GOSTA (1994) 'Budgets and Democracy: Towards a Welfare State in Spain and Portugal 1960–1986', in Ian Budge and David MacKay (eds), *Developing Democracy.Comparative Research in Honour of Jean Blondel* (London: Sage), pp. 112–27.

ESTEVES, ANTONIO JOAQUIM and STEPHEN R. STOER (eds) (1992) *Sociologia na Escola. Professores, Educação e Desenvolvimento* (Lisbon: Edicoes Afrontamento).

EUROPEAN COMMISSION (1994a) *Competitiveness and Cohesion: Trends in the Regions. Fifth periodic report on the social and economic situation and development of the regions in the Community* (Luxembourg: Office of the Official Publications of the European Communities).

EUROPEAN COMMISSION (1994b) *Interregional and cross-border cooperation in Europe. Proceedings of the Conference on Interregional Cooperation – Regions in Partnership. Brussels, 14 and 15 December 1992* (Luxembourg: Office of the Official Publications of the European Communities).

EUROPEAN PARLIAMENT (1991) *Committee of Inquiry on Racism and Xenophobia in Europe. Report*, rapporteur Glyn Ford (Luxembourg: Office of the Official Publications of the European Communities).

FARIA, ISABEL HUB, MARIA JOSÉ GROSSO and ROSA LOPES (1986) 'Dez Anos de Auto-Referência: Que Transformação na Orientação para o Significado da Mulher na Assembleia da República?', *Revista Crítica de Ciencias Sociais*, nos 18–20 (February), pp. 213–24.

FERNANDES, HÉLIO (1990) 'The Modernization of Portuguese Civil Service', unpublished manuscript (Lisbon: Secretariado para a Modernizaçao Administrativa).

FERREIRA, GONCALVES F. A. (1985) *Quinze Anos da Historia Recente de Portugal (1970–1984)* (Lisbon).

FERREIRA, JOSÉ MEDEIROS (1983) *Ensaio Histórico sobre a Revoluçao do 25 de Abril. O Período Pré-Constitucional* (Lisbon: Imprensa Nacional-Casa da Moeda).

FERREIRA, JOSÉ MEDEIROS (1989) 'Um corpo perante o Estado: militares e instituições politicas, in Coelho (1989), pp. 427–51.

FIGUEIREDO, ANTÓNIO DE (1976) *Portugal: Cinquenta Anos de Ditadura* (Lisbon: Dom Quixote).

FIGUEIREDO, EURICO (1988) *Conflito de Gerações, Conflito de Valores*, Vol. II of *Portugal os próximos 20 Anos* (Lisbon: Fundação Calouste Gulbenkian).

FRANCO, ANTÓNIO DE SOUSA (1993) *O Controlo da Administração Pública em Portugal* (Lisbon: Tribunal de Contas).

FURLONG, PAUL (1993) *Modern Italy* (London: Routledge).

GALLAGHER, TOM (1983) *Portugal. A Twentieth Century Interpretation* (Manchester: Manchester University Press).

GALLAGHER, TOM (1988) 'Goodbye to Revolution: The Portuguese Election of July 1987', *West European Politics*, vol. 11 (January), pp. 139–45.

GALLAGHER, TOM (1990) 'The Portuguese Socialist Party: the Pitfalls of Being First', in Tom Gallagher and Allan Williams (eds), *Southern European Socialism* (Manchester: Manchester University Press), pp. 12–32.

GALTUNG, JOHAN (1975) *Strukturelle Gewalt. Beitraege zur Friedens- und Konfliktforschung* (Frankfurt: Rowohlt).

GAGO, MARIA AMÉLIA CORREA, PEREIRA, LUZ VALENTE (1990) *Informacao Sócio-Economica para planeamento municipal. A Perspectiva de Algumas Municipalidades Sobre a Promoção do Desenvolvimento* (Lisboa: Laboratório de Engenharia Civil).

GARNHAM, NICHOLAS and RAYMOND WILLIAMS (1990) 'Pierre Bourdieu and the Sociology of Culture. An Introduction', in Nicholas Garnham (ed.), *Capitalism and Communication. World Culture and the Economics of Information* (London: Sage), pp. 70–88.

GASPAR, CARLOS (1990) 'O Processo Constitucional e a Estabilidade do Regime', *Análise Social*, vol. xxv, nos 105–6, pp. 9–29.

GASPAR, JORGE (1985) '10 Anos de Democracia: Reflexos na Geografia Politica', in *Conflict and Change in Portugal, 1974–1984* (Lisbon: Teorema), pp. 135–55.

GASPAR, JORGE (1990) 'Portugal Between Centre and Periphery', in *The World Economy and the Spatial Organization of Power* (Aldershot: Avebury), pp. 219–32.

GASPAR, VITOR (1991) 'Budgetary Deficits and Debt Policy: Preliminary Assessment of the Portuguese Case', in José Silva Lopes and L. M. Beleza (eds), *Portugal and the Internal Market of the EEC. Proceedings of the International Conference held in Lisbon on October 6 and 7, 1989* (Lisbon: Banco de Portugal), pp. 73–83.

GIDDENS, ANTHONY (1993) *Modernity and Self-Identity. Self and Society in the Late Modern Age* (Oxford: Polity Press).

GOMES, JOAO SALIS (1982) 'Alianca Democrática. Análise de uma Coligacao', in *Perspectivas* April, no. 10, 11, 12, pp. 19–40.

GRAHAM, LAWRENCE (1982) 'O Estado Português visto a partir de baixo', *Análise Social*, vol. XVIII, nos 72–74, pp. 959–74.

GRAHAM, LAWRENCE (1985) 'A Administração Pública central e local: continuidade e mudança', *Análise Social*, vol. XXI, nos 87–89, pp. 903–24.

GRAHAM, LAWRENCE (1991) 'Centre–Periphery Relations', in Kenneth Maxwell and Michael H. Hatzel (eds), *Ancient Country, New Democracy* (Washington: Woodrow Wilson Center Press), pp. 24–36.

GRAHAM, LAWRENCE (1992) 'Redefining the Portuguese Transition to Democracy', in Richard Gunther and S. Higley (eds), *Elites and Democratic Consolidation in Latin America and Europe* (Cambridge: Cambridge University Press), pp. 282–94.

GRAHAM, LAWRENCE (1993) *The Portuguese Military and the State. Rethinking Transitions in Europe and Latin America* (Boulder, Colo.: Westview Press).

GUIBENTIF, PIERRE (1985) 'Discursos e aparelhos nas transformações políticas – o caso da segurança social', *Análise Social*, vol. XXI, nos 87–9, pp. 945–59.

GUIBENTIF, PIERRE (1989) 'Rechtskultur und Rechtsproduktion: Das Beispiel Portugal', *Zeitschrift fuer Rechtssoziologie*, vol. 2, pp. 148–69.

GUZZINI, STEFANO (1994) 'La longue nuit de la Prémiere Republique. L'implosion clienteliste en Italie', *Revue Française de Science Politique*, vol. 44, no. 6 (December), pp. 979–1013.

HABERMAS, JÜRGEN (1986) *Die Theorie des Kommunikativen Handelns*, 2 vols (Frankfurt: Suhrkamp).

HAGE, JERALD and JEFFREY Z. SHI (1993) 'Alternative Strategies for the Reconstruction of the State During Economic Reform', *Governance*, vol. 6, no. 4, pp. 463–91.

HALL, MARK (1994) 'Industrial Relations and the Social Dimension of European Integration: Before and After Maastricht', in Richard Hyman and Anthony Fenner (eds), *New Frontiers in European Industrial Relations* (Oxford: Blackwell), pp. 281–311.

HARSGOR, MIKHAEL (1975) *La Naissance D'Un Nouveau Portugal* (Paris: Editions du Seuil).

HARVIE, CHRISTOPHER (1994) *The Rise of Regional Europe* (London: Routledge).

HARVEY, ROBERT (1978) *Portugal: Birth of a Democracy* (London: Macmillan).

HEIMER, FRANZ-WILHELM, JORGE VALA and JOSÉ MANUEL LEITE VIEGAS (1990a) 'Cultura Política. Uma leitura interdisciplinar', *Sociologia. Problemas e Prácticas*, no. 8, pp. 9–28.

HEIMER, FRANZ-WILHELM, JORGE VALA and JOSÉ MANUEL LEITE VIEGAS (1990b) 'Padrões de Cultura Politica e Portugal: Atitudes Face à Democracia', *Análise Social*, vol. XXV, no. 105–6, pp. 31–56.

HEINRICH, HANS-GEORG (1985) 'Sinn und Grenzen des politikwissenschaftlichen Ost-West Vergleichs', in *Osteuropa In Blickpunkt. 30 Jahre Gesellschaft fuer Ost- und Suedostkunde* (Linz: Gesellschaft fuer Ost- und Sudostkunde).

HESPANHA, A. M. (1986) 'As Transformações Revolucionárias e o Discurso dos Juristas' in *Revista Critica de Ciencias Sociais*, nos 18, 19, 20, pp. 312–41.

HINE, DAVID (1991) 'Italy and Europe: The 1990 Presidency and the Domestic Management of European Community Affairs', *Italy, The European Community and the 1990 Presidency: Policy Trends and Policy Performance*, Occasional Paper no. 3, June (Bristol: Centre for Mediterranean Studies), pp. 17–38.

HIX, SIMON (1994) 'The Study of the European Community: The Challenge to Comparative Politics', *West European Politics*, vol. 17, no. 1, pp. 1–30.

HORKHEIMER, MAX (1987) *Zur Kritik der instrumentellen Vernunft* (Frankfurt: Fischer).

HUDSON, MARK (1994) 'The Portuguese Economy, 1974–1993', paper presented at the University of Reading, Workshop on Portugal, 18 February.

HUNEEUS, CARLOS (1987) 'From Diarchy to Polyarchy: Prospects for Democracy in Chile', in Enrique A. Baloyra (ed.), *Comparing New Democracies* (Boulder and London: Westview Press), pp. 109–52.

HUNTINGTON, SAMUEL P. (1968) *Political Order in Changing Societies* (New Haven, CT: Yale University Press).

HUNTINGTON, SAMUEL P. (1991) *The Third Wave: Democratization in the Late Twentieth Century* (Norman: University of Oklahoma Press).

'International Organisations and Democracy' (1994) *Journal of Democracy*, no. 3 (July), pp. 3–69.

ISHYAMA, JOHN T. (1993) 'Founding Elections and the Development of Transitional Parties: The Cases of Estonia and Latvia, 1990–1992', *Communist and Post-Communist Studies*, vol. 26, no. 3 (September), pp. 277–99.

ITURRA, RAUL (1990) *A Construcao Social do Insucesso Escolar. Memoria e Aprendizagem in Vila Ruiva* (Lisbon: Escher).

JACOBS, FRANCIS (1989) *European Political Parties* (London: Bowker-Saur).

KATSELI, LOUKA L. (1992) 'The Internalisation of Southern European Economies', paper presented at the Conference 'Economic Change in Southern Europe', organised by the Social Science Research Council, Subcommittee on Southern Europe, Sintra, 9–12 July 1992.

KAY, HUGH (1971) *Die Zeit steht still in Portugal. Hintergrund eines politischen Systems* (Bergisch-Gladbach: Gustav Luebbe Verlag).

KINTIS, ANDREAS, MAGONE, JOSÉ (1996) *Environmental Policy in Europe*. Working Paper, European Studies Research Institute (Manchester: University of Salford).

KIRCHNER, EMIL (1986) 'The Relationship Between Interest Groups in Greece, Spain and Portugal and Their European Counterparts', *Revista de Ciência Politica*, no. 3, pp. 61–9.

KIRCHNER, EMIL (1994) 'Is the European Community a Transnational Democracy?', in Ian Budge and David McKay (eds), *Developing Democracy. Essays in Honour of Jean Blondel* (London: Sage), pp. 253–66.

KOLM, SERGE-CHRISTOPHE (1975-6) 'Portugal: Quelle Revolution, Vers Quelle Societé? Dynamique du changement des structures de proprieté dans le Portugal actuel', *Les Temps Modernes*, vol. 31, no. 353, pp. 881–97.

KOLM, SERGE-CHRISTOPHE (1977) *La Transition Socialiste. La Politique Economique de Gauche* (Paris: Les Editions du Cerf).

KRAUS, PETER A. (1990) 'Elemente einer Theorie post-autoritarer

Demokratisierungsprozesss im sudeuropaischen Kontext', *Politische Vierteljahresschrift*, vol. 31, no. 2, pp. 191–213.

LADRECH, ROBERT (1993) 'Parliamentary Democracy and Political Discourse in EC Institutional Change', *Journal of European Integration*, vol. XVII, no. 1 (Autumn), pp. 53–70.

LANE, JAN ERIK and SVANTE ERSSON (1994) *Comparative Politics. An Introduction and a New Approach* (Oxford: Polity Press).

LANGE, PETER (1993) 'Maastricht and the Social Protocol: Why Did They Do It', *Politics and Society*, vol. 21, no. 1, pp. 3–6.

LAVDAS, KOSTAS and MENDRINOU, MARIA (1995) 'Competition Policy and Institutional Politics in the European Community: State Aid Control and Small Business Promotion', *European Journal for Political Research*, 38, pp. 171–201.

LEAL, ANTÓNIO DA SILVA (1985) 'As políticas sociais no Portugal de hoje', *Análise Social*, vol. XXI, nos 87–9, pp. 925–943.

LECHER, WOLFGANG (ed.) (1994) *Trade Unions in the European Community. A Handbook* (London: Lawrence and Wishart).

LEMARCHAND, RENÉ and KEITH LEGG (1972) 'Political Clientelism and Development. A Preliminary Analysis', *Comparative Politics* (January), pp. 149–78.

LEMOS, P. (1988) 'Associativismo e Defesa do Ambiente em Portugal', in *Actas do I.Congresso Luso-Galego de Conservação e Ambiente*, Braga, Outubro 1987 (Lisbon: GEOTA), pp. 285–7.

LEWIS, J. R. and WILLIAMS, A. M. (1984) 'Social Cleavages and Electoral Performance: The Social basis of Portuguese Political Parties 1976–83' in Geoffrey Pridham (ed.), *The New Mediterranean Democracies. Regime Transition in Spain, Greece and Portugal* (London: Frank Cass), pp. 119–37.

LIBERATO, PEDRO NUNES (1992) 'Desenvolvimento e Ambiente', *Administração, Dirigentes e Técnicos do Estado*, Janeiro–Fevereiro, pp. 29–35.

LIGTHART, HENK and HENK REITSMA (1988) 'Portugal's semiperipheral middleman role in its relations with England, 1640–1760', *Political Geography Quarterly*, vol. 4 (October), pp. 353–62.

LIMA, MARINÚS PIRES DE (1986) 'Transformações das Relaçoes de Trabalho e Acção Operária nas Industrias Navais (1974–1984)', *Revista Critica de Ciências Sociais*, nos 18–20 (February), pp. 537–46.

LIMA, MARINÚS PIRES DE (1991) 'Relações de Trabalho, Estratégias Sindicais e Emprego (1974–1990)', *Análise Social* vol. XXVI, pp. 905–43.

LIMA, MARINÚS PIRES DE (1993) 'A Europa Social: Questões e Desafios', *Análise Social*, vol. XXVIII, nos 123–4, pp. 835–67.

LINZ, JUAN (1978) *Crisis, Breakdown, and Reequilibration. The Breakdown of Democratic Regimes*, vol. 1 (Baltimore and London: Johns Hopkins University Press).

LIPOVETSKY, GILLES (1983) *L'Ere du Vide. Essais sur l'individualisme contemporain* (Paris: Gallimard).

LIPSET, SEYMOUR MARTIN (1963) *Political Man. The Social Basis of Politics* (Garden City, NY: Anchor).

LIPSET, SEYMOUR MARTIN, SEONG, KYOUNG, RYUNG, TORRES and JOHN CHARLES (1993) 'Une Analyse Comparative des Prérequis Sociaux de la Democratie' in *Revue Internationale des Sciences Sociales*, vol. 136, Mai, pp. 181–205.

LIPSET, SEYMOUR MARTIN (1994) 'The Social Requisites of Democracy Revisited. 1993 Presidential Address', *American Sociological Review*, vol. 59, pp. 1–22.

LOBO, ISABEL DE SOUSA (1985) 'Estrutura social e produtiva e propensao à subterraneidade no Portugal de hoje', *Análise Social*, vol. XXI, nos 87–9, pp. 527–62.

LOPES, FERNANDO FARELO (1994) *Poder Politico e Caciquismo na la Republica Portuguesa* (Lisbon: Editorial Estampa).

LOPES, JOSÉ DA SILVA (1991) *Portugal and the Internal Market, 1991* (Lisbon: Fundação Calouste Gulbenkian), pp. 1–16.

LOPES, PEDRO SANTANA and MANUEL BARROSO (1980) *Sistema de Governo e Sistema Partidário* (Lisbon: Livraria Bertrand).

LOPES, VICTOR SILVA (1976) *Constituição da Republica Portuguesa 1976 (anotada)* (Lisbon: Editus).

LOUÇÃ, FRANCISCO (1985) 'A "Vertigem Insurrecional": Teoria e Politica do PCP na Viragem de Agosto de 1975', in *Revista Critica de Ciencias Sociais*, nos 15, 16, 17, pp. 149–62.

LOURENÇO, EDUARDO (1984) *O Complexo de Marx* (Lisbon: Publicacoes Europa–América).

LUCENA, MANUEL DE (1976) *A Evolução do Sistema Corporativo*, 2 vols (Lisbon: Perspectivas e Realidades).

LUCENA, MANUEL DE (1985) 'Neocorporativismo? – Conceito, interesses e aplicação ao caso português', *Análise Social*, vol. XXI, nos. 87–9, pp. 819–65.

LUCENA, MANUEL DE (1989) 'A herança de duas revoluções: continuidade e rupturas no Portugal post-salazarista', in Coelho (1989), pp. 505–55.

LUCENA, MANUEL DE and CARLOS GASPAR (1991) 'Metamorfoses corporativas? – Associações de interesses económicos e institucionalização da democracia em Portugal (I)', *Análise Social*, vol. XXVI, pp. 847–903.

LUCENA, MANUEL DE and CARLOS GASPAR (1992) 'Metamorfoses corporativas? – Associações de interesses económicos e institucionalização da democracia em Portugal (II)', *Análise Social*, vol. XXXVII, no. 115, pp. 135–87.

MACPHERSON, C. B. (1967) *The Political Theory of Possessive Individualism. From Hobbes to Locke* (Oxford: Clarendon).

MACPHERSON, C. B. (1973) *Democratic Theory: Essays in Retrieval* (Oxford: Clarendon).

MAGONE, JOSÉ (1991) 'Politische Kultur in der Europaeischen Semiperipherie (1910–1990)', *Oesterreichische Zeitschrift für Entwicklungspolitik* vol. 4, pp. 93–107.

MAGONE, JOSÉ (1993) 'The Impact of the European Community on the New Iberian Democracies (1974–1993). An Empirical Contribution Towards a Theory of Regional Monitoring of Democratic Transition and Consolidation Processes', *Insight* (newsletter of the Centre for European Union Studies), no. 1, pp. 11–17.

MAGONE, JOSÉ (1994) 'Democratic Consolidation and Political Corruption in the Southern European Semi-Periphery: Some Research Notes on the

Portuguese Case, 1974–1993', in Patrick Dunleavy and Jeffrey Stanyer (eds), *Contemporary Political Studies 1994. Proceedings of the Annual Conference held at the University of Wales Swansea, March 29th–31st* (Belfast: Political Studies Association), pp. 751–64.

MAGONE, JOSÉ (1995a) 'Party Factionalism in New Small Southern European Democracies: Some Comparative Findings from the Portuguese and Greek Experiences', *Democratization*, vol. 2, no. 1, pp. 90–101.

MAGONE, JOSÉ (1995b) 'The Portuguese Assembleia da República: Discovering Europe', *Journal of Legislative Studies*, vol. 1, no. 3, pp. 152–65.

MAGONE, JOSÉ (1996a) 'Portugal', in Juliet Lodge (ed.), *Euro-elections 1994* (London: Pinter).

MAGONE, JOSÉ (1996b) *The Changing Architecture of Iberian Politics (1974–92). An Investigation on the Structuring of Democratic Political Systemic Culture in Semiperipheral Southern European Societies* (Lewiston, NY: Edwin Mellen Press).

MAGONE, JOSÉ and ANDREAS KINTIS (1994) 'The Mediterranean Entente', *European Brief*, October.

MAIA, FERNANDO (1986) 'Seguranca Social', in Silva (1986), pp. 167–91.

MAJONE, GIANDOMENICO (1991) 'Cross-National Sources of Regulatory Policy-Making in Europe and the United States', *Journal of Public Policy*, vol. 11, no. 1, pp. 79–106.

MAKLER, HARRY (1979) 'The Portuguese Industrial Elite and Its Corporative Relations: A Study in Compartmentalization in the Authoritarian Regime', in Lawrence S. Graham and Harry Makler (eds), *Contemporary Portugal. The Revolution and Its Antecedents* (Austin and London: Texas University Press), pp. 123–65.

MALLE, SILVANA (1994) 'From Market to Capitalism: the Building of Institutional Ethics', *Journal for Public Policy*, vol. 14, no. 1, pp. 1–16.

MANUEL, PAUL CHRISTOPHER (1995) *Uncertain Outcome. The Politics of the Portuguese Transition to Democracy* (Lanham, NY: University Press of America).

MARKS, GARY (1993) 'Structural Policy and Multilevel Governance in the European Community', in Allan W. Calfruny and Glenda C. Rosenthal (eds), *The State of the Community. Vol. 2: The Maastricht Debates and Beyond* (Boulder, Colo.: Lynne Rienner Publishers), pp. 391–410.

MARQUES, GUILLERMINA (1990) 'L'integration des Groupes d'Interet Portugais au Niveau Europeen', in *L'Europe du Sud dans la Communauté Européenne. Analyse comparative des groupes d'interet et de leur insertion dans le réseau communautaire* (Geneva: Presses Universitaires de France), pp. 185–201.

MARQUES, OLIVEIRA H. (1980) *A Primeira República Portuguesa* (Lisbon: Livros Horizonte).

MARQUES, OLIVEIRA H. (1981) *História de Portugal. Vol. III: Das Revolucoes Liberais aos Nossos Dias* (Lisbon: Palas Editora).

MARQUES, VIRIATO SOROMENHO (1993) 'O Problema da Decisão em Política do Ambiente', *Revista Crítica de Ciências Sociais*, no. 36 (February), pp. 27–38.

MARTINS, HERMINIO (1968) 'Portugal', in S. J. Woolf (ed.), *European Fascism* (London: Weidenfeld and Nicolson).

MATOS, LUIS SALGADO DE (1983) 'Significado e consequências da eleição do presidente por sufrágio universal – o caso português', *Análise Social*, vol. XIX, no. 76, pp. 235–59.

MATOS, LUIS SALGADO (1994) 'The Portuguese Political System and the EC: An Interaction Model', in José da Silva Lopes (ed.), *Portugal and the EC Membership Evaluated* (London: Pinter) pp. 157–72.

MELO, JOANAZ DE and CARLOS PIMENTA (1992) *O Ambiente em Portugal 1992 e o futuro* (Oeiras: Instituto Naçional de Administração.

MELO, JOANAZ DE and CARLOS PIMENTA (1993) *O Que é a Ecologia* (Lisbon: Difusão Cultural).

MEDEIROS, FERNANDO (1994) 'A Teoria, do Dualismo Revisitada nos Paises de Industrialização sem Modernização' in *Análise Social*, nos 125–26, pp. 81–119.

MENDES, ARMINDO RIBEIRO (1989) 'O Conselho da Revolução e a Comissão Constitucional na fiscalização da constitucionalidade das leis' in Mário Baptista Coelho (ed.), *Portugal. O Sistema Político e Constitucional 1974–87* (Lisbon: Instituto de Ciencias Sociais, Universidade de Lisboa), pp. 925–40.

MENDES, A. J. MARQUES (1994) 'The Development of the Portuguese Economy in the Context of the EC', in José Silva Lopes (ed.), *Portugal and EC Membership Evaluated* (London: Pinter), pp. 7–29.

MENDRINOU, MARIA (1994) 'European Community Fraud and the Politics of Institutional Development', *European Journal for Political Research*, vol. 26, no. 1 (July), pp. 81–101.

MENDRINOU, MARIA (1995) 'Non-compliance and the European Commission's Role for Integration', in Joni Lovenduski and Jeffrey Stanyer (eds), *Contemporary Political Studies 1995. Proceedings of the Annual Conference held at the University of York, April 18th–20th 1995* (Belfast: Political Studies Association), pp. 1317–32.

MINISTÉRIO DA ADMINISTRAÇÃO E RECURSOS NATURAIS (MARN) (1993a) *Análise Temática, Propostas de Seguimento em Portugal das Conclusoes da CNUAD, organizadas Accões e Medidas de Ambiente de Cada Área Temática* (Lisbon: MARN).

MINISTÉRIO DA ADMINISTRAÇÃO E RECURSOS NATURAIS (MARN) (1993b) *Sintese Estratégica, Aspectos mais relevantes para o seguimento em Portugal das conclusões da CNUAD* (Lisbon: MARN).

MINISTÉRIO DO PLANEAMENTO E ADMINISTRAÇÃO DO TERRITÓRIO (MPAT) (1989) *Portugal. Plano de Desenvolvimento Regional 1989–93*, 2 vols (Lisbon: MPAT).

MINISTÉRIO DO PLANEAMENTO E ADMINISTRAÇÃO DO TERRITÓRIO (MPAT) (1993) *Preparar Portugal para o Século XXI. Plano de Desenvolvimento Regional 1994–99* (Lisbon: MPAT).

MINISTRY OF FOREIGN AFFAIRS (1991) *Setting Course for European Union. The Portuguese Presidency in the first half of 1992. Maastricht Consolidation – Strengthened Links with the World – Enlargement in Perspective* (Lisbon: Ministry of Foreign Affairs).

MISHLER, WILLIAM and RICHARD ROSE (1994) 'Support for Parliaments and Regimes in the Transition Towards Democracy in Eastern Europe', *Legislative Studies Quarterly*, vol. XIX, no. 1 (February), pp. 5–32.

MÓNICA, MARIA FILOMENA (1994) 'A lenta morte da Câmara dos Pares (1878–1896)', *Análise Social*, vol. XXIX, pp. 121–52.

MOREIRA, ADRIANO (1989) 'O regime: Presidencialismo do Primeiro Ministro', in Coelho (1989), pp. 31–7.

MORLINO, LEONARDO (1986) 'Consolidamento Democratico: Alcuni Ipotesi Esplicative', *Rivista Italiana di Scienza Politica*, vol. XVI, no. 3 (December), pp. 439–59.

MORLINO, LEONARDO (1987) 'Democratic Establishments: A Dimensional Analysis', in Enrique A. Baloyra (ed.), *Comparing New Democracies* (Boulder and London: Westview Press), pp. 53–78.

MORLINO, LEONARDO (1995) 'Political Parties and Democratic Consolidation in Southern Europe', in Richard Gunther, P. Nikiforos Diamandouros and Hans-Juergen Puhle (eds), *The Politics of Democratic Consolidation* (Baltimore: Johns Hopkins University Press) pp. 315–88.

MORRISON, RODNEY (1981) *Portugal: Revolutionary Change In An Open Economy* (Boston, Mass.: Auburn House).

MOZZICAFREDDO, JUAN, ISABEL GUERRA, MARGARIDA A. FERNANDES and JOÃO G. P. QUINTELA (1991) *Gestão e Legitimidade no Sistema Político Local* (Lisbon: Escher).

MÜLLER, WOLFGANG C. and VINCENT WRIGHT (1994) 'Reshaping the State in Western Europe: The Limits of Retreat', in Wolfgang Muller and Vincent Wright (eds), *The State in Western Europe*, special issue of *West European Politics*, pp. 1–11.

MUNSLOW, BARRY and FRANCOIS EKANGA EKOGO (1995) 'Is Democracy Necessary for Sustainable Development?', *Democratization*, vol. 2, no. 2, (Summer), pp. 158–78.

NETHERLANDS ECONOMIC INSTITUTE (1993) *New Location Factors for Mobile Investment in Europe* (Luxembourg: Office of the Official Publications of the European Communities).

NOGUEIRA, TERESA FIDELIS and PAULO PINHO (1988) 'Estudos de Impacte Ambiental e Processos de Tomada de Decisão', in Carlos Borrego *et al.* (eds), *La Conferencia Nacional sobre a Qualidade do Ambiente* (Aveiro: Universidade de Aveiro), pp. 94–108.

NOGUEIRA, TERESA FIDELIS (1993) 'The Environmental Policy in Portugal: The Implementation of the EC EIA Directive', paper presented at the conference of the European Consortium of Political Research, University of Leiden, April.

NOSTY, B. DIAZ (1975) *Mário Soares. O Chanceler Portugues* (Lisboa: Liber).

NOTTERMAN, TON (1993) 'The Abdication from National Policy Autonomy: Why the Macroeconomic Policy Regime Has Become So Unfavourable to Labor', *Politics and Society*, vol. 21, no. 2 (June), pp. 133–67.

O'DONNELL, GUILLERMO and PHILIPPE SCHMITTER (1986) *Transitions from Authoritarian Rule. Tentative Conclusion about Uncertain Democracies* (Baltimore and London: Johns Hopkins University Press).

OECD (1993) *Portugal. Annual Survey 1994* (Paris: OECD).

OLIVEIRA, CÉSAR (1975) *O Operariado e a Republica Democratica* (Lisbon: Seara Nova).

O'NULLAIN, COLM (ed.) (1985) *The Presidency of the European Council of Ministers* (London: Croom Helm).

OPELLO, WALTER C. (1985) *Portugal's Political Development. A Comparative Approach* (Boulder, Colo.: Westview Press).

OPELLO, WALTER C. (1991) *Portugal. From Monarchy to Pluralist Democracy* (Boulder, Colo.: Westview Press).

OPTENHOGEL, UWE and ALAN STOLEROFF (1985) 'The Logics of Politically Competing Trade Union Confederations in Portugal 1974–1984', in Eduardo de Sousa Ferreira and Walter C. Opello (eds), *Conflict and Change in Portugal 1974–1984* (Lisbon: Teorema), pp. 179–90.

OS SUV em Luta, (1975) *Manifestos. Entrevistas. Comunicados* (Lisboa).

OVERBEEK, HENK (1990) *Global Capitalism and National Decline. The Thatcher Decade in Perspective* (London: Unwin and Hyman).

OZBUDUN, ERGUN (1981) 'Turkey: The Politics of Political Clientelism', in S. N. Eisenstadt and René Lemarchand, *Political Clientelism Patronage and Development* (Beverly Hills: Sage Publications), pp. 249–68.

PAIS, JOSÉ MACHADO (1990) Lazeres e sociabilidades juvenis-um ensaio de análise etnográfica', *Análise Social*, vol. XXV, nos 108–9, pp. 591–644.

PAIS, JOSÉ MACHADO (1991) 'Emprego Juvenil e mudança social: velhas teses, novos de vida', *Análise Social*, vol. XXVI, no. 114, pp. 945–87.

PAREKH, BIKHU (1992) 'The Cultural Particularity of Liberal Democracy', in 'Prospects for Democracy', edited by David Held, *Political Studies*, special issue, pp. 160–75.

PARTIDO SOCIALISTA (1974) *Declaração de Principios, Programa e Estatutos. Aprovado no Congresso do PS, em Dezembro* (Lisbon).

PARTIDO SOCIALISTA (1986) *Declaração de Principios, Programa e Estatutos. Aprovado no VI Congresso do PS* (Lisbon).

PASSOS, MARCELINO DOS (1987) *Der Niedergang des Faschismus in Portugal. Zum Verhaeltnis von Okonomie, Gesellschaft und Staat. Politik in einem europaeischen Schwellenland* (Marburg: Verlag für Arbeiterbewegung und Gesellschaftswissenschaft).

PASQUINO, GIANFRANCO and DIMITRIS SOTIROPOULOS (forthcoming) 'Bureaucratic Reform and Political Control of the Bureaucracy in the New Southern Europe', in Richard Gunther, Nikiforos Diamandouros, Gianfranco Pasquino (eds), *The Changing Functions of the State* (Manchester: Manchester University Press).

PATEMAN, CAROLE (1970) *Democratic Theory and Participation* (Manchester: Manchester University Press).

PEREIRA, JOSÉ PACHECO (1982) *Conflitos Sociais Nos Campos do Sul* (Lisbon: Europa–América).

PEREIRA, JOSÉ PACHECO (1983) 'O P.C.P. na I. República: Membros e Direcção', in *Estudos sobre o Comunismo*, nr. 1, Sept.–Dec., pp. 2–21.

PEREIRINHA, JOSÉ (1993) 'Social Exclusion in Portugal', in José Silva Lopes (ed.), *Portugal and EC Membership Evaluated* (London: Pinter), pp. 225–39.

PEREZ-DIAZ, VICTOR (1993) *The Return of Civil Society. The Emergence of Democratic Spain* (New Haven, CT: Yale University Press).

PESSOA, VICTOR (1986) 'Regionalização e Poder Local', in Silva (1986), pp. 503–18.

PETERSON, JOHN (1995) 'Decision-Making in the European Union: Towards a Framework of Analysis', *Journal of European Public Policy*, vol. 2, no. 1, pp. 69–93.

206   *References*

PINTO, JAIME NOGUEIRA (1989) 'A Direita e o 25 de Abril: Ideologia, Estratégia e Evolucao Politica', in Mário Baptista Coelho (ed.), *Portugal. O Sistema Politico e Constitucional 1974–1987* (Lisbon: Instituto de Ciencias Sociais, Universidade de Lisboa).

PINTO, MÁRIO (1991) 'Trade Union Action and Industrial Relations in Portugal', in Guido Baglioni and Colin Crouch (eds), *European Industrial Relations. The Challenge of Flexibility* (London: Sage), pp. 243–63.

POLANYI, KARL (1944) *The Great Transformation* (New York: Rinehart).

POLLACK, MARK A. (1994) 'Creeping Competence: The Expanding Agenda of the European Community', *Journal of Public Policy*, vol. 14, part 2, pp. 95–145.

PORTAS, NUNO, and SERRAS GAGO (1980) 'Some Preliminary Notes on the State in Contemporary Portugal', in Richard Scase (ed.), *The State in Western Europe* (London: Croom Helm), pp. 230–40.

PORTAS, PAULO and VASCO PULIDO VALENTE (1990) 'O Primeiro-Ministro: Estudo Sobre o Poder Executivo em Portugal', *Análise Social*, vol. XXV, no. 107, pp. 333–49.

PORTO, MANUEL CARLOS LOPEZ (1989) 'La Politica Regionale Portoghese e i fondi strutturali della communita europea', in *Mercato Commune e sviluppo regionale. Spagna, Portogallo e Grecia* (Padova: Centro di Documentazine e Studi Sulle Communitá Europee, Universitá degli Studi di Ferrara), pp. 159–215.

POZNANSKI, KAZIMIERZ L. (ed.) (1992) *Constructing Capitalism. The Reemergence of Civil Society and Liberal Economy in the Post-Communist World* (Boulder, Colo.: Westview Press).

PRAÇA ÁFONSO, ALBERTINO ANTUNES, ANTONIO AMORIM, CESÁRIO BORGA and FERNANDO CASCAIS (eds) (1974) *25 de Abril. Documento* (Lisbon: Casa Viva Editora).

PRIDHAM, GEOFFREY (ed.) (1984a) *The New Mediterranean Democracies. Democratic Transitions in Portugal, Spain and Greece* (London: Frank Cass).

PRIDHAM, GEOFFREY (1984b) 'Comparative Perspectives on the New Mediterranean Democracies: A Model of Regime Transition?', in Pridham (1984a), pp. 1–29.

PRIDHAM, GEOFFREY (1991) *The International Dimension of Democratic Transition*, Occasional Paper no. 1 (Bristol: Centre for Mediterranean Studies, University of Bristol).

PRIDHAM, GEOFFREY and JOSÉ MAGONE (forthcoming) 'Environmentalism and Democratization: Comparative Policy Perspectives on the Politics of the New Southern Europe', in Richard Gunther, Nikiforos Diamandouros and Gianfranco Pasquino (eds), *The Changing Functions of the State* (Baltimore: Johns Hopkins University Press).

PRZEWORSKI, ADAM (1988) 'Democracy as a Contingent Outcome of Conflicts', in John Elster and Rune Slagstad (eds), *Constitutionalism and Democracy* (New York and New Rochette: Cambridge University Press).

PRZEWORKSKI, ADAM (1991) *Democracy and the Market. Political and Economic Reforms in Eastern Europe and Latin America* (Cambridge: Cambridge University Press).

PRZEWORSKI, ADAM (1992) 'Games of Transition', in Scott Mainwaring, Guillermo O'Donnell and Samuel J. Valenzuela (eds), *Issues in Democratic*

Consolidation. The New South American Democracies in Comparative Perspective (Notre Dame: University of Notre Dame), pp. 105–52.
PUTNAM, ROBERT D., LEONARDI, ROBERT, NANETTI, RAFFAELLA Y; (1993) *Making Democracy Work. Civic Traditions in Modern Italy* (Princeton, New Jersey: Princeton University Press).
RABY, D. L. (1988) *Fascism and Resistance in Portugal. Communists. Liberals and Military Dissidents in the Opposition to Salazar, 1971–74* (Manchester: Manchester University Press).
RADAELLI, CLAUDIO M. (1995) 'The role of knowledge in the policy process', *Journal of European Public Policy*, vol. 2, no. 2 (June), pp. 159–83.
RAJEVSKA, FELICIANA (1994) 'The Social Dimension of the Transition from a Command to a Market Economy in Latvia', paper presented at the Political Studies Association Annual Conference, March.
RAVET, VINCENT (1992) *Les politiques regionales dans l'opinion publique* (Luxembourg: Commission des Communautés Européennes).
REIS, JOSÉ (1985) 'Modos de industrialização, força de trabalho e pequena agricultura. Para uma análise da articulação entre acumulação e a reprodução', *Revista Critica de Ciencias Sociais*, nos 15–17, pp. 225–60.
'Rethinking Civil Society', (1994) *Journal of Democracy*, vol. 5, no. 3 (July), pp. 2–56.
RIBEIRO, ANTÓNIO SOUSA (1986) 'O Povo e o Público. Reflexões sobre a Cultura em Portugal no Pós – 25 de Abril', in 'Colóquio Portugal 1974–1984. Dez Anos de Transformação Social', *Revista Crítica de Ciências Sociais*, nos 18–20 (February), pp. 11–26.
RIBEIRO, MARIA EDUARDA (1993) 'Employment and vocational training', in José Silva Lopez, *Portugal and EC Membership Evaluated* (London: Pinter), pp. 193–202.
RODIN, MICHAIL (1994) 'Political Trust in Baltic States', paper presented at the Political Studies Association Annual Conference, University College Swansea, Department of Politics, 29–31 March.
RODRIGUES, MARIA JOÃO (1985) 'O mercado de trabalho nos anos 70: das tensoes aos metabolismos', *Análise Social*, vol. XXI, nos 87–9, pp. 679–733.
RODRIGUES, MARIA JOÃO (1988) *O Sistema de Emprego em Portugal. Crise and Mutações* (Lisbon: Dom Quixote).
RODRIGUES, MARIA JOÃO (1991) *Competividade e Recursos Humanos. Dilemas de Portugal na Construcao Europeia* (Lisbon: Publicacoes Dom Quixote).
ROSÁRIO, EUGÉNIA ARRIS DO, MIGUEIS, JORGE (1991) 'Assembleia da República-Resultados Eleitorais (1976–1991)', in *Eleições, revista de assuntos eleitorais*, no. 2, Dezembro, pp. 37–42.
ROSETA, AGOSTINHO (1985) 'Dos Grémios à Confederação Nacional do Patronato: Hesitaçoes e Ambiguidades', *Análise Social*, vol. XXI, nos 87–9, pp. 785–99.
ROTHER, BERND (1984) 'Wirtschaftspolitik von Sozialisten in der Krise: Der Fall Portugal', *Vierteljahresschrift*, vol. 25, no. 2, pp. 156–68.
ROTHER, BERND (1985) *Der verhinderte Übergang zum Sozialismus. Die sozialistische Partei Portugals im Zentrum der Macht (1974–1978)* (Frankfurt: Materialis).
RUIVO, FERNANDO (1993) 'Estado e Poder Relacional: A Intervenção Informal

dos Governos Locais em Portugal', in *Portugal Retrato Singular* (Porto: Afrontamento), pp. 402–37.

RUSTOW, DANKWART (1970) 'Transitions to Democracy. Towards a Dynamic Model', *Comparative Politics*, vol. 2, pp. 337–63.

SANTISO, JAVIER (1994) 'La Démocratie Incertaine. La theorie des choix rationels et la démocratisation en Amérique Latine', *Revue Française de Science Politique*, vol. 43, no. 6, pp. 970–93.

SANTOS, BOAVENTURA DE SOUSA (1984) 'A crise e a Reconstituicao do Estado em Portugal (1974–1984)', *Revista Critica de Ciencias Sociais*, vol. 14, pp. 7–29.

SANTOS, BOAVENTURA DE SOUSA (1985) 'Estado e sociedade na semiperiferia do sistema mundial: o caso português', *Análise Social*, vol. XXI, nos 87–9, pp. 869–701.

SANTOS, BOAVENTURA DE SOUSA (1986) 'Social Crisis and the State', in Kenneth Maxwell (ed), *Portugal in the 1980s. Dilemmas of Democratic Consolidation* (New York: Greenwood), pp. 168–95.

SANTOS, BOAVENTURA DE SOUSA (1990) *Estado e Sociedade em Portugal (1974–1988)* (Lisbon: Edicoes Afrontamento).

SANTOS, BOAVENTURA DE SOUSA (1993) 'O Estado, As Relacões salariais e Bem-Estar Social na Semiperiferia: O Caso Português', in Boaventura de Sousa Santos (ed.), *Portugal. Um Retrato Singular* (Porto: Edicoes Afrontamento), pp. 16–56.

SANTOS, JOSÉ ALBERTO LOUREIRO DOS (1980) *Forças Armadas, Defesa Nacional e Poder Político* (Lisbon: Imprensa Nacional-Casa da Moeda).

SCHLOSBERG DAVID (1995) 'Communicative Action in Practice: Intersubjectivity and New Social Movements', *Political Studies*, vol. 43, no. 2 (June), pp. 291–311.

SCHMIDT, MARIA LUISA (1985) 'A evolução da imagem pública da juventude portuguesa: 1974–84', *Análise Social*, vol. XXI, nos 87–9, pp. 1053–66.

SCHMIDT, MARIA LUISA (1990) 'Jovens: familia, dinheiro, autonomia', *Análise Social*, vol. XXV, nos 108–9, pp. 645–73.

SCHMITTER, PHILIPPE (1975) *Corporatism and Public Policy in Authoritarian Portugal* (London: Sage).

SCHMITTER, PHILIPPE (1993) *Some Propositions about Civil Society and the Consolidation of Democracy* (Vienna: Institut für Hoehere Studien. Forschungsberichte 10, September).

SCHNEIDER, CHRISTINE (1990) *Norwegische Gleichstellungspolitik am Beispiel der Frauenforderung im Öffentlichen Dienst*, Diplomarbeit aus Politikwissenschaft zur Erlangung des Magistergrades an der Grund- und Integrativwissenschaftlichen Fakultät der Universitat Wien, Juni.

SCHWARTZMAN, KATHLEEN (1985) 'The PostWar Democratic Economy of Portugal', in Eduardo de Sousa Ferreira and Walter C. Opello (eds), *Conflict and Change in Portugal 1974–1984* (Lisbon: Teorema), pp. 41–57.

SCHWARTZMAN, KATHLEEN (1987) 'Instabilidade Democrática Nos Países Semiperiféricos. A Primeira República Portuguesa', in *O Estado Novo. Das Origens Ao Fim da Autarcia, 1926–1959*, vol. I (Lisbon: Fragmentos).

SCHWARTZMAN, KATHLEEN (1989) *The Social Origins of Democratic Collapse. The First Republic in the Global Economy* (Kansas City: University Press of Kansas).

SECRETARIADO PARA A MODERNIZACÃO ADMINISTRATIVA (SMA) (1990) 'Réponse portugaise au questionnaire sur les fonctions publiques européennes', *Revue Française d'Administration Publique*, no. 55 (July–Sept.)

SECRETARIADO PARA A MODERNIZACÃO ADMINISTRATIVA (SMA) (1992) 'How to Provide Better Services. Administration–Citizen Relationship. Evolution over the last ten years (1982–1992)', unpublished manuscript.

SECRETARIADO PARA A MODERNIZACÃO ADMINISTRATIVA (SMA) (1993) 'Portugal: Regulatory Management and Reform at a Glance', mimeo (Lisbon: Secretariado para a Modernização Administrativa).

SECRETARIADO PARA A MODERNIZACÃO ADMINISTRATIVA (SMA) (1995a) *Plano de Actividades 1995* (Lisbon: Secretariado para a Modernização Administrativa).

SECRETARIADO PARA A MODERNIZACÃO ADMINISTRATIVA (SMA) (1995b) 'Portuguese initiatives on Administrative Modernization', mimeo (Lisbon: Secretariado para a Modernização Administrativa).

SECRETARIADO TÉCNICO DOS ASSUNTOS PARA O PROCESSO ELEITORAL (STAPE) (1986) *Caracterização dos Eleitos para as Autarquias Locais 1982* (Lisbon: STAPE).

SECRETARIADO TÉCNICO DOS ASSUNTOS PARA O PROCESSO ELEITORAL (STAPE) (1980–94) *Eleiçoes para os Orgãos das Autarquias Locais 1979–93*, several volumes (Lisbon: STAPE).

SECRETARIADO TÉCNICO DOS ASSUNTOS PARA O PROCESSO ELEITORAL (1992) *Eleição para a Assembleia da República 1991* (Lisbon: STAPE).

SECRETARIADO TECNICO DOS ASSUNTOS PARA O PROCESSO ELEITORAL ELEITORAL (STAPE) (1993) *Caracterização dos Eleitos para as Autarquias Locais 1989* (Lisbon: STAPE).

SECRETARIADO TÉCNICO DOS ASSUNTOS PARA O PROCESSO ELEITORAL (STAPE) (1994) *Eleiçoes Autárquicas 1976/93. Atlas Eleitoral* (Lisbon: STAPE).

SEMANIS, EINARS (1994) 'The Development of Political Regime in Latvia', paper presented at the Political Studies Association Annual Conference, University College Swansea, Department of Politics, 29–31 March.

SERTÓRIO, MANUEL (1978) 'A Luta Contra o Fascismo no Exilio', in: Sertório, Manuel, *Humberto Delgado 70 Cartas Inédita* (Lisbon).

SHIN, DON CHULL (1994) 'On the Third Wave, of Democratization. A Synthesis and Evaluation of Recent Theory and Research', in *World Politics*, 47, pp. 135–70.

SIDJANSKI, DUSAM, AYRBECK, URAL (1990) 'Le nouveau visage des groupes d' interet communautaires'. In Dusam Sidjanski and Ural Ayrbeck (eds), *L'Europe Du Sud dans la communauté européenne. Analyse comparative des groupes d' interet et leur insertion dans le reseau communautaire* (Geneve: Presses Universitaires de France), pp. 42–82.

SILVA MANUELA (ed.) (1986) *Portugal Contemporâneo. Problemas e Perspectivas, 1986* (Lisbon: Instituto Nacional de Administração).

SILVA MANUELA (1993) 'Social Security', in José Silva Lopes (ed.), *Portugal and EC Membership Evaluated* (London: Pinter), pp. 216–20.

SILVA, MANUEL CARLOS (1993) 'Camponeses, mediadores e Estado', *Análise Social*, vol. XXVIII, pp. 489–521.

SOARES, MÁRIO (1975a) *Democratização e Descolonização. Dez Meses no Governo Provisório* (Lisbon: Dom Quixote).

SOARES, MÁRIO (1975b) *Democracia Sim, Ditadura Nâo! Relatório Aprovado Pelo I Congresso do PS na Legalidade* (Lisbon: Empresa do Jornal do Comércio).

SOARES, MÁRIO (1976) *Portugal. Que Revolucâo?* Diálogo com Dominique Pouchin (Lisbon: Perspectivas e Realidades).

SOARES, M. CANDIDAM (1986) 'Emprego, Formação Profissional e Condições de Trabalho', in Silva (1986), pp. 127–66.

SOBRAL, JOSÉ MANUEL and PEDRO GINESTAL DE ALMEIDA (1982–3) 'Caciquismo e Poder Político. Reflexoes em Torno das Eleicoes de 1901', *Analise Social*, vol. XVIII, nos 72–4), pp. 649–71.

SPINOLA, ANTÓNIO (1974) *Portugal e o Futuro. Análise da Conjuntura Nacional* (Lisbon: Arcadia).

STALLINGS, BARBARA (1981) 'Portugal and the IMF: The Political Economy of Stabilization', in Jorge Braga de Macedo and Simon Serfaty (eds), *Portugal Since the Revolution. Economic and Political Perspectives* (Boulder, Colo.: Westview Press) pp. 101–35.

STEEN, ANTON (1995) 'Change of Regime and Political Recruitment. The Parliamentary Elites in the Baltic States', paper presented at the European Consortium for Political Research, Joint Sessions, Bourdeaux, 27 April to 2 May.

STERNBERG, ERNST (1993) 'Justifying Public Intervention Without Market Externalities: Karl Polanyi's Theory of Planning on Capitalism', *Public Administration Review*, vol. 53, no. 3 (March–April), pp. 100–9.

STEWART, JENNY (1994) 'Corporatism, Pluralism and Political Learning: A Systems Approach', *Journal of Public Policy*, vol. 12, no. 3, pp. 243–55.

STIEFFEL, MATTHIAS and THOMAS WOLFE (1994) *A Voice to the Excluded* (Geneva: Zed Books).

STOCK, MARIA JOSÉ (1984) 'Sistema de Partidos e Governabilidade (Um Estudo Comparado)', *Economia e Sociologia*, no. 37, pp. 43–84.

STOCK, MARIA JOSÉ (1985a) 'A Base Social de Apoio e o Recrutamento dos lideres do PSD e do CDS', *Revista de Ciência Politica*, no. 1, pp. 103–21.

STOCK, MARIA JOSÉ (1985b) 'O Centrismo Politico em Portugal: Evolução do Sistema de Partidos, Genese do 'Bloco Central' e análise dos parceiros de coligação', *Analise Social*, vol. XXI, no. 85, pp. 45–82.

STOCK, MARIA JOSÉ (1988) 'A imagem dos partidos e a consolidação democrática em Portugal – Resultados de um Inquérito', *Análise Social*, vol. XXIV, no. 100, pp. 151–61.

STOCK, MARIA JOSÉ (1989a) 'Elites, Façoes e Conflito Intra-partidário – O PPD/PSD e o Processo Politico Português de 1974 a 1985', unpublished doctoral thesis in Political Sociology, Universidade de Évora.

STOCK, MARIA JOSÉ (1989b) 'O centrismo politico e os partidos do poder em Portugal', in Coelho (1989), pp. 147–79.

STOCK, MARIA JOSÉ (1992) 'Portugal', in *European Data Yearbook 1992*, special issue of *European Journal for Political Research*.

STOCK, MARIA JOSÉ (1993) 'Portugal', in *European Data Yearbook 1993*, special issue of *European Journal for Political Research*.

STOCK, MARIA JOSÉ and JOSÉ MAGONE (1994) 'Portugal', in *European*

References   211

Data Yearbook 1994, special issue of European Journal for Political Research.
STOCK, MARIA JOSÉ and JOSÉ MAGONE (1995) 'Portugal', in European
  Data Yearbook 1994, special issue of European Journal for Political Research.
STOER, STEPHEN (1986) Educação e Mudanca Social em Portugal 1970–1980.
  Uma década de transição (Porto: Edicoes Afrontamento).
STOLEROFF, ALAN D. (1992) 'Between Corporatism and Class Struggle: the
  Portuguese Labor Movement and the Cavaco Silva Governments', West
  European Politics, vol. 15, no. 4 (October), pp. 118–50.
SYRETT, STEPHEN (1993) 'Local Power and Economic Policy: Local Authority
  Economic Initiatives in Portugal', Regional Studies, vol. 28, no. 1, pp. 53–67.
SYRETT, STEPHEN (1994) Local Development. Restructuring Locality and
  Economic Initiative (Aldershot: Avebury).
TARROW, SIDNEY (1978) 'Introduction', in Sidney Tarrow, Peter J. Katzenstein
  and Luigi Graziano (eds), Territorial Politics in Industrial Nations (New York
  and London: Praeger), pp. 1–27.
THOMASHAUSEN, ANDRÉ (1981a) Verfassungs und Verfassungswirklichkeit
  in Portugal (Cologne: Nomos).
THOMASHAUSEN, ANDRÉ (1981b) 'Portugal', in Frank Wende (ed.), Lexikon
  zur Geschichte der Parteien in Europa (Stuttgart: Kroner), pp. 495–515.
TOCQUEVILLE, ALEXIS DE (1981) De la Democratie en Amerique, 2 vols
  (Paris: Flammarion).
TRIBUNAL DE CONTAS (1990–4) Relatório. de Actividades e Contas (Lisbon:
  Tribunal de Contas).
TRIBUNAL DE CONTAS (1992) Origem e Evolução do Tribunal de Contas
  de Portugal (Lisbon: Tribunal de Contas).
TRIBUNAL DE CONTAS (1994) O Sistema de Controlo Sucessivo do Tribu-
  nal de Contas (Lisbon: Tribunal de Contas).
VALA, JORGE (1989) 'Identidades Sociais e Representações Sociais sobre o
  Poder: Para um Entendimento das Culturas Políticas em Portugal', paper
  presented at the IV International Meeting on Portugal, University of New
  Hampshire, Durham, 21–24 September.
VASCONCELOS, ALVARO (1991) 'Portuguese Defence Policy: Internal Politics
  and Defence Commitments', in John Chipman (ed.), Nato's Southern Allies:
  Internal and External Allies (London and New York: Routledge), pp. 86–139.
VENEZA, ANA (1986) 'O Poder Local, 1976–1984: Da Indefinição à
  (Des)centralização Estatal', Revista Crítica de Ciencias Sociais, nos 18–20,
  pp. 693–708.
VESTER, MICHAEL (1986) 'A Reforma Agrária Portuguesa como Processo
  Social', Revista Crítica de Ciências Sociais, nos 18–20, (February), pp. 481–526.
VIDIGAL, LUIS (1988) Cidadania, Caciquismo e Poder (Lisbon: Livros
  Horizonte).
VIEGAS, JOSÉ MANUEL LEITE (1986) 'Cultura e comportamentos políticos
  em meios sociais de predominância rural – Revisão critica de literatura sobre
  Portugal', Revista de Ciência Politica, no. 4, pp. 37–48.
VIEGAS, JOSÉ MANUEL LEITE and MANUELA REIS (1988) 'Campesinato
  e Regime Democrático. Uma Cultura Política em Transformação?', Sociologia.
  Problemas e Prácticas, no. 5, pp. 78–105.
VIRILIO, PAUL (1986) Speed and Politics: An Essay on Dromology (New York:
  Columbia University Press).

WALLACE, HELEN (1986) 'The British Presidency of the Council of Ministers. The Opportunity to Persuade', *International Affairs*, no. 4 (Autumn), pp. 83–99.

WALLERSTEIN, IMMANUEL (1974–89) *The Modern World System* (New York: Academic Press).

WEFFORT, FRANCISCO C. (1993) 'Les "démocraties nouvelles": analyse d'un phenomene', *Revue Internationale des Sciences Sociales*, vol. 136 (May) pp. 289–302.

WHEELER, DOUGLAS L. (1978) *Republican Portugal. A Political History, 1910–1926* (Madison: University of Wisconsin).

WHITEHEAD, LAURENCE (1992) 'The Alternatives to "Liberal Democracy": a Latin American Perspective', in 'Prospects for Democracy', edited by David Held, special issue of *Political Studies*, vol. XL, pp. 146–59.

WORLD COMMISSION ON ENVIRONMENTAL DEVELOPMENT (1987) *Our Common Future* (Oxford: Oxford University Press).

WRIGHT, VINCENT (1994) 'Reshaping the State: The Implications for Public Administration', in 'The State in Western Europe', edited by Wolfgang C. Mueller and Vincent Wright, special issue of *West European Politics*, pp. 102–110.

ZENHA, FRANCISCO SALGADO (1976) *Por uma politica de concórdia e grandeza nacional* (Lisbon: Perspectivas e Realidades).

Index

Index

215

Index

217

Sá Carneiro, Francisco   28, 40, 97
Salazar, Antonio Oliveira   18–20
salaries   136
Sampaistas   93
saneamentos   122
*Secretaria do Estado do Ambiente e
   Recursos Naturais
   (SEARN)*   138
*Secretaria de Estado para a
   Integração Europeia*   166
Semipresidentialism   29, 40–2
SIC, private television   42
sindicatos   111
Soares, Mário   23, 29, 30, 31, 32,
   35, 41–3, 45, 92–5, 184
Soaristas   93–4
social market economy   8–10, 147
Socialist Party   *see Partido
   Socialista*
Social-democratic Party   *see
   Partido Social-democrata*
*Sociedade para os Estudos de
   Desenvolvimento Económico e
   Social* (SEDES)   95
social security   129–31
Soldados Unidos Vencerão (SUV)   25
sustainable development   15, 137,
   139
Supreme Administrative Court   *see
   Supremo Tribunal
   Administrativo (STA)*

*Supremo Tribunal Administrativo
   (STA)*   53
stabilisation   28
   economic   28
   political   30–3
state   5–6
   competition   5–6
structural funds   162, 174–5
structural violence   11

*União Democrática Popular
   (UDP)*   26, 28, 108
*União Geral dos Trabalhadores
   (UGT)*   114, 115, 119–21
*Union de Centro Democrático
   (UCD)*   3
Union of the Industries of the
   European Community
   (UNICE)   117

tangentopoli ('kick-back city')   9
tráfico de influencias   124, 178
Transnational corporations
   (TNCs)   4
Tribunal de Contas   53
tripartite agreement   114–16

West European Union (WEU)   144

youth   148–9, 178–9